The Psychology of Tipping

Michael Lynn

The Psychology of Tipping

Scientific Insights for Services Customers, Workers, and Managers

Michael Lynn
School of Hotel Administration
Cornell University
Ithaca, NY, USA

ISBN 978-3-032-09532-9   ISBN 978-3-032-09533-6 (eBook)
https://doi.org/10.1007/978-3-032-09533-6

© The Editor(s) (if applicable) and The Author(s), under exclusive license to Springer Nature Switzerland AG 2026

This work is subject to copyright. All rights are solely and exclusively licensed by the Publisher, whether the whole or part of the material is concerned, specifically the rights of translation, reprinting, reuse of illustrations, recitation, broadcasting, reproduction on microfilms or in any other physical way, and transmission or information storage and retrieval, electronic adaptation, computer software, or by similar or dissimilar methodology now known or hereafter developed.
The use of general descriptive names, registered names, trademarks, service marks, etc. in this publication does not imply, even in the absence of a specific statement, that such names are exempt from the relevant protective laws and regulations and therefore free for general use.
The publisher, the authors and the editors are safe to assume that the advice and information in this book are believed to be true and accurate at the date of publication. Neither the publisher nor the authors or the editors give a warranty, expressed or implied, with respect to the material contained herein or for any errors or omissions that may have been made. The publisher remains neutral with regard to jurisdictional claims in published maps and institutional affiliations.

Cover credit by eStudioCalamar

This Springer imprint is published by the registered company Springer Nature Switzerland AG
The registered company address is: Gewerbestrasse 11, 6330 Cham, Switzerland

If disposing of this product, please recycle the paper.

Dedicated to all past, present and future tipped workers, but especially to one particular former waitress (Ann), whose support as my partner and wife helped me pursue this career-long research passion. Thank you Dear.

Contents

1 **More Than Small Change (Who Cares About Tipping? Why? What Should They Know?)**   1
   Consumers   2
   Service Workers   3
   Business Firms   4
   Government Agents   4
   Sources of Answers About Tipping   5
   Author's Qualifications   6
   References   8

2 **Beyond Gratitude and Gratuity (Why Do, or Don't, People Tip?)**   11
   Reasons for Tipping   12
   Reasons for Not Tipping   19
   Implications for…   21
   Conclusion   26
   References   26

3 **Big-Tippers and Stiffers (Who Gives the Best, and Worst, Tips?)**   31
   Tipping Propensities of Different Demographic Groups   32
   Tipping Propensities of Different Behavioral-Trait Groups   41
   Tipping Propensities of Different Personality Types   44

	Summary Thoughts	46
	References	47
4	**A Time for Tipping (When Do People Tip More? … or Less?)**	**51**
	Time-of-Day Effects	52
	Day-of-Week Effects	54
	Seasonal Effects	57
	Holiday Effects	59
	Conclusions	60
	References	60
5	**A Place for Tipping (How and Why Does Tipping Vary Across Geographic Areas?)**	**63**
	Urban/Rural Differences	64
	State Differences	64
	National Differences	74
	Summary	83
	References	84
6	**Perk of the Job (Why Do We Tip Some Service Occupations and not Others?)**	**87**
	More Efficient Incentives	88
	Greater Concerns About Envy/Harm	89
	More Convenient Tipping	90
	Enhanced Extrinsic Tipping Motives	91
	Stronger Intrinsic Tipping Motives	92
	Greater Offense at Being Offered Tips	94
	Summary and Conclusion	95
	References	97
7	**Unequal Pay (Who Gets the Best Tips and Who Gets the Worst?)**	**99**
	Do Men Get Larger (or Smaller) Tips Than Women?	101
	Does a Worker's Age Affect His or Her Tip Sizes?	105
	Do Ethnic Minorities Get Smaller Tips?	107
	Do Physically Attractive Workers Get Larger Tips?	108
	Do Workers with Certain Personalities Get Larger Tips?	109
	Do More Experienced Servers Get Larger Tips?	110
	Do Service Workers with a Better Work Attitude Get Larger Tips?	111

	Summary and Conclusions	111
	References	112
8	**Mega Tips (How Can Servers Get Larger Tips?)**	117
	Maximizing Sales	118
	Delivering Better Service	119
	Mega Tips for Workers	120
	Concluding Remarks About Server Tactics	143
	Managerial Tactics for Increasing Tips	144
	Display Larger Digital Tipping Options (Within Normative Expectations)	148
	Concluding Remarks About Managerial Tactics	149
	Concluding Note to Skeptics	149
	References	151
9	**Winners a Losers (Who Does Tipping Benefit and How? Who Does It Harm and How?)**	157
	Pros and Cons of Tipping from a Consumer Perspective	158
	Pros and Cons of Tipping from a Worker Perspective	169
	Pros and Cons of Tipping from a Business Perspective	180
	Conclusions	189
	References	190
10	**Cornucopia of Controversies (What Controversies Arise from Tipping? What Should People Know About Them?)**	197
	Disagreement About the Ethics of Tipping	197
	Disagreement About Social Obligation to Tip	201
	Disagreement About the Tipped Minimum Wage	203
	Disagreement About Mandatory Tip Sharing	208
	Disagreement About Taxing Tips	209
	Disagreement About Digital Tipping	211
	References	217
11	**Past as Prologue (When and Where Did Tipping Arise? How Might It Change Going Forward?)**	223
	Origins of the Word "Tip"	223
	Origins of Tipping	224
	History of Tipping in the U.S.	225
	Future of Tipping	228
	References	231

1

More Than Small Change (Who Cares About Tipping? Why? What Should They Know?)

Every day, millions of consumers around the world give voluntary payments of money (called "tips," "propinas," and "trinkgelds," among other names) to service providers such as baristas, bartenders, concierges, deliverymen, doormen, haircutters, hotel maids, masseurs, porters, sommeliers, street musicians, taxi drivers, tour guides, and waiters (Lynn, 2016). In some cases, these tips are just small change, but in many other cases they amount to 10–20% of the contracted payments for services. In rare cases, individual tips can reach truly astronomical sizes as happened when a 16-year-old cashier at a Missouri pizza restaurant, Ryheem Lumpkins, was given a $2500 tip by a generous customer who was impressed by his attitude and demeanor (Fuoco-Karasinski, 2023).

Precise measures of aggregated tips do not exist, but estimates place the amount tipped to restaurant workers in the United States alone at over $45 billion a year (Azar, 2011), so the total amount tipped worldwide must be enormous. This pervasive and substantial phenomenon is important to consumers, service workers, business firms, and government officials, each of whom would benefit from a better understanding of the psychology underlying it. Why tipping is important to these groups, as well as what kinds of information about tipping would benefit them, and how, are briefly discussed below.

Consumers

To consumers, tipping is primarily a monetary expense that buys a variety of social benefits. However, many consumers misperceive the potential benefits of (or motivations for) tipping. For example, few consumers think that they tip in restaurants for the server's social approval even though research (described later in this book) suggests that it is the strongest motivation for restaurant tipping (Lynn, 2015). A fuller understanding of the potential benefits/motivations underlying tipping would allow those consumers to make more deliberate and rewarding decisions about whom, when, and how much to tip.

Some of the benefits sought from tipping are positional in nature. That is, some tippers strive to improve their service, social status, and/or self-image relative to other consumers while some strive to avoid losses of service, status, and/or self-image relative to other consumers. This motivation was humorously illustrated in an episode of Curb Your Enthusiasm in which Larry David and Jason Alexander go to a restaurant and split the bill. At the end of the meal, Larry suggests that they "coordinate the tip" by both leaving $12 for the waiter. With a smile on his face, Jason encourages Larry to leave the $12 while ostentatiously writing his tip on the credit slip, putting it in the check folder so Larry cannot read what he wrote, and handing it to the server with generous verbal praise for the service. Later, Larry interrogates the waiter and learns to his chagrin that Jason tipped over $30. Clearly, both Larry and Jason view tipping as a competition for the server's esteem—with one wanting to win and the other not wanting to lose. Of course, this is a fictional scene but it is funny because it captures a motivation and a social dynamic that is all too real. Many consumers compete for tip recipients' esteem and that competition is with all other tippers not just their immediate companions (Lynn, 2015). Knowing how much others generally tip in different service settings and how those amounts are affected by the characteristics of the consumer, the service worker, and the service encounter would help such tippers gauge the size of tip that is necessary and sufficient to get the positional benefits they seek in various situations.

As the source of tips, consumers are also the targets of tip-enhancing strategies and tactics (Lynn, 2011, 2018). A greater awareness of what those strategies and tactics are, as well as how they work, would help consumers identify and perhaps resist these manipulative attempts to part them from their money. For example, many tip-enhancing tactics—like calling customers by name and touching customers—work by communicating the server's liking of the customer and, thereby, increasing the customer's perceptions of rapport with the worker (Lynn, 2011). Knowing about these tactics would allow consumers to resist impulses to generously tip the servers employing those tactics by encouraging the consumers to be more questioning and discerning judges of how genuine these signals of liking really are.

Finally, as customers and voters, consumers can support (or oppose) business and government tipping policies they believe are beneficial (or harmful). Consumers' evaluations of tipping policies require the same information that businesses and government agents need to make and revise those policies, so consumers share the informational needs of those groups as described below.

Service Workers

To service workers, tipping is primarily a source of income and feedback about job performance. Tipped workers have a vested interest in assessing their potential tip income from various jobs, maximizing the tips they receive, and properly interpreting the meaning of those tip amounts they receive. A greater knowledge about any and all of the factors that affect tipping would help them do each of these tasks better. For example, knowing who gets the biggest and the smallest tips would help workers better anticipate their own tip earning potential when deciding whether or not to accept tipped jobs and might provide some understanding and solace if they find that co-workers make more than them in tips. In addition, knowing who are big and who are small tippers would help service workers select jobs with more of the latter customers and might help workers more profitably allocate the time they devote to different customers. Finally, knowing why people tip and what server behaviors cause them to tip more or less would help service workers pull the right motivational levers and employ the right tactics to increase their tip take.

Many servers may believe they already know all they need to about tipping, and perhaps some do, but research suggests that many do not. For example, many servers over-estimate group differences and under-estimate individual differences in tipping and, consequently, inappropriately discriminate in service delivery to individual members of those groups they perceive to be bad tippers (Brewster & Nowak, 2019). In addition, many servers fail to engage in simple behaviors, such as writing "Thank You" on checks and touching customers on the arm or shoulder, that have been proven to substantially increase tips (Lynn, 2011). Clearly, these servers could benefit from a more extensive knowledge and understanding of the psychology of tipping.

Business Firms

To businesses, tipping is a form of both consumer pricing and employee compensation. Business managers want to adopt tipping policies, and to communicate tipping expectations and options to consumers in ways, that increase their employees' incomes and incentives to do a good job as well as their customers' satisfaction and return intentions. A few notable examples of businesses grappling with these concerns include:

- Marriott's 2014 Envelope Please campaign, which asked guests to tip the maids $1 to $5 using envelopes in the hotel's rooms (Hsu, 2014),
- Uber's 2016 decision to allow in-app tipping of its drivers (Mohammed, 2016),
- Frontier Airlines' 2019 adding tipping requests to its digital payment devices used when passengers pay for in-flight food or drinks (Berger, 2019), and
- DoorDash's 2023 warnings to customers that failing to leave a digital pre-service tip would result in delays delivering their orders (Walrath-Holdridge, 2023).

All of these companies tried to increase tips to their employees and they faced varying degrees of consumer backlash for doing so. Knowledge about the psychology of tipping, and (especially) about how various tipping policies/practices affect consumers' emotions, perceptions of expensiveness, service expectations, and tipping behavior, would help firms like these better achieve their tipping-related goals.

Government Agents

To government officials and policymakers, tipping is an economic activity to be taxed and regulated. Tip income is easy to hide and the United States' Internal Revenue Service (IRS) estimates that less than half of it is declared. Thus, tax authorities would benefit from better prediction of total tip amounts received by individual workers, the firms they work for, and the service industry as a whole. That is why the IRS has periodically hired outside vendors, such as the Survey Research Laboratory at the University of Illinois (in the 1980s) and the marketing research firm Fors Marsh Group (in the 2010s), to help it better estimate and predict tipping. Obviously, such estimation and prediction of tipping would be facilitated by a greater knowledge about the psychology of tipping and the factors affecting consumer tipping behavior.

As an economic activity impacting consumers, workers, and firms, tipping raises numerous questions relevant to government policymakers. For example, federal lawmakers and regulators in the United States have decided (c.f., Department of Labor, 2024) that:

- Tips are income not gifts,
- Tipped workers can be paid hourly wages substantially below the regular minimum wage as long as they get at least $30 a month in tips and those tips bring their total pay up to the regular minimum wage,
- Tipped workers receiving subminimum wages can be forced to share their tips only with other traditionally tipped workers (e.g., waiters can be forced to share tips with bartenders and busboys but not cooks or dishwashers), and
- Tipped workers receiving the standard minimum wage can be forced to share their tips with all other hourly workers not in supervisory positions.

These regulatory decisions are based on numerous assumptions and value judgments, but some of those assumptions are about tippers' expectations, intentions, and motivations concerning tipping. Information about the validity of those assumptions would allow policymakers to more effectively design and/or modify regulations in pursuit of their policy goals.

Sources of Answers About Tipping

Consumers, service workers, service businesses, and government agents are all interested in tipping as something to be managed (as described above). However, there is another group of people who are interested in tipping as a phenomenon to be studied and explained, namely academics. One subset of this group (i.e., economists) finds tipping particularly mysterious and puzzling because it goes against their assumptions about how people behave. As the Harvard economist Greg Mankiw (2007) wrote in an online blog, "*Economists do not have a good theory of tipping. Normally, we assume that consumers pay as little as they have to when buying the products they want. Yet, when buying meals, haircuts and taxi services, most consumers voluntarily pay more than they are legally required. Why does this happen? Why is it more true for some services than for others? Why do tipping customs vary from country to country? I have no idea.*" Psychologists and other scholars in allied disciplines such as hospitality management, human resources management, marketing, and sociology are less baffled by tipping than are economists, but they still find it a practically important and theoretically rich topic of study.

As a result, there are now hundreds of academic articles and studies examining the psychology underlying various aspects of this phenomenon (for academic reviews, see Azar, 2007, 2020; Lynn, 2015, 2017, 2018). Researchers have studied: why people tip, what characteristics differentiate big tippers from less generous ones, what characteristics cause some service workers to get larger tips than others, what specific behaviors servers can engage in to increase their tips, what situations lead to larger and smaller tips, why some occupations are more likely than others to get tipped, why tipping is more common in some countries than others, and how various tipping policies and practices affect the perceptions, sentiments, and behaviors of employees and customers. In other words, we now have a lot of answers to the questions that consumers, service workers, service businesses, and government agents are asking themselves. However, most of those answers are locked away in academic journals not easily accessible to the general public. The popular press does occasionally cover some of this research in magazine, newspaper, and online articles or in podcasts and radio and television news programs, but that coverage tends to be both narrow in scope and shallow in depth. There is no easily accessible source covering both the breadth and depth of what is known about tipping. This book attempts to correct that state of affairs; it integrates and summarizes much of what academics have learned about the psychology of tipping using easily understood, everyday language without the jargon and complicated statistics that heretofore have obfuscated it.

Author's Qualifications

Curious and critical readers, of which I hope there will be many, will want to know what my qualifications for writing such a book are, so I conclude this chapter with a brief description of the journey that led me to be typing these words.

I do not remember my first conscious encounter with tipping, but it was undoubtedly in a restaurant observing my father leave money on the table as we departed and him explaining that it is customary to give waiters and waitresses additional money amounting to 15 to 20 percent of the bill as an expression of gratitude, and as a reward, for having done a good job. Thus, like almost everyone else, I first approached tipping in the role of customer and tipper. Of course, that is a role I continue to play today.

A major shift in my relationship with tipping occurred right after my freshman year in college. My father had intended to fully pay for my college education, but he was audited by the IRS my freshman year and ended up owing a lot of money in back taxes. He still covered most of my expenses, but explained that I needed to contribute my share by getting and holding jobs in the summer and during the school year. I quickly realized that the best paying jobs I could get with my limited skills and qualifications were in restaurants, so I began working at them and came to rely on tips as a source of income. That summer, I began working at Pizza Hut, where I was a cook during the day and waiter at night. The next year at college (the University of Texas), I got a job as a busboy at LaTour, a fancy French restaurant on the top of the Westgate building in Austin. Soon I was promoted to back waiter, a job in which I wore a tuxedo and not only delivered food to tables but often prepared those foods (like Ceasar's Salad and Bananas Foster) tableside. I held that job until the restaurant closed. I then moved to a more traditional waiter job at the Headliner's Club in Austin, where I worked until my graduation. I continued working part time at various restaurants and private clubs for many years and eventually added bartending to my resume. Thus, I have seen tipping from the perspective of a worker in several different jobs and at downscale, mid-scale, and upscale establishments.

Another change in my relationship with tipping occurred my first year as a graduate student in Social Psychology at the Ohio State University. I moved to Columbus before the start of the school year and got a job as a restaurant bartender to support myself until my research fellowship began later that year. Once school started, my fellowship required me to quit my outside job. However, I would not see the first fellowship check for a month, so I asked my advisor, Bibb Latane, for permission to keep the job until then. He agreed that I could keep the bartending job, but only if I used it as an opportunity to come up with some research project in that setting. I never did end up doing research at that particular restaurant, but I did start thinking of tipping as a potential topic of research (not just as a source of income). Bibb had done some research a few years earlier finding that large groups of diners tipped less than small groups of diners (Freeman et al., 1975) and I decided to test different explanations for that effect for my thesis. I soon found myself standing outside of an International House of Pancakes restaurant near campus interviewing departing customers about their dining experience and tipping behavior. Thus began my career studying the psychology of tipping.

A few years after getting my PhD, my research on tipping gave me an opportunity to work as a professor of consumer psychology at the famed Cornell Hotel School. That job gave me yet another perspective on tipping as I was supposed to do research that was relevant to hospitality management. I began to study not just why people tip and what determines whom and how much they tip, but also how tipping affects worker behavior and how both customers and workers respond to businesses' tipping policies and practices. Eventually, I also became interested in how government regulations regarding tipping affected consumers, workers, and businesses.

Today, as I type these words, I remain a professor at the Cornell Hotel School, where I continue a forty plus year career studying tipping. I have written over 80 academic papers on almost every aspect of the topic and published those papers in the journals of such varied disciplines as economics, hospitality management, human resources, marketing, social psychology, and sociology. Now, I want to share what I and my fellow tipping researchers have learned with a wider audience. Whoever you are and whatever your relationship with tipping, I believe that you will find the insights in this book both interesting and practically useful.

References

Azar, O. H. (2007). The social norm of tipping: A review. *Journal of Applied Social Psychology, 37*(2), 380–402.

Azar, O. H. (2011). Business strategy and the social norm of tipping. *Journal of Economic Psychology, 32*(3), 515–525.

Azar, O. H. (2020). The economics of tipping. *Journal of Economic Perspectives, 34*(2), 215–236.

Berger, S. (2019, January 11). This airline is asking passengers to tip their flight attendants. https://www.cnbc.com/2019/01/11/budget-airline-frontier-asks-passengers-to-tip-their-flight-attendant.html. Accessed February 1, 2024.

Brewster, Z. W., & Nowak, G. R. (2019). Racial prejudices, racialized workplaces, and restaurant servers' hyperbolic perceptions of black–white tipping differences. *Cornell Hospitality Quarterly, 60*(2), 159–173. https://doi.org/10.1177/1938965518777221

Department of Labor. (2024). Fact Sheet #15: Tipped employees under the Fair Labor Standards Act (FLSA). https://www.dol.gov/agencies/whd/fact-sheets/15-tipped-employees-flsa. Accessed February 1, 2024.

Freeman, S., Walker, M. R., Borden, R., & Latane, B. (1975). Diffusion of responsibility and restaurant tipping: Cheaper by the bunch. *Personality and Social Psychology Bulletin, 1*(4), 584–587.

Fuoco-Karasinski, C. (2023, June 2). Mo. Teen cashier "speechless" after getting $2,500 tip from customer for all his "hard work". https://people.com/missouri-teen-cashier-speechless-gets-tip-customer-hard-work-7507397. Accessed February 1, 2024.

Hsu, T. (2014, October 4). Marriott hotel chain pushes the envelope on housekeeper tipping. https://www.latimes.com/business/la-fi-hotel-tipping-20141003-story.html. Accessed February 1, 2024.

Lynn, M. (2011). Mega Tips 2: Twenty tested techniques to increase your tips. *Cornell Hospitality Tools, 2*(1), 4–22. https://ecommons.cornell.edu/handle/1813/71274. Accessed November 30, 2021.

Lynn, M. (2015). Service gratuities and tipping: A motivational framework. *Journal of Economic Psychology, 46*, 74–88.

Lynn, M. (2016). Why are we more likely to tip some service occupations than others? Theory, evidence, and implications. *Journal of Economic Psychology, 54*, 134–150.

Lynn, M. (2017). Should US restaurants abandon tipping? A review of the issues and evidence. *Psychosociological Issues in Human Resource Management, 5*(1), 120–159.

Lynn, M. (2018). Are published techniques for increasing service-gratuities/tips effective? P-curving and R-indexing the evidence. *International Journal of Hospitality Management, 69*, 65–74.

Mankiw, G. (2007, October 1). No, really, it's up to you. https://gregmankiw.blogspot.com. Accessed February 1, 2024.

Mohammed, R. (2016, May 5). Uber's new tipping policy is a mistake. https://hbr.org/2016/05/ubers-new-tipping-policy-is-a-mistake. Accessed February 1, 2024.

Walrath-Holdridge, M. (2023, November 3). Customers who don't tip DoorDash drivers will wait longer for deliveries, company warns. https://www.usatoday.com/story/money/2023/11/01/no-tip-orders-delivered-slower-doordash/71409399007/. Accessed February 1, 2024.

2

Beyond Gratitude and Gratuity (Why Do, or Don't, People Tip?)

Tips are voluntary payments given after services have been delivered and often going to complete strangers we will never meet again. Why do we do it? What motivations underlie this behavior? You may think that you already know the answers to these questions because you know why you yourself tip. However, different people often have different motivations, so our self-insights may or may not apply to others. Furthermore, psychologists have found that people's awareness of the factors and motives underlying their own behavior is incomplete at best (Nisbett & Wilson, 1977). We are all driven by internal and external factors whose effects are beyond our awareness, so we cannot give a complete account of why we do the things we do and the accounts we can and do give may explain less than we believe. To fully understand what motivates our own and others tipping, we need to supplement self-insights with logical inferences from the factors known to affect tipping. This chapter draws upon research about tipping to make such inferences and to more fully explain why we do, or do not, tip.

Based on surveys of consumers and knowledge of the existing research on tipping, I believe this behavior can be best understood as the result of a mental tug of war between five pro-tipping and two anti-tipping motives (see Fig. 2.1). On the pro-tipping side are consumers' desires to: (i) reward service workers' efforts and performance, (ii) help service workers make a decent living, (iii) gain or keep preferential service in future encounters, (iv) gain or keep the approval, liking, and/or esteem of tip recipients and other onlookers, and (v) fulfill a sense of obligation or duty to tip. In other words, the main motivational drivers of tipping are gratitude/reciprocity, altruism, future service, social esteem, and duty. Opposing these motives for tipping

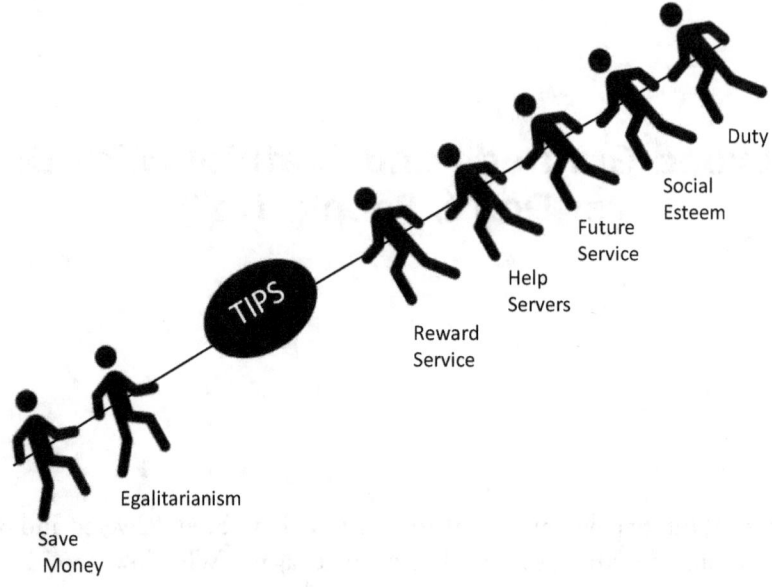

Fig. 2.1 Motivational tug of war over tipping

are consumers' desires to save the money for other uses and their dislike of tipping's power and status implications. These pro- and anti-tipping motives are not equally strong in all people or situations. In some cases, one or more of the motives may not come into play at all. Nevertheless, some subset of these motives underlay all or nearly all cases of tipping and they help explain much of the variability in tipping across consumers, servers, occupations, service encounters, and other situations (Lynn, 2015b). Accordingly, each of these motives is discussed further in the sections that follow.

Reasons for Tipping

Reward Service

Tips are traditionally thought to be an incentive and reward for good service. For example, Charlotte Ford's *Book of Modern Manners* says: "A tip is a gesture of appreciation for service; the percentage of the tip isn't an absolute, so consider the quality of service before deciding on the amount you will leave" (Ford, 1980). Thus, it should not be surprising that 83 percent of a large sample of U.S. consumers said they tipped to reward service (Lynn, 2009). Consistent with these traditions and self-perceptions, researchers have found that consumers' tips increase with both the quality and quantity of services provided. Specifically, restaurant customers tip more when servers make more trips to the table and when those customers rate the service more highly (Bodvarsson & Gibson, 1994; Lynn, 2001). In other service contexts, tips increase with the number of in-room service activities performed by hotel bellmen (Lynn & Gregor, 2001), the speed of restaurant delivery services (Kerr & Domazlicky, 2009), the safer driving behaviors of Uber drivers (Chandar et al., 2019), and the length and timeliness of answers to questions provided by online researchers working at Google Answers (Regner, 2014). In addition, restaurant servers with more positive service attitudes (Lynn et al., 2011) and Uber drivers with higher lifetime ratings (Chandar et al., 2019) have been found to earn more in tips than do less service-oriented and less highly rated workers. Finally, after controlling for occupational status, occupations that provide customized services are more likely to be tipped than are occupations that provide more standardized services (see Fig. 2.2)—presumably because consumers are more motivated to reward workers for services that go beyond the standard care given to everyone (Lynn, 2016).

While the evidence supports our belief that we tip to reward good service, it also suggests that we tend to over-estimate the importance of this motive. Many people report that rewarding service is the main reason they tip, but the effects on tipping of differences in service across situations, workers, and establishments are too small for this to be true (Lynn, 2003). For example, restaurant customers' ratings of service account for only about 5% of the

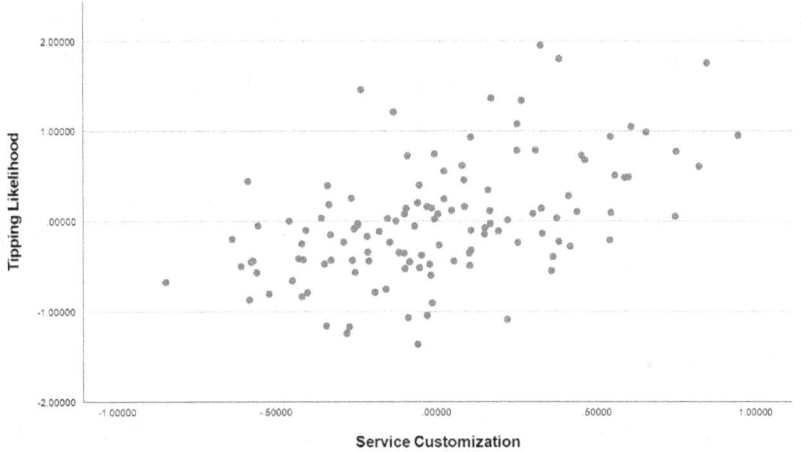

Fig. 2.2 Controlling for occupational status, people are more likely to tip occupations that provide customized services than to tip occupations that provide standardized services ($r = 0.51$, $n = 122$, $p < 0.001$: data from Lynn, 2016)

variability (or differences) in the tip percentages they leave (Lynn & McCall, 2000). Other factors combined have nearly 20 times the impact of service ratings on restaurant tip percentages!

Altruism

Service jobs in the hospitality, personal-care, and tourism industries generally pay low wages. In the United States, some of these jobs are even allowed to pay below the standard minimum wage as long as the wage shortfall is covered by tips. For example, many restaurant servers in the U.S. make only $2.13 an hour in wages even though the federal minimum wage is currently $7.25. As a result, one reason people give for tipping is that they want to financially help out these low wage workers. In fact, this is the second most commonly given reason for tipping—with 72% of a large U.S. sample saying that they tip to "help servers" (Lynn, 2009).

Consistent with this claimed motivation, research has found that increasing the salience and/or importance of helping motives increases tips. For example, restaurant customers in the U.S. tip more in states with lower tipped wages (Lynn, 2020, 2022a) and when they have past experience working for tips (Parrett, 2011). Furthermore, restaurant customers tip more when: (i) songs with pro-social lyrics are played in the restaurant (Jacob et al., 2010a, 2010b), (ii) an altruistic quotation is printed on the check (Jacob et al., 2013), and (iii) the bill is presented on a heart-shaped dish (Guéguen, 2013). In addition, workers in low-income/status occupations are more likely to be tipped in the U.S. than are workers in higher-income/status occupations and this occupational income/status effect is stronger among consumers who report stronger altruistic motives for tipping (Lynn, 2016, 2021b). Finally, unpublished data indicates that coffee shop and taxi tips are higher in states whose populations score higher on kindness (see Fig. 2.3). None of these findings by itself is conclusive proof that people tip to help servers, but such an altruistic motive is the most parsimonious explanation for this collective set of findings.

Future Service

To economists, the only logical reason for tipping is to ensure better future service and approximately 60% of U.S. consumers in one survey claimed that this motive underlies their own tipping (Lynn, 2009). However, research suggests that this motive drives tipping far less than is commonly believed.

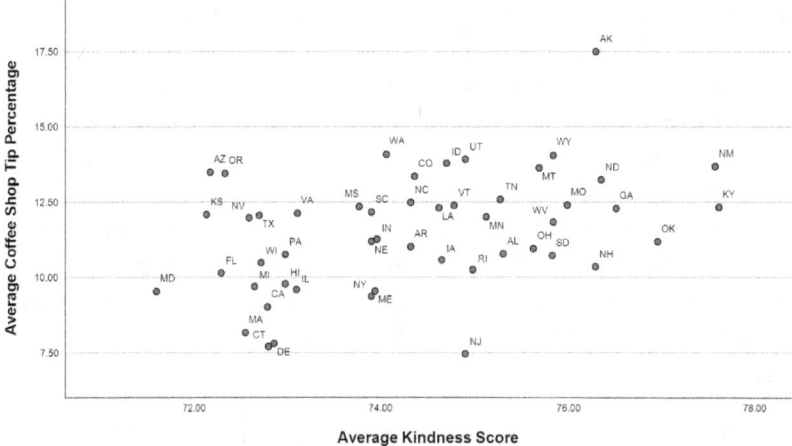

Fig. 2.3 States whose populations score higher on kindness also tip more in coffee shops ($r = 0.40$, $n = 50$, $p < 0.005$; data from Curry et al., 2021; Lynn, 2020)

One way that tipping can motivate better future service is if servers believe their tips are contingent on the quality of the services they deliver. This suggests that frequent patrons of an establishment can buy better future service by establishing a reputation for tipping more when service is excellent than when it is not. Contrary to such a strategy, however, researchers have found no evidence that regular restaurant patrons vary their tips with service quality any more than do infrequent patrons (Lynn & McCall, 2000).

A second way that tipping can motivate better future service is if servers feel an obligation to repay past tipping generosity with better current service. This suggests that frequent patrons of an establishment can buy better future service by tipping generously even if current service is not as good as hoped for. Consistent with this strategy, researchers have found that regular restaurant patrons do tip more than infrequent patrons (Lynn & McCall, 2000). However, this patronage frequency effect on tipping could have nothing to do with future service. Instead, frequent patrons may tip more than infrequent ones because the former are wealthier, more satisfied with the dining experience, more concerned about the server's opinion of them, and/or have more empathy for the server.

There is some evidence that people who report stronger future-service motives for tipping are more likely than others to tip outside of restaurant settings (Lynn, 2009), but even the meaning of this effect is suspect because it is not stronger in situations where it should be. Tips should be used to buy future service more when the frequency of server-customer interactions is high and when service customization allows workers to give better service to some customers than to others. Contrary to these expectations, future-service motives do not predict tipping likelihood more strongly for occupations involving higher patronage frequency, higher likelihood of customers getting the same server across service encounters, or higher service customization (Lynn, 2021a, 2021b). I have no doubt that desires for good future service motivate some tipping, but the occasions on which it does so appear to be rare. That is bad news for economists who see future service as the only rational reason for tipping, but is good news for tipped workers and their managers, because this motivation offers few levers that servers can pull to increase their tip incomes and have few implications of consequence to managers.

Social Esteem

Few people believe they tip to buy social approval or esteem. In fact, only 27% of U.S. consumers in one survey agreed that they tip to impress the server, only 18% agreed that they tipped to avoid appearing poor or cheap, and only 14% agreed that they tipped to impress other people (Lynn, 2009). Nevertheless, research makes it clear that desires for social approval, liking, and esteem are major drivers of most consumers' tipping. In U.S. restaurants, the strongest predictor of dollar and cent tip amounts is bill size; it accounts for twice as much of the variability in restaurant tip amounts as all other factors combined (Lynn & McCall, 1999)! Much of bill sizes' predictive power comes from the fact that it defines the socially expected tip amount in accordance with the 15–20% tipping norm. Furthermore, people tip what they are expected to tip in large part to gain the approval and esteem of those holding the expectation. Supporting this claim is the fact that bill size predicts tip amount more strongly among frequent than infrequent patrons and at expensive than inexpensive restaurants—both of which are conditions likely to increase consumers' concern about the servers' esteem (Lynn & McCall, 1999).

In addition, people in the U.S. are more likely to tip occupations for whom the service encounter and, hence, act of tipping is visible to other customers, but only when tipping that occupation is normative (Lynn, 2016). Furthermore, researchers have found that tipping is more common and widespread in countries whose populations are more concerned with impression management (Lynn & Starbuck, 2015) and more highly value social status and recognition (see Fig. 2.4). and more highly value social status and recognition (Lynn & Starbuck, 2015). Finally, unpublished data indicates that restaurant and hair salon tips are higher in U.S. states with a

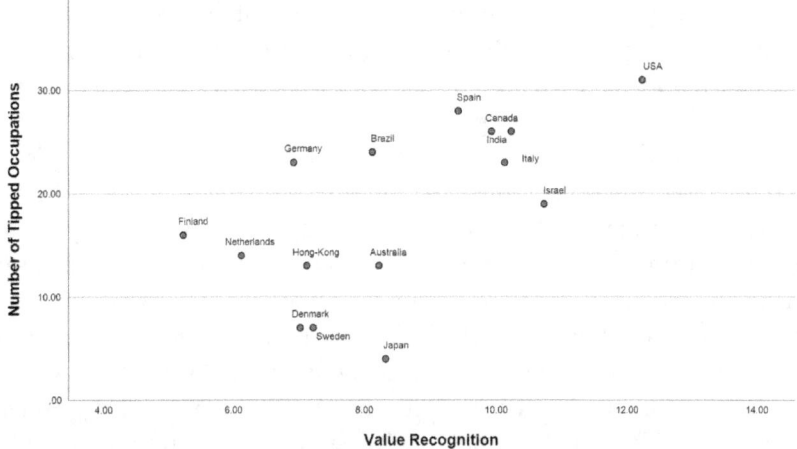

Fig. 2.4 Nations whose populations value "recognition" more tip a greater number of service providers (*source* Lynn, 1997)

stronger interest in status goods as reflected in Google searches for "Cartier," "Gucci," and "Rolex."[1] Thus, the evidence suggests that tippers are motivated by impression management concerns to a far greater degree than they want to admit.

Duty

To many consumers, tipping is simply a duty created by internalized tipping norms. In general, people comply with social expectations and norms to gain or keep social esteem as discussed previously, but also to feel satisfaction or pride from doing what is right and to avoid guilt from failing to do right. These latter motivations also drive tipping—50% of U.S consumers in a large survey said they tip to feel satisfaction from doing right and nearly 20% said they tip to avoid guilt (Lynn, 2009).

Such duty-based motivations for tipping differ from the other tipping motives in a way worth noting. Larger tips provide servers with more rewards and help and they buy the tippers better future service and more social esteem, so strengthening these motives should increase tips with no logical cap on the resulting tip amount. In contrast, only minimally normative tips

---

[1] For restaurants $r = 0.25$ ($n = 49$, $p < 0.09$) and for hair salons $r = 0.47$ ($n = 50$, $p < .001$). Restaurant tip data are from Lynn (2022a, 2022b) and hair salon tip data are from Risen (2016). Interest in status goods was measured by averaging the percentages in each state searching these terms from 2004 to 2021 as reflected in a Google Trends search by the author.

are necessary to gain satisfaction or avoid guilt by fulfilling obligations. Thus, duty motives for tipping should increase normative tipping (i.e., tipping the people and amounts called for by tipping norms), but strengthening those motives should not increase tipping outside of normative dictates.

Consistent with this reasoning, research has found that individuals with stronger duty motives for tipping report a greater likelihood both of leaving restaurant tips in the 15–20% range and of tipping across a variety of other traditionally tipped service settings. Similarly, states with more duty motivated tippers leave a higher proportion of restaurant tips that are 15–20% of the bill (see Fig. 2.5; Lynn, 2022b). Duty motivated individuals do not, however, leave larger amounts on average when they do tip than do others (Lynn, 2015a, 2021a, 2021b). Despite this, it is customary to tip a greater number of service providers and to give larger tip amounts to restaurant servers in nations whose populations are more motivated by a sense of duty (Lynn & Starbuck, 2015). This later finding suggests that while duty motives may not motivate individuals to leave super-normative tips, they do facilitate the development of larger customary tip amounts. More research is needed to explain this apparent paradox, but perhaps competition for status and future service drives customary tip sizes upward and duty-oriented tippers are more willing than others to accept the elevation in tips as the new norm.

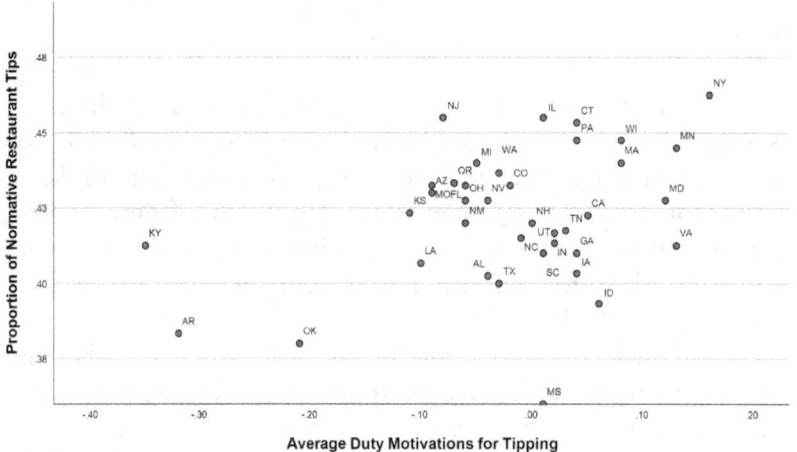

Fig. 2.5 States whose populations have stronger duty motives for tipping leave more tips in the 15–20% range ($r = 0.35$, $n = 38$, $p < 0.03$; data from Lynn, 2022b)

Reasons for Not Tipping

To Save Money

Money spent on tips is not available for other uses and common sense suggests this should reduce peoples' willingness to tip. This is the reason that most economists regard tipping as irrational and mysterious—they see it as an unnecessary loss of limited resources (aka, a cost). If concerns about costs do constrain tipping, then wealthier people, who are presumably less concerned about those costs, should tip more than others. Consistent with this expectation, the size of restaurant tips and the likelihood of tipping outside of restaurants both increase with consumers' incomes (Lynn, 2009). In addition, ride-share and taxicab passengers picked up from wealthier neighborhoods tip their drivers more than do passengers from less wealthy neighborhoods (Chandar et al., 2019; Conlisk, 2022). Finally, average restaurant tips are higher in states with larger median incomes (Lynn, 2020). Of course, wealthy people and states differ from less wealthy ones in many ways—not just in lower concerns about costs—so these effects of individual and state differences in income are not conclusive evidence for cost constraints on tipping.

Stronger evidence of cost constraints on tipping is provided by research showing that externally caused increases and decreases in wealth have parallel effects on tipping. In one study, researchers found that stock market fluctuations had corresponding effects on the tips given to NYC taxi drivers—with stronger effects observed among those passengers whose wealth was more likely to be affected by stock market returns (Tan & Zhang, 2021). Another study found that the COVID-19 pandemic, which economically hurt working-class people while economically benefitting more wealthy ones, decreased Chicago taxi passengers' likelihood of tipping their drivers more when the passengers came from poor neighborhoods and increased the size of those tips given to the drivers more when the passengers came from wealthy neighborhoods (Conlisk, 2022). More research on how changes in wealth affect tipping is needed, but these existing findings are in line with expectations that gains in wealth increase tipping while losses of wealth decrease tipping.

While income and income-change effects on tipping suggest that monetary cost considerations do constrain tipping, other research findings suggest that those constraints are rather loose. First, although income affects tip amounts, it does not appear to affect the sensitivity of tips to service quality (Lynn et al., 2012). Within the income ranges observed at most restaurants, better service increases the tips left by both the rich and poor alike, so cost constraints do not keep people from rewarding better service with larger tips.

Second, restaurant, taxicab, hair salon, and laundry delivery tips all increase with bill size at a constant rate as bill sizes go from small to large (Alexander et al., 2021; Lynn & Sturman, 2003). Larger bill sizes deplete consumer resources and budgets more than do smaller bill sizes, so if tipping were highly sensitive to monetary costs, then tips should increase less when bill size goes from $91 to $100 than when bill size goes from $1 to $10. However, that does not happen—the effects of bill size on tip amount are linear rather than marginally decreasing.

Third, a study I did with a restaurant magician found that doubling the tips customers gave him (via a manipulation to be discussed later) had no effects on the tips those customers gave the waiter or waitress who subsequently served them (Frank & Lynn, 2020). Giving bigger tips to the magician used up more of the tippers' monetary resources, so it should have decreased the amount they tipped other service providers if tips are highly sensitive to monetary costs. The failure to observe such an effect suggests that they are not.

Finally, studies have found that a "no-tipping" policy together with a 15% increase in menu prices increases the perceived expensiveness of restaurants even though the higher menu prices are offset by the elimination of tipping (Lynn & Wang, 2013; Wang & Lynn, 2007). This suggests that people are less sensitive to changes in expected tips than they are to comparable changes in menu prices. Together, these findings suggest that consumers' tipping budgets are fairly large and/or easily expanded and that cost considerations have relatively weak effects on consumers' tipping decisions. Once again, economists assumptions about human behavior are wrong—not only do economists under-emphasize the importance of intangible and psychological benefits, but they over-estimate the importance of economic costs!

Egalitarianism

Tipping involves giving people money, which seems like something the recipient would be happy about. However, there is a history of some people viewing tips as demeaning to the tip recipient. For example, William Scott (1916) wrote a book titled "The Itching Palm" in which he argued that tipping was un-American because it put service personnel in the position of having to be servile in order to get adequately paid for their work. More recently, Harvard economist David Hemenway (1992) has argued that tipping can be seen as demeaning to its recipients because it: (i) gives the consumers direct power over service workers who have no recourse if their efforts are not adequately remunerated, (ii) implies that the worker is untrustworthy and will not do a good job without the threat of withholding a tip, and (iii) carries the aura of charity for the poor.

The effects of these perceptions on the tipping of individual consumers have been under-studied, but it only stands to reason that people would be reluctant to tip someone they thought might be insulted by it. Certainly, such concerns prevented me from offering a tip to the tour guide I had on a trip to the Australian Outback. He was a great guide and I wanted to give him a tip, but never did because I was uncertain how he would interpret it given that tipping is rare in Australia. Going beyond this anecdote, the idea that some people may refrain from tipping out of fear of giving offense may explain why people are less likely to tip high status than low status occupations in the U.S. (Lynn, 2016), because workers in high status occupations are more likely to be offended by tips than are low status workers. In addition, concerns about creating and highlighting status and power differences between consumers and service workers may explain why tipping is less common in countries with more egalitarian values (see Fig. 2.6; Lynn et al., 1993). More research needs to be done on these issues, but it seems likely that the status and power inequalities fostered by tipping make egalitarian consumers reluctant to leave tips and that the fear of those status implications giving offense to tip recipients makes even non-egalitarian consumers reluctant to leave tips when tipping norms are unclear.

Implications for…

What does all of this information about the motivational drivers of, and impediments to, tipping mean for the stakeholders described in Chap. 1? Let's consider them one at a time—starting with consumers.

Consumers

As we have seen, consumers over-estimate the importance of reward and future-service motives for tipping while under-estimating the importance of social-approval motives. On a personal level, consumers can use this information to reassert deliberate control over their own tipping behavior. Awareness of how little reward and future-service motives affect the tip amounts they leave can help tippers genuinely wanting to reward past service or secure future service to change their behavior appropriately. At the same time,

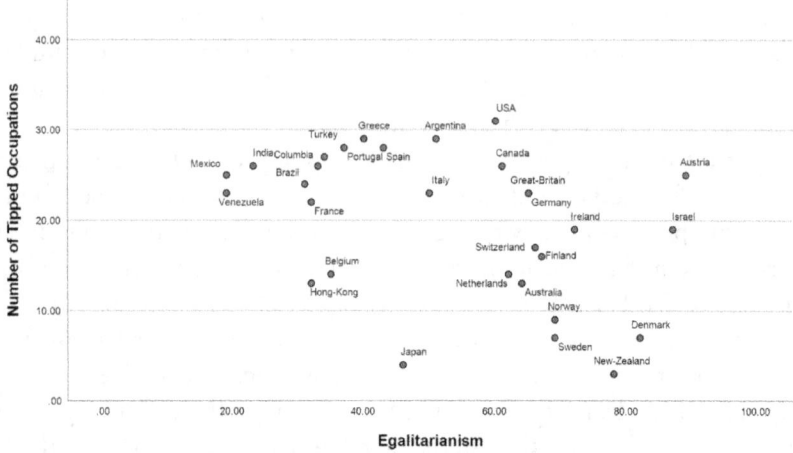

Fig. 2.6 More egalitarian nations tip fewer occupations than do those with greater tolerance of status and power differences between people ($r = -0.40$, $n = 30$, $p < 0.03$, data from Lynn et al., 1993). *Note* Egalitarianism = 100-Hofstede's Power Distance Index

increased appreciation of their own impression management concerns can help tippers resist giving in to unwanted social pressures.

At a collective level, consumers can use this information to motivate and inform tipping reform efforts. Weak reward and future-service motives for tipping weaken its traditional role as an incentive/reward. Strong social-approval motives create a competition that increases tipping rates over time and create what economists called an "externality" that requires many consumers to tip more simply to avoid social disapproval (Lynn, 2015a, 2015b). In that way, they decrease consumer satisfaction and, perhaps, overall social welfare. Indeed, both of these collective effects can be seen in the current phenomena of ***tip-creep*** to low-service and even self-service contexts and of ***tip-flation*** to levels above the previous maximum of 20% of the bill, which have resulted in a new wave of consumer antipathy toward tipping (see Shon et al., 2023). Spreading information about the weakness of reward and future-service motives and about the strength of social-approval motives for tipping would support and might help fuel tipping reform efforts. Past tipping reform efforts (like those of the American Anti-Tipping Association in the early 1900s and Tipper's International in the late 1900s) failed (Seagrave, 1998), but modern communications technology and social media may make future efforts more successful.

Service Workers

Knowledge about consumer motivation for tipping is useful to servers primarily because it gives them insight into what levers they can pull to increase tips. For example, parking valets may want to jog rather than walk when retrieving cars for guests, or at least to do so when in the guests' line of sight, to be seen as more hustling, prompt, and deserving of a large reward. In addition, workers who are college students or moms, might want to casually mention that fact during interactions with customers in the hope that those customers will be more willing to help struggling students and/or parents with large tips. Finally, waitresses can increase their male customers' desires to impress them with large tips by looking as attractive as possible and/or being flirtatious.

Similarly, the idea that consumer tipping is constrained by resource limits and associated cost considerations suggests that tipped workers can expect to get better tips working at establishments with wealthier clientele. However, the fact that those constraints are fairly loose means that even less wealthy customers can and will tip more for better service, so tipped workers should not ignore some customers just because they appear to be less well-off than others. The looseness of resource-constraints on tipping also means that tipped workers need not view themselves as being in competition with their employer or with other servers over limited customer budgets. The tips workers get are unlikely to be reduced by their customers' accrual of larger bill sizes or by their customers' tips to another worker.

Businesses

The preceding information about consumer motivations for tipping also have numerous implications for firms and managers seeking to increase their employees' incomes and incentives to do a good job as well as their customers' satisfaction and return intentions. First, the idea that consumers tip to reward service suggests that managers can use tipping as a means of motivating servers to do a good job and as a measure of their performance. Indeed, economists argue that this is the main reason that tipping exists—because it is more efficient for firms to allow customers to monitor and reward server performance than to have managers to do so (Azar, 2004; Jacob & Page, 1980). The fleeting, intangible, and customized nature of many services makes it hard for managers or other third parties to tell if service workers are doing a good job, but customers can easily assess how well service workers are satisfying their needs and desires. On the other hand, the fact that this motive has weak effects on tip amounts means that managers should not rely on tips alone as the primary incentive for, and measure of, their tipped workers' job performances. Buyer monitoring via tipping needs to be supplemented with server evaluations based on managerial monitoring, customer satisfaction surveys, and/or mystery diners.

Second, the fact that a desire to reward and to help workers motivates tipping informs firm and managerial efforts to expand consumer tipping to new categories of workers, as with digital tipping requests in many retail establishments today (Burke, 2023). Specifically, it helps explain why we are more likely to tip occupations involving customized services, low pay, and workers who are less happy than their customers (Lynn, 2016, 2021a, 2021b) and suggests that managerial efforts to expand tipping to occupations without these characteristics are likely to fail—because consumers will see little need to reward or help those workers with tips. Conversely, managerial attempts to implement "No-Tipping" service-inclusive pricing policies need to be accompanied by public assurances that workers are well compensated and intrinsically motivated. Otherwise, many customers may continue tipping even though they are paying higher service-inclusive menu prices.

Third, the fact that consumers tip to reward and to help the workers serving them also suggests that many consumers will be opposed to business policies and practices requiring those workers to share their tips with others. In fact, research has found such a negative consumer sentiment toward tip sharing and pooling that is particularly strong among more altruistic and reciprocity motivated tippers (Lynn & Ni, 2022). Managers need to consider this consumer sentiment before adopting tip sharing or tip pooling policies. If they adopt such policies any way, then managers should try broadening consumers' reciprocity and altruism motives to include those other workers. For example, perhaps they could remind consumers how much back-of-house and other staff contribute to their service-experience and how sharing in tips helps these workers support their families.

Fourth, the idea that consumers use tipping to manage impressions has conflicting implications for service managers. On the one hand, managers can help workers capitalize on this motivation by communicating high tip expectations to consumers. For example, businesses could print larger tip suggestions at the bottom of bills or present larger amounts as one-touch tip options on digital screens (see Alexander et al., 2021). On the other hand, such manipulations of this motivation for tipping are likely to be perceived as unwanted social pressure that reduces customer satisfaction (Warren et al., 2021a).

The optimal way to balance these competing effects of explicit tip requests on employee income and customer sentiment is unclear and probably differs across specific situations. However, there is some research suggesting that tipping guidelines feel less like social pressure when they are presented or explained as tip-calculation assistance or as data entry conveniences rather than tip expectations (Cabano & Attari, 2023) and when digital suggestions are presented on spacious (as opposed to crowded) pages (Fan et al., 2024). Thus, managers should seriously consider incorporating these elements into tipping guidelines they present to customers. There is also some evidence that tip requests and/or suggestions will induce feelings of social pressure and irritation more in the absence of other motivations for tipping (Karabas et al., 2020; Warren et al., 2021b), so managers should be particularly wary of making tip requests and suggestions in pre-service contexts or other contexts involving standard service and/or well-paid workers.

Finally, the idea that many people tip in order to comply with tipping norms they accept as legitimate suggests that businesses may want to educate their customers about those norms. A representative national survey I had conducted back in 2003 asked respondents: "Thinking about tipping overall, and not your own practices, how much is it customary for people in the United States to tip waiters and waitresses?" In one of the most surprising (to me) findings of my career, only about 71% of White and 37% of Black respondents gave an answer that fit within the then widely accepted normative range of 15–20% of bill size (Lynn, 2004). Restaurant servers are among the most frequently tipped service providers (Lynn, 2016), so there can be little doubt that awareness of other tipping norms is even lower than this surprising level. It is hard to imagine an unawkward and low-pressure way for servers to educate their customers about tipping norms, but managers can certainly do so by posting educational messages—such as: "Gratuities of $1–$5 for valet parking are customary and appreciated" or "It is customary to tip 15 to 20% of the bill in U.S. restaurants"—on claim stubs, menus, bills, and signs. The available evidence suggests that such signs are needed everywhere, but that is particularly true for businesses with a large minority or foreign clientele (Lynn, 2011, 2014; Shrestha, 2014).

Government Agents

Finally, information about the motives underlying tipping can inform and improve the design, implementation, and/or modifications of government tipping policies and regulations. For example, the idea that people tip to help service workers make a decent living probably helps explain the widespread public support for the idea that tips be exempted from income taxation (see Jackson & Mendez, 2024) and suggests that an important criteria to be used in the design and adoption of such a policy is how much it would benefit poor workers. Similarly, the idea that people tip to buy the tip recipient's approval and esteem probably helps explain why consumers prefer that service workers be able to keep all of the tips they receive (DeSilver & Lippert, 2023; Lynn & Ni, 2022), because consumers care less about the approval of service workers they do not directly encounter. In turn, this raises questions about the desirability of recent regulatory changes expanding the acceptability of mandatory tip sharing policies.

Conclusion

As this chapter has made clear, tipping is a complex economic and social behavior with many motivational underpinnings. People tip to reward good service, financially help poorly paid workers, acquire or keep good future service, gain or keep social approval, and fulfill a sense of duty or obligation to comply with tipping norms. People tip smaller amounts and/or refrain from tipping altogether in order to save money for other purposes and to avoid the negative power and status implications of the practice. The information about these motives and their relative strengths in this chapter should help consumers, service workers, businesses, and government regulators and policymakers alike achieve their respective goals regarding tipping. They should also help readers of this book to mentally organize, understand, and remember the myriad factors affecting tipping that we will cover in subsequent chapters. So keep this chapter in mind as you read the rest of this book.

References

Alexander, D., Boone, C., & Lynn, M. (2021). The effects of tip recommendations on customer tipping, satisfaction, repatronage, and spending. *Management Science, 67*(1), 146–165.

Azar, O. H. (2004). Optimal monitoring with external incentives: the case of tipping. *Southern Economic Journal, 71*(1), 170–181. https://doi.org/10.1002/soej.v71.1.10.1002/j.2325-8012.2004.tb00632.x

Bodvarsson, Ö. B., & Gibson, W. A. (1994). Gratuities and customer appraisal of service: Evidence from Minnesota restaurants. *The Journal of Socio-Economics, 23*(3), 287–302.

Burke, M. (2023, July 6). 70% of consumers are tired of tipping and it's pushing our most valuable customers away: Here's how to respond. https://www.capterra.com/resources/tip-fatigue/. Accessed February 9, 2024.

Cabano, F. G., & Attari, A. (2023). Don't tell me how much to tip: The influence of gratuity guidelines on consumers' favorability of the brand. *Journal of Business Research, 159*, Article 113754.

Chandar, B., Gneezy, U., List, J. A., & Muir, I. (2019). *The drivers of social preferences: Evidence from a Nationwide tipping field experiment* (No. w26380). National Bureau of Economic Research.

Conlisk, S. (2022). Tipping in crises: Evidence from Chicago taxi passengers during COVID-19. *Journal of Economic Psychology*, 102475.

Curry, O., Wilkinson, J., & Krasnow, M. (2021). *Getting the measure of kindness*. Unpublished manuscript, Oxford University.

DeSilver, D., & Lippert, J. (2023, November 9). Tipping culture in America: Public sees a changed landscape. Pew Research Center. Available at: https://www.pewresearch.org/wp-content/uploads/2023/11/SR_23.11.09_tipping-culture_report.pdf. Accessed October 10, 2024.

Fan, A., Wu, L., & Liu, Y. (2024). To display tip suggestion or not? Examining tip suggestion's impact in technology-facilitated preservice tipping encounters. *Journal of Hospitality & Tourism Research, 48*(1), 32–57.

Ford, C. (1980). *Charlotte Ford's book of modern manners*. Simon and Schuster.

Frank, D. G., & Lynn, M. (2020). Shattering the illusion of the self-earned tip: The effect of a restaurant magician on co-workers' tips. *Journal of Behavioral and Experimental Economics, 87*, Article 101560.

Guéguen, N. (2013). Helping with all your heart: The effect of cardioid dishes on tipping behavior. *Journal of Applied Social Psychology, 43*(8), 1745–1749.

Hemenway, D. (1992). *Prices and choices: Microeconomic vignettes*. Revised edition. University Press of America.

Jackson, C., & Mendez, B. (2024). Proposed policy to end federal income tax on tips has bipartisan support. https://www.ipsos.com/en-us/proposed-policy-end-federal-income-tax-tips-has-bipartisan-support. Accessed December 6, 2024.

Jacob, N. L., & Page, A. N. (1980). Production, information costs, and economic organization: The buyer monitoring case. *The American Economic Review, 70*(3), 476–478.

Jacob, C., Guéguen, N., Ardiccioni, R., & Sénémeaud, C. (2013). Exposure to altruism quotes and tipping behavior in a restaurant. *International Journal of Hospitality Management, 32*, 299–301.

Jacob, C., Guéguen, N., & Boulbry, G. (2010a). Effects of songs with prosocial lyrics on tipping behavior in a restaurant. *International Journal of Hospitality Management, 29*(4), 761–763.

Jacob, C., Guéguen, N., Boulbry, G., & Ardiccioni, R. (2010b). Waitresses' facial cosmetics and tipping: A field experiment. *International Journal of Hospitality Management, 29*(1), 188–190.

Karabas, I., Orlowski, M., & Lefebvre, S. (2020). What am I tipping you for? Customer response to tipping requests at limited-service restaurants. *International Journal of Contemporary Hospitality Management, 32*(5), 2007–2026.

Kerr, P. M., & Domazlicky, B. R. (2009). Tipping and service quality: Results from a large database. *Applied Economics Letters, 16*(15), 1505–1510.

Lynn, M. (1997). Tipping customs and status seeking: a cross-country study. *International Journal of Hospitality Management, 16*(2), 221–224. https://doi.org/10.1016/S0278-4319(97)00007-8

Lynn, M., & McCall, M. (1999). *Beyond gratitude and gratuity: A meta-analytic review of the predictors of restaurant tipping.* Unpublished manuscript, Cornell University.

Lynn, M. (2001). Restaurant tipping and service quality: A tenuous relationship. *Cornell Hotel and Restaurant Administration Quarterly, 42*(1), 14–20.

Lynn, M. (2003). Tip levels and service: An update, extension, and reconciliation. *Cornell Hotel and Restaurant Administration Quarterly, 44*(5–6), 139–148.

Lynn, M. (2004). Ethnic differences in tipping: A matter of familiarity with tipping norms. *Cornell Hotel and Restaurant Administration Quarterly, 45*(1), 12–22.

Lynn, M. (2009). Individual differences in self-attributed motives for tipping: Antecedents, consequences, and implications. *International Journal of Hospitality Management, 28*(3), 432–438.

Lynn, M. (2011). Race differences in tipping: Testing the role of norm familiarity. *Cornell Hospitality Quarterly, 52*(1), 73–80.

Lynn, M. (2014). The contribution of norm familiarity to race differences in tipping: A replication and extension. *Journal of Hospitality & Tourism Research, 38*(3), 414–425.

Lynn, M. (2015a). Explanations of service gratuities and tipping: Evidence from individual differences in tipping motivations and tendencies. *Journal of Behavioral and Experimental Economics, 55*, 65–71.

Lynn, M. (2015b). Service gratuities and tipping: A motivational framework. *Journal of Economic Psychology, 46*, 74–88.

Lynn, M. (2016). Why are we more likely to tip some service occupations than others? Theory, evidence, and implications. *Journal of Economic Psychology, 54*, 134–150.

Lynn, M. (2020). The effects of minimum wages on tipping: A state-level analysis. *Compensation & Benefits Review, 52*(3), 98–108.

Lynn, M. (2021a). Effects of the Big Five personality traits on tipping attitudes, motives and behaviors. *International Journal of Hospitality Management, 92*, Article 102722.

Lynn, M. (2021b). The effects of occupational characteristics on the motives underlying tipping of different occupations. *Journal of Behavioral and Experimental Economics, 95*, Article 101783.

Lynn, M. (2022a). How tip credits affect consumer tipping behavior. *International Journal of Hospitality Management, 103*, Article 103214.

Lynn, M. (2022b). State differences in tipping attitudes and behavior: Attributable to state differences in tipping motivations? *Review of Regional Studies, 52*(3), 367–386.

Lynn, M., & Gregor, R. (2001). Tipping and service: The case of hotel bellmen. *International Journal of Hospitality Management, 20*(3), 299–303.

Lynn, M., Jabbour, P., & Kim, W. G. (2012). Who uses tips as a reward for service and when? An examination of potential moderators of the service–tipping relationship. *Journal of Economic Psychology, 33*(1), 90–103.

Lynn, M., Kwortnik, R. J., Jr., & Sturman, M. C. (2011). Voluntary tipping and the selective attraction and retention of service workers in the USA: An application of the ASA model. *The International Journal of Human Resource Management, 22*(9), 1887–1901.

Lynn, M., & McCall, M. (2000). Gratitude and gratuity: A meta-analysis of research on the service-tipping relationship. *The Journal of Socio-Economics, 29*(2), 203–214.

Lynn, M., & Ni, X. (2022). The effects of tip distribution policies: Servers' keeping vs sharing/pooling tips affects tippers' sentiments but not tip-giving. *International Journal of Hospitality Management, 100*, Article 103087.

Lynn, M., & Starbuck, M. (2015). Tipping customs: The effects of national differences in attitudes toward tipping and sensitivities to duty and social pressure. *Journal of Behavioral and Experimental Economics, 57*, 158–166.

Lynn, M., & Sturman, M. C. (2003). It's simpler than it seems: An alternative explanation for the magnitude effect in tipping. *International Journal of Hospitality Management, 22*(1), 103–110.

Lynn, M., & Wang, S. (2013). The indirect effects of tipping policies on patronage intentions through perceived expensiveness, fairness, and quality. *Journal of Economic Psychology, 39*, 62–71.

Lynn, M., Zinkhan, G. M., & Harris, J. (1993). Consumer tipping: A cross-country study. *Journal of Consumer Research, 20*(3), 478–488.

Nisbett, R. E., & Wilson, T. D. (1977). Telling more than we can know: Verbal reports on mental processes. *Psychological Review, 84*(3), 231.

Parrett, M. (2011). Do people with food service experience tip better? *The Journal of Socio-Economics, 40*(5), 464–471.

Regner, T. (2014). Social preferences? Google answers! *Games and Economic Behavior, 85*, 188–209.

Risen, T. (2016, June 22). Where Americans tip the most. https://www.usnews.com/news/articles/2016-06-22/where-americans-tip-the-most. Accessed July 2, 2024.

Scott, W. F. (1916). *The itching palm: A study of the habit of tipping in America*. Penn Publishing Company.

Seagrave, K. (1998). *Tipping: An American social history of gratuities*. McFarland Publishing.

Shon, S., Flanagan, G. L., & Frankel, R. S. (2023, November 14). More places are asking for tips, and it's tiring Americans out. https://www.usatoday.com/money/blueprint/credit-cards/tipping-fatigue-growing-in-america/. Accessed February 24, 2024.

Shrestha, J. (2014). *Tipping differences of domestic and foreign customers in casual dining restaurants: An investigation of customers' and servers' perception.* Oklahoma State University.

Tan, W., & Zhang, J. (2021). Good days, bad days: Stock market fluctuation and taxi tipping decisions. *Management Science, 67*(6), 3965–3984.

Wang, S., & Lynn, M. (2007). The effects on perceived restaurant expensiveness of tipping and its alternatives. *Center for Hospitality Research Report, 7*(3), Cornell Hotel School.

Warren, N. B., Hanson, S., & Yuan, H. (2021a). Who's in control? How default tip levels influence customer response. *Marketing Science Institute Working Paper Series, 21*(126).

Warren, N., Hanson, S., & Yuan, H. (2021b). Feeling manipulated: How tip request sequence impacts customers and service providers? *Journal of Service Research, 24*(1), 66–83.

3

Big-Tippers and Stiffers (Who Gives the Best, and Worst, Tips?)

Visit online forums for restaurant servers (like r/Serverlife), or simply ask a sample of servers, and you will find no shortage of opinions about what types of people leave the best tips and what types leave the worst tips. Commonly nominated for the former category are regular customers, rich people, men, and smokers while foreigners, Blacks, Hispanics, teenagers, and the elderly are often nominated for the latter category (Harris, 1995; McCall & Lynn, 2009). At first glance, you might think that these perceptions must be valid. After all, service workers have direct experience getting tips and should know who their good and bad tips come from. However, that trust in server's opinions would be misplaced.

Server's perceptions of who are good and bad tippers *may* be accurate, but we cannot just take their word for it because they (like us) are subject to biases in perceptions, inferences, and memory that can lead them to see relationships that are not there (Bott et al., 2021; Van Dessel et al., 2021). Thus, we need to turn to empirical data to determine which of server's perceptions of good and bad tippers are accurate and which are not. We might also want to ask about the tipping propensities of psychologically as well as demographically and behaviorally defined groups. Who really does leave the best, and the worst, tips? Most importantly, how big are the differences in tips left by various groups?

The answers to these questions are obviously important to service workers—whose frequent discussion of them we noted above. Those answers would tell servers whether their strategic avoidances of jobs with specific clientele they consider poor tippers, and/or their allocations of more attention to groups of customers they consider good tippers, are justified or misplaced.

The answers to these questions can also be used by managers to help correct their employees' misperceptions and/or more effectively deploy policies, practices, and messages meant to address the business problems posed by poor tippers. Finally, the answers to these questions can be used by consumers to better assess their own relative standing as tippers as well as to draw fairer inferences about other tippers they observe.

Accordingly, this chapter reviews what we know about individual and group differences in tipping. It begins with an examination of potential demographic predictors of tipping such as age, sex, race, religion, income, and nationality. Then it moves on to potential behavio ral-trait predictors such as smoking, patronage frequency, and work history. Finally, it ends with an examination of potential personality differences in tipping. As you will see, almost none of these predictors have consistent relationships with tipping across all studies. I will not go into a detailed review of every study and its strengths or weaknesses here, because to do so would overwhelm readers. Instead, I will summarize the main takeaways from my own critical review of the literature (including unpublished data I have collected) and will highlight what I perceive to be some of the key studies and findings.

Tipping Propensities of Different Demographic Groups

The most obvious differences between customers are their demographic characteristics. Servers can easily see differences in their customers' age, sex, and race/ethnicity and can reasonably infer their customers' wealth and nationality from observable characteristics such as clothing and accents. As described in the introduction to this paper, all of these demographic characteristics are perceived by servers as predictors of tipping. How inaccurate some of those perceptions are will surprise many.

Age

As previously mentioned, many restaurant servers believe that teenagers and the elderly are poor tippers. Unfortunately, servers' perceptions of the former group cannot be verified or falsified, because there is too little data on teenagers' tipping. On the other hand, there is a lot of data on how adults of varying ages tip, so server's perceptions of elderly tippers can be empirically tested. To make sense of these data, it is necessary to look separately at age effects on tipping likelihood and on tip size when a tip is left, so that is what is done below.

Age Effects on Tipping Likelihood. Existing studies are largely consistent in finding that older consumers claim to tip commonly tipped service providers—such as waiters/waitresses, food delivery people, haircutters, hotel maids, and taxi/ride-share drivers—more frequently than do younger consumers (see Lynn, 2009, 2015a, 2021a). In addition, older consumers reliably claim to tip rarely tipped service providers—such as furniture/appliance delivery workers, home repair providers, teachers, and trash/recycling collectors—less frequently than do younger consumers.[1] See Fig. 3.1 for a graph of some of this data. On the whole, these findings contradict waiters' and waitresses' claims that the elderly tip them poorly, but it appears that less commonly tipped service providers can truthfully make that claim.

Age Effects on Tip Size. The data is less consistent about age differences in the size of tips when tips are given, but a number of studies have found that older consumers report tipping smaller amounts—to waiters/waitresses, baristas, bartenders, haircutters, hotel maids, and/or pizza delivery drivers—than do younger consumers (e.g., Conlin et al., 2003; Lynn, 2009, 2015a; Lynn & Katz, 2013; Schwer & Daneshvary, 2000). This negative relationship

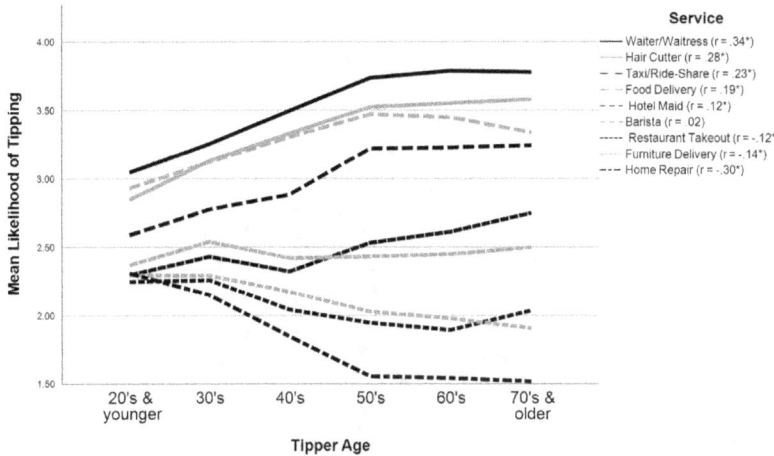

Fig. 3.1 Older consumers are more likely to tip commonly tipped workers but less likely to tip rarely tipped workers [*This previously unpublished data comes from two surveys of over 5000 respondents in the U.S. conducted by YouGov for Creditcards.com in 2022 and 2023. Likelihood of tipping was measured: never = 1, only sometimes = 2, most of the time = 3, always = 4. Correlations with asterisks are larger than would be expected by chance*]

is also supported by a large unpublished dataset of credit card transactions from a large restaurant chain that permitted me to test age effects on actual tip size (see Fig. 3.2). Although negative, the relationship in this data (and in most other studies) is very weak. Tips declined by only 1/10th of a percent of bill size for every additional 10 years the tipper had lived and this relationship explained less than one percent of the variance in percent tip. Thus, the data simply do not support many servers' claims that the elderly are generally bad tippers. To be sure, some elderly tip poorly, but so do some members of other groups.

Age Effects on Tipping Knowledge and Motivation. What underlies the age differences in tipping noted above? It is hard to say for sure, but age differences in awareness of tipping norms and in tipping attitudes and motives may play a role. Research on this is limited, but unpublished analyses of one of my studies suggests that awareness of tipping norms/expectations generally increases with consumer age—though this is more true for some services than for others (see Fig. 3.3). In addition, two of my published studies indicate that older consumers like tipping a little more than do younger consumers, have slightly stronger intrinsic (altruistic and reciprocity) motivations for tipping, have slightly weaker extrinsic (future-service and social-esteem) motives for tipping, and have similar duty motives for tipping

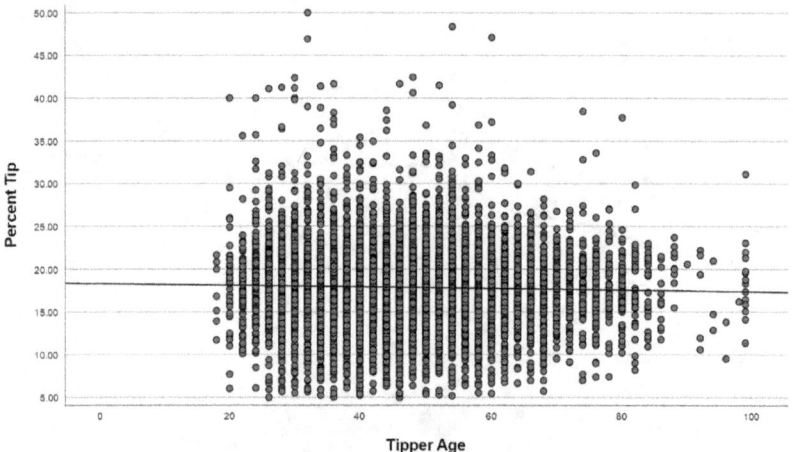

Fig. 3.2 Older restaurant customers tip slightly smaller percentages of their bill amounts than do younger customers [*The data, provided to me by a point-of-sale technology company called Gazelle in 2001, are over 18,000 anonymized charge sales records from the top customers of a large, Italian restaurant chain along with demographic information about those anonymous customers. Only tips between 5 and 50% were included in this analysis. Multiple transactions by the same customer were averaged to get one observation per customer*]

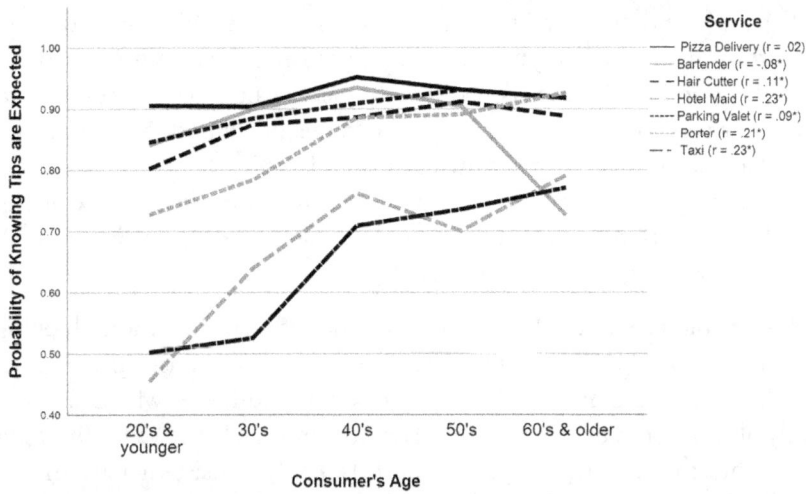

Fig. 3.3 Older restaurant customers are more likely than younger ones to be aware of tipping norms/expectations, though the effect varies in size across service contexts [*The data are from a sample of 831 Zoomerang panel members as described in Lynn (2009, 2011). Correlations with asterisks are larger than would be expected by chance*]

(Lynn, 2009, 2021a). These age differences in attitudes, beliefs, and motivations are likely to be at least partially responsible for observed age differences in tipping.

Sex

Restaurant servers also tend to consider men better tippers than women (McCall & Lynn, 2009). Evidence on this point is decidedly mixed, with some studies finding that men tip more frequently or larger amounts than do women (Chandar et al., 2019; Jahan, 2018; Lynn, 2009), other studies finding the opposite (Boyes et al., 2004; Cho, 2014; Lynn, 2023), and still others finding no sex differences in tipping (Ayres et al., 2004; Jewell, 2008; Lynn, 2021a, 2021b). Again, it is helpful to consider the effects of tipper sex on tipping likelihood and on tip size separately.

Sex Effects on Tipping Likelihood. Published research on sex differences in tipping likelihood shows all three patterns of effects described above—sometimes men tip more often than women, sometimes women tip more often, and sometimes they tip with similar frequencies or likelihoods. Recent unpublished surveys by YouGov have also found all three of these effect patterns—with different effects being observed for different service providers (see Fig. 3.3). In those surveys, men reported (i) a greater likelihood of tipping furniture/appliance deliverymen and home repairers than did women, (ii) a lower likelihood of tipping hairdressers/barbers, waiters/waitresses, and food delivery drivers, and (iii) essentially the same likelihood of tipping hotel maids, baristas, restaurant takeout, and taxi/ride-share drivers. However, note that when they exist, the sex differences tend to be small. The sex of tipper typically accounts for 1 percent or less of the variance (or differences) in tipping reported by different individuals.

Sex Effects on Tip Size. The picture is a little different for studies looking at sex differences in tip size; most of those studies find no statistically significant sex differences and there is no consistency across studies in which sex is even slightly ahead of the other (c.f., Brewster & Lynn, 2014; Jewell, 2008; Lynn, 2021a; Shrestha, 2014). However, one reasonably consistent pattern in the literature is that observed sex differences in tip size depend on the sex of the service provider. Not surprisingly, tips involving opposite-sex tippers and tippees tend to be higher than tips involving same-sex tippers and tippees (Conlin et al., 2003; Gourlay & Brewster, 2023; Lynn & McCall, 2000; Lynn et al., 2016). Thus, sex differences in tip size do exist, but neither sex appears to consistently tip more than the other.

A particularly notable exception to the some of the conclusions described above is an unpublished study of charge tips given to Uber drivers that involved over 40 million trips (Chandar et al., 2019). This study found that male riders were more likely than female riders to tip and tipped larger amounts when they did tip. Overall, men tipped about 17% more than did women in this context. Furthermore, male riders tipped drivers of both sexes more than did female riders. The huge sample size and use of actual (not just self-reported) tip amounts in this study mean that we can conclude with high confidence that male Uber riders are generally better tippers than female Uber riders even though other studies do not find a similar sex difference in tipping outside this context (see Fig. 3.4).

Sex Differences in Tip Knowledge and Motivation. What underlies the sex differences in tipping noted above? Research on this is limited, but unpublished analyses of one of my studies (see Lynn, 2011) found that women are less likely than men to be aware that tipping taxicab drivers is expected ($r = -0.07$, $n = 802$, $p < 0.04$) and more likely to be aware that tipping hairdressers/barbers is expected ($r = 0.09$, $n = 818$, $p < 0.02$). This might explain the sex differences in tipping of Uber drivers and haircutters noted above. Another of my studies found that women have slightly stronger intrinsic (altruistic and reciprocity) and duty motivations for tipping, but slightly

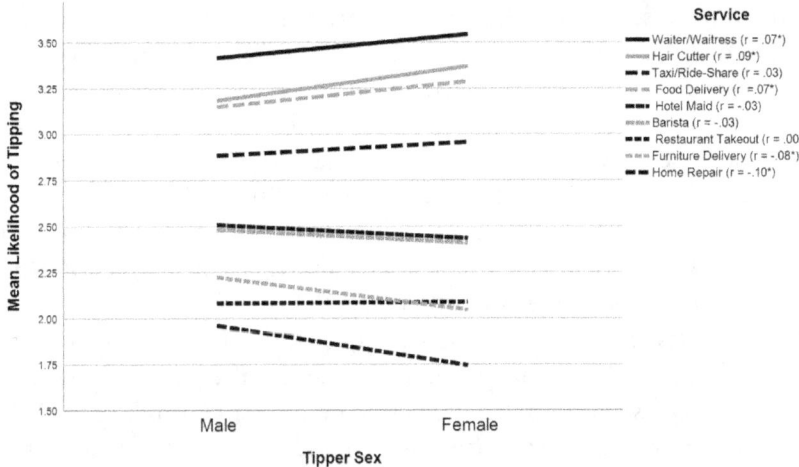

Fig. 3.4 Men are more likely than women to tip some service providers, less likely to tip other service providers, and equally likely to tip still others [*This previously unpublished data comes from two survey of over 5000 respondents in the U.S. conducted by YouGov for Creditcards.com in 2022 and 2023. Likelihood of tipping was measured: never = 1, only sometimes = 2, most of the time = 3, always = 4. Correlations with asterisks are larger than would be expected by chance*]

weaker extrinsic (future-service and social-esteem) motives for tipping (Lynn, 2021a). Research indicates that the motivations for tipping vary across service contexts/providers (Lynn, 2021b), so perhaps sex differences in tipping motivations help explain why women are more likely to tip some service providers and less likely to tip other service providers than are men.

Race/Ethnicity

Talking about racial/ethnic differences in tipping risks being labeled as prejudiced, but the issue is too important to ignore. Many restaurant servers perceive Blacks and Hispanics to be poor tippers (McCall & Lynn, 2009) and this perception colors the service they provide to those groups (Brewster, 2015). How to best address the resulting service discrimination depends in part on the validity of servers' perceptions about racial/ethnic differences in tipping. If those perceptions are invalid, then servers need to be educated about the reality of racial/ethnic differences in tipping. If those perceptions are valid, then ethnic minority consumers may need to be educated about tipping norms and expectations (Lynn & Brewster, 2015). Accordingly, I venture into politically fraught territory and review the evidence about race and ethnic differences in tipping below.

Perhaps because it is so politically fraught, relatively few people other than myself and my collaborators have examined race and ethnic differences in tipping. Nevertheless, I have collected enough evidence to conclude that, on average, Blacks and Hispanics do tip less than Whites in restaurants as well as in some other service settings (Lynn & Thomas-Haysbert, 2003; Lynn, 2004, 2006a, 2006b, 2013, 2014; Lynn & Brewster, 2015). However, Hispanic-White differences in tipping are typically smaller and less consistently found than Black-White differences (see Fig. 3.5 and Lynn, 2014), so subsequent discussion will focus on the later differences.

Blacks are less likely than Whites to tip many commonly tipped service providers, but more likely than Whites to tip some infrequently tipped service providers and these race differences persist even after controlling for income and other demographic factors (see Fig. 3.5 and Lynn, 2004). Blacks are also less likely than Whites to be aware of mainstream tipping norms and expectations and this helps explain at least part of the observed differences in tipping likelihood (Lynn, 2011).

In restaurants, Blacks are more likely than Whites to (i) stiff (not tip) servers, (ii) tip a flat dollar amount rather than a percentage of the bill, and

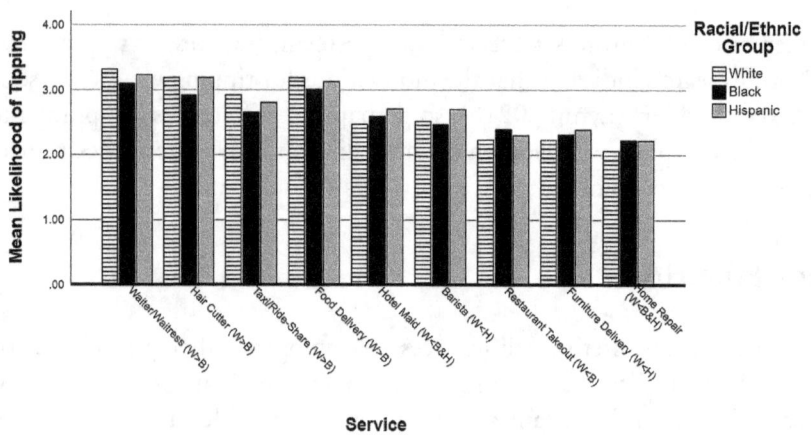

Covariates appearing in the model are evaluated at the following values: What is your age? = 42.65

Fig. 3.5 Blacks and Hispanics tip some service providers less often and others more often than do Whites [*This previously unpublished data comes from surveys of over 5000 total respondents in the U.S. conducted by YouGov for Creditcards.com in 2022 and 2023. Likelihood of tipping was measured as: never = 1, only sometimes = 2, most of the time = 3, always = 4. Differences from Whites that are larger than expected by chance (at 0.05 level) are noted in parentheses. These data and analyses statistically control for the tipper's age, sex, and income*]

(iii) leave below average tip amounts (Lynn, 2006a, 2006b; Lynn & Brewster, 2015; Lynn & Thomas-Haysbert, 2003). Black-White differences in stiffing and flat tipping, but not in tip size, decrease with consumer socio-economic status (Lynn et al., 2012a, 2012b). That is NOT to say that these differences are caused by race differences in socio-economic status—only that they are smaller among high SES consumers than among lower SES consumers. Black-White differences in restaurant tip sizes average about 3 percent of the bill size and persist even when the server is Black and when the quality of service is comparable for both Whites and Blacks (Brewster & Nowak, 2019; Lynn, 2006a, 2006b). They are, however, diminished in size by about one-half after controlling for (eliminating race differences in) perceptions of the restaurant tipping norm, so restaurateurs should consider educating and reminding their customers about that norm (Lynn & Brewster, 2015).

In acknowledging the reality of Black-White differences in restaurant tipping, it is important to note two things. First, the differences between racial groups are dwarfed by differences within each group (see Fig. 3.6), so race is not a reliable indicator of how a particular patron will tip. Second, servers who react to Black-White differences in tipping by giving their Black customers less service effort, or fewer non-verbal displays of friendliness and liking, can only increase the likelihood of getting the poor tip they are expecting. Animosity and service discrimination against Black customers are not only unjustified but also likely to backfire and reduce tip income.

Religion

Jesus Christ commanded his followers to "Love your neighbor as yourself" (Mark 12:31). Since helping is a manifestation of love, you can be forgiven for assuming that the followers of Christ are particularly generous tippers. Surprisingly, restaurant servers have the opposite impression; many of them perceive Christians to be poor tippers (Lynn, 2015b). It turns out that neither position is accurate. My studies (many unpublished) have found few differences in the tips of Christians and non-Christians (c.f., Lynn & Katz, 2013; Lynn, 2015a, 2021a). I believe that the few differences that I have found are chance effects—what scientists call Type 1 errors—but even if they are real and Christians do tip slightly less often or slightly smaller amounts that non-Christians, it would not justify categorizing Christians as poor tippers. The majority of Americans (64% according to the Pew Center, 2022) are Christians, so they are the average American and it would make more sense to describe non-Christians as particularly good tippers than to describe Christians as unusually bad tippers.

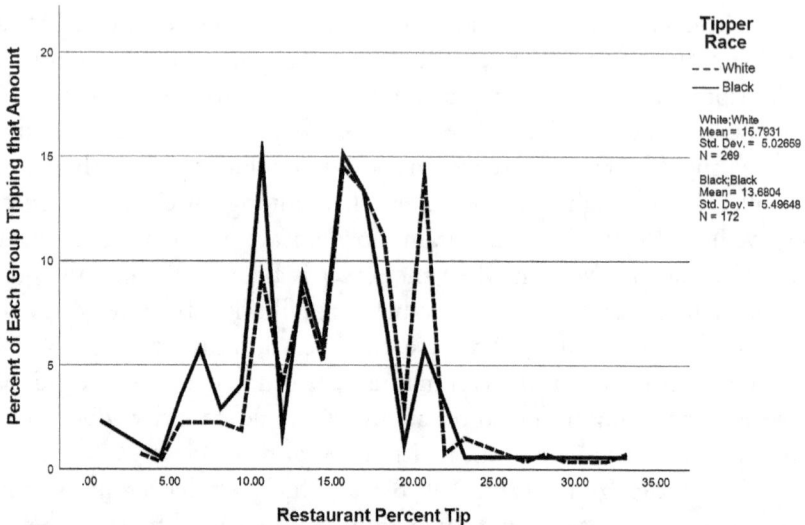

Fig. 3.6 Black-White differences in restaurant tipping are small compared to individual differences within each racial group [*Previously unpublished graph of data analyzed and reported in* Lynn & Brewster, 2015]

Thus, religion is yet another case where server's perceptions of good and bad tippers are not really supported by the data. Where do such misperceptions come from? I do not think there is one answer to this question. The origins of servers' mistaken beliefs about good and bad tippers probably differs with the particular group involved and I am not sure what all of those origins might be. However, the idea that Christians are bad tippers may come from the Sunday after church lunch crowd.

There is good evidence that restaurant tips are lower on Sundays than other days of the week (Maynard & Mupandawana, 2009) and that this effect is larger at lunch than at other times and in more religious counties (Ali et al., 2024). Thus, it appears that the Sunday after church lunch crowd really are poor tippers. The problem is that servers misattribute this group's tipping to their religion even though that group does not represent all Christians or all restaurant dining situations. The Sunday after church crowd's poor tipping could have nothing to do with their religion. For example, it could be that poor families with kids reserve their dining-out for Sundays after church, so the low tips observed at this time could stem from the economic and family status of this particular crowd rather than its faith. Simply put, it is more accurate to say that Sunday lunch diners are poor tippers than to say that Christians are.

Income

The overwhelming majority of findings indicate that both tipping likelihood and tip amounts increase with tipper income across a variety of service contexts (c.f., Conlisk, 2022; Jahan et al., 2023; Lynn, 2009, 2023; Thomas-Haysbert, 2002). This income effect on tipping may be attributable to income effects on the perceived costs or sacrifice of tipping and on awareness of tipping norms. Unreported analyses of one of my studies (Lynn, 2011) indicates that high-income consumers are less sensitive to the costs of restaurant dining ($r = -0.14$, $n = 804$, $p < 0.001$) and more aware that people are generally expected to tip service providers such as bartenders, haircutters, hotel maids, porters, parking valets, pizza delivery drivers, and taxi drivers (all r's > 0.12 and < 0.18, all p's < 0.001) than are low-income consumers. Another study indicated that awareness of the 15–20% restaurant tipping norm also increases with income (Lynn, 2006a, 2006b).

Nationality

Although many of servers' perceptions of who are good and bad tippers appear to be incorrect, their often-expressed belief that foreigners tend to tip poorly is supported by the available data. Research in both Canada and the United States has found that foreigners tip less in restaurants than do native born residents of those countries (Fong, 2005; Jahan, 2018; Shrestha, 2014). One study also found that foreigners were less familiar with U.S tipping norms and that those foreigners who were aware of U.S. norms tended to tip amounts closer to those left by native born Americans (Shrestha, 2014). Thus, managers in destinations frequented by foreign tourist should consider posting notices about U.S. tipping customs on menus, checks, signs, or other communications as a way of boosting their employees' tips.

Tipping Propensities of Different Behavioral-Trait Groups

Among those groups of customers that many servers include on lists of good tippers are smokers, regular customers, and current or former servers (Harris, 1995; McCall & Lynn, 2009; Waiter, 2022). Let's examine the accuracy of these perceptions next.

Smokers

Are server's perceptions of smoking and non-smoking tippers accurate? Should workers volunteer to work in smoking sections of establishments and risk the hazards of second-hand smoke in the hopes of taking in larger tips? The evidence suggests not—studies in the U.S. (Bryant & Smith, 1995; Jewell, 2008; Sánchez, 2002) and in other countries (Künzli et al., 2003; Kvasnička & Szalaiová, 2015) have failed to find significant differences in the bill-adjusted tip amounts left by smokers and non-smokers.

Work Experience

What about servers' perceptions of their current and former colleagues? I am aware of no studies comparing the tipping of current tipped workers with that of others, but several published and unpublished studies have compared the tips of those with and without past food-service, hospitality, or tipped work experience. While many of these studies have failed to find significant differences in the tipping of these two groups (c.f., Cho, 2014; Lynn & Brewster, 2015; Mok & Hansen, 1999; Parrett, 2006), others have found that people with experience working for tips are more likely to tip at least some service providers (see Fig. 3.7) and that they tip waiters and waitresses larger amounts than do those without such experience (Lynn et al., 2012a, 2012b; Lynn, 2021a). However, even when the effects are found, they tend to be small. For example, Lynn (2021a) found that those with experience working for tips said they would tip a waitress only about 29 cents more on a $15.73 bill (only about 1.8% of the bill more) than did those who had never worked for tips. That difference was trivial compared to the differences between individual tippers within each group (see Fig. 3.8).

Regular Patrons

Finally, what about regular customers? Do familiar faces leave bigger tips than unfamiliar faces? For restaurant servers, the answer is yes. Though some studies have failed to find an effect (Boyes et al., 2004; Lynn, 2003; Parrett, 2006), many others have found that frequent patrons of a restaurant do tip better than infrequent patrons (Brewster & Lynn, 2014; Conlin et al., 2003; Lynn et al., 2008; Lynn & McCall, 2000; Sánchez, 2002). Similar effects were observed for tipping of Uber drivers—tips to drivers increased with the number of times the passenger and driver encountered one another (Chandar

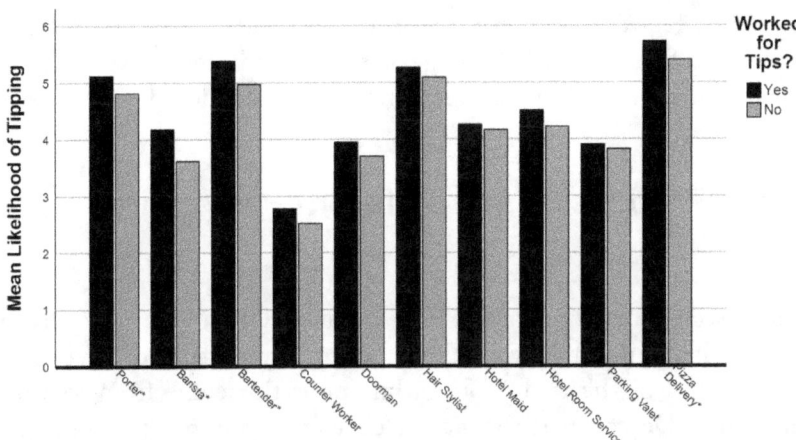

Fig. 3.7 People with experience working for tips are more likely than those without such experience to tip some (but not all) service providers [*This is unreported analysis of a data set described and analyzed in* Lynn (2021a). *Likelihood of tipping was measured as: very unlikely = 1, unlikely = 2, somewhat unlikely = 3, somewhat likely = 4, likely = 5, very likely = 6. Differences between the two groups that are larger than expected by chance (at 0.05 level) are noted with an asterisk*]

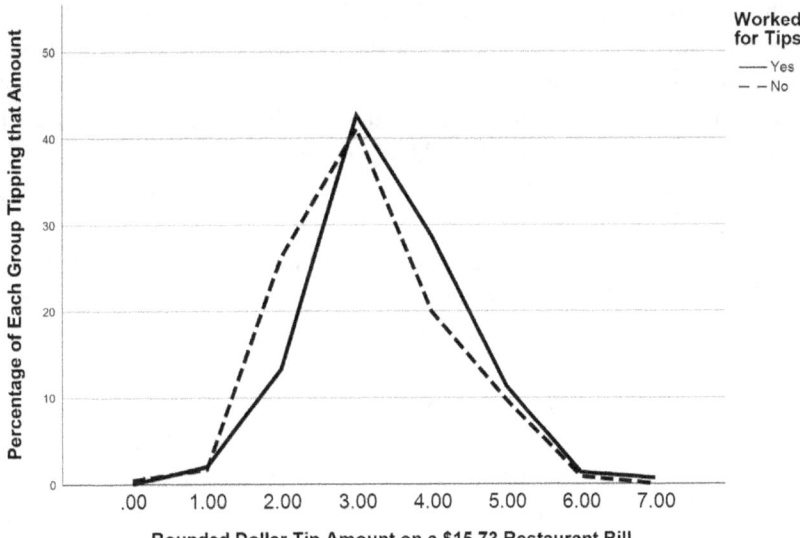

Fig. 3.8 Frequency distributions of dollar and cent tip amounts (on a $15.73 restaurant bill) are similar for those with and without experience working for tips—with a difference in means of only 29 cents [*This is a previously unreported analysis of a data set described and analyzed in* Lynn (2021a)]

et al., 2019). However, care must be taken not to over generalize these findings, because Square's (2014) charge sales data indicate that regular coffee shop patrons tip about 20 percent less (not more) than do infrequent patrons.

Tipping Propensities of Different Personality Types

We have seen that demographic and behavioral traits are generally poor predictors of tipping, but what about personality traits? Do big tips come from kind and big-hearted people while poor tips come from selfish and miserly ones? Do other personality or character traits predict tipping? The answers to these questions cannot really help servers identify those expected to give a good tip, because psychological traits are not visible or easily inferred like demographic and behavioral traits. Nevertheless, those answers are important.

Servers along with many other people have a tendency to assume that good tippers are good people while bad tippers are bad people. Servers may use such attributions to justify to themselves the poor service they give to known or suspected bad tippers. Other people may base hiring or other relationship decisions on the tipping behavior of their prospective employee, friend, or spouse—as the actress Kaley Cuoco did when she dumped a famous boyfriend for being a bad tipper (Abrahamson, 2018; Young, 2018). Such people would benefit from knowing how much tipping really reflects the soul or character of the tipper.

Again, the scientist in me yearns for more data on this point, but the data we already have makes it pretty clear that tipping is not a good measure of someone's personality or character. Some studies have found that extraverts and those high in agreeableness and conscientiousness tip more than do their counterparts, but these effects are not always observed and are very weak even when present (Cho, 2014; Lynn, 2008, 2021a; Lynn et al., 2012a, 2012b). One of the stronger relationships found between tipping and personality is depicted in Fig. 3.9 and, as you can plainly see, both high and low extraversion scores can be seen at every level of tipping. Tip amounts convey very little information about the tippers' personality.

I have found slightly stronger correlations between character strengths and average likelihood of tipping various service workers in some unpublished research examining these relationships. People who more strongly rate kindness, social intelligence, fairness, forgiveness, and gratitude as describing themselves report a greater average likelihood of tipping bartenders, taxi

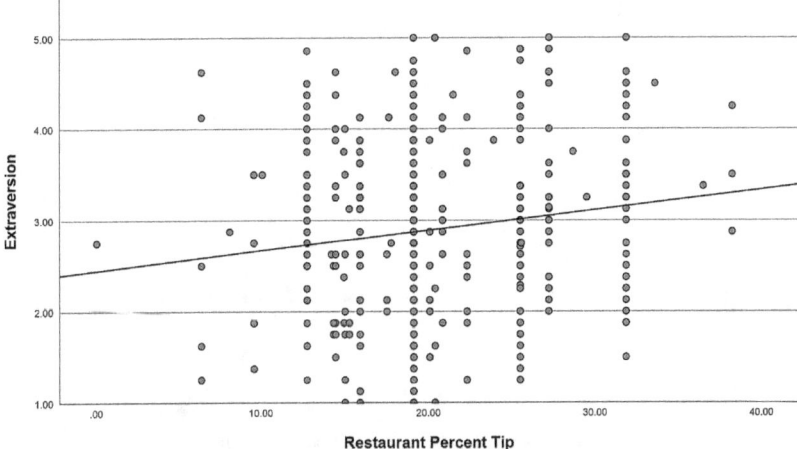

Fig. 3.9 The more people tip the more extraverted they are likely to be, but the relationship is too weak to provide a good indication of the tipper's level of extraversion [*Graph of the extraversion-tipping relationship reported in* Lynn (2021a). *Each dot represents one or more survey respondents having the depicted extraversion score and reported tipping intention*]

drivers, parking valets, hotel bellmen, hotel doormen, motel maids, pizza delivery drivers, and restaurant waiters ($0.11 <$ all r's < 0.26, n's ≈ 407, p's < 0.02). However, even these character strengths predict tipping likelihood too weakly to provide a good indication of the tipper's character. Figure 3.10 depicts the strongest observed relationship, which was with fairness. Note that both high and low fairness scores can be seen at every level of tipping.

The relatively weak effects of personality and character traits on tipping behavior may surprise some readers, but it actually makes sense when you consider the multi-faceted nature of tipping and tipping motivations. Greater altruistic motivations may lead kind people to tip more than unkind ones; greater reward motivations may lead fair-minded people to tip more than those who are less fair-minded; greater future-service motives may lead extraverts (who like social attention) to tip more than introverts; greater social approval motives may lead agreeable people to tip more than disagreeable ones; and greater duty motivations may lead conscientious people to tip more than unconscientious ones. However, each of these relationships should be weak because a dispositional deficit in one tipping motivation may be made up for by a surfeit in another and vice versa. Furthermore, circumstances may increase or decrease tipping motivations and behaviors even more strongly than do dispositions. For example, knowing that many restaurant servers make only $2.13 an hour in wages may make even the most hard-hearted feel a need to help servers with a generous tip. Conversely, being pressured by an

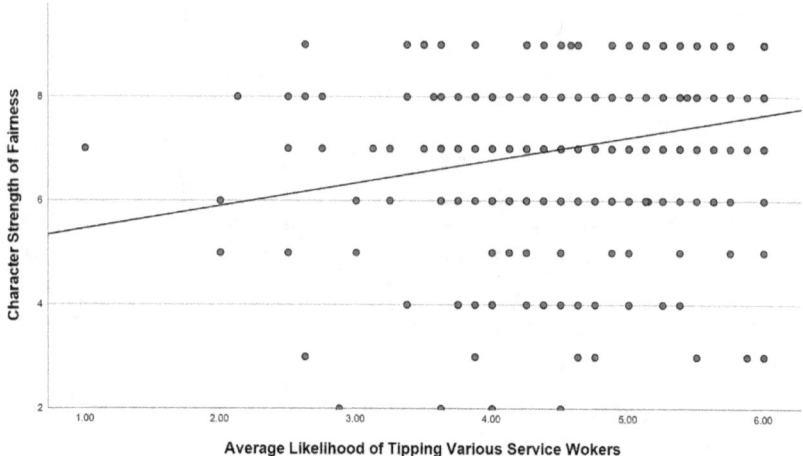

Fig. 3.10 The more likely people are to tip various traditionally tipped workers, the more they claim fairness as a character strength, but the relationship is too weak to provide a good indication of the tipper's level of fairness [*Data are from an unpublished study I did in 2014. The correlation between variables is 0.25, n = 407, p < 0.001. Each dot represents one or more survey respondents having the depicted combination of fairness score and average reported likelihood of tipping*]

employee and/or digital screen to tip 20 or 30% may prompt even the kindest and most fair-minded to reconsider their initial inclinations to tip generously. Given the diversity of tipping motives and circumstances, it is simply not reasonable to expect differences in personality (or other stable individual differences for that matter) to explain substantial variance in tipping behavior.

Summary Thoughts

Many (but not all) of servers' beliefs about who are good and bad tippers have some basis in reality. However, demographic, behavioral-trait, and personality differences in tipping are small. Tipping varies far more across individuals within groups than it does between groups, so group membership says very little about how much a particular customer will tip. Punishing with poor service an individual customer for his or her group's tendency to tip less than other groups is unfair to that customer. Moreover, it can only be expected to lower the customer's tip from whatever it might have been had service been better. Thus, service workers should avoid discriminating in service to those groups thought to be bad tippers. Managers of tipped workers should use the facts in this chapter to educate their employees and dissuade them from engaging in such discriminatory service. Customers should refrain from using their group membership to justify leaving small tips—even if your sex, age, race, income, or other group does tip less than the general population, that does not give you license to join them. Finally, no one should judge another person's character on the basis of their tipping behavior alone.

Notes

1. Based on my unpublished analyses of 2019 and 2023 survey data collected by YouGov for Creditcards.com.

References

Abrahamson, R. P. (2018, April 3). Kelly Cuoco dumped a famous actor because he was a bad tipper: "I was horrified". https://www.usmagazine.com. Accessed March 2, 2024.

Ali, F., Olson, C. C., Pantzalis, C., Park, J. C., Robinson, D., & Wang, P. (2024). *Why are tipping rates lower on weekends?* Unpublished manuscript, University of South Florida.

Ayres, I., Vars, F. E., & Zakariya, N. (2004). To insure prejudice: Racial disparities in taxicab tipping. *Yale LJ, 114*, 1613.

Bitchy Waiter. (2022, July 21). Servers say these are the 5 best tippers. Are you one of them? https://brokeassstuart.com. Accessed February 20, 2024.

Bott, F. M., Kellen, D., & Klauer, K. C. (2021). Normative accounts of illusory correlations. *Psychological Review, 128*(5), 856.

Boyes, W. J., Stewart Mounts, Jr., W., & Sowell, C. (2004). Restaurant tipping: free-riding, social acceptance, and gender differences. *Journal of Applied Social Psychology, 34*(12), 2616–2625.

Brewster, Z. W. (2015). Perceptions of intergroup tipping differences, discriminatory service, and tip earnings among restaurant servers. *International Journal of Hospitality Management, 46*, 15–25.

Brewster, Z. W., & Gourlay, K. (2021). The "Mask Effect" on the tips that customers leave restaurant servers. *International Journal of Hospitality Management, 99*, Article 103068.

Brewster, Z. W., & Lynn, M. (2014). Black-White earnings gap among restaurant servers: A replication, extension, and exploration of consumer racial discrimination in tipping. *Sociological Inquiry, 84*(4), 545–569.

Brewster, Z. W., & Nowak, G. R., III. (2019). Racial prejudices, racialized workplaces, and restaurant servers' hyperbolic perceptions of black–white tipping differences. *Cornell Hospitality Quarterly, 60*(2), 159–173.

Bryant, P. G., & Smith, M. (1995). *Practical data analysis: Case studies in business statistics*. Richard D. Irwin Publishing.

Chandar, B., Gneezy, U., List, J. A., & Muir, I. (2019). *The drivers of social preferences: Evidence from a nationwide tipping field experiment* (No. w26380). National Bureau of Economic Research.

Cho, S. B. (2014). Factors affecting restaurant consumers' tipping behavior. *Journal of the Korean Society for Quality Management, 42*(1), 15–32.

Conlin, M., Lynn, M., & O'Donoghue, T. (2003). The norm of restaurant tipping. *Journal of Economic Behavior & Organization, 52*(3), 297–321.

Conlisk, S. (2022). Tipping in crises: Evidence from Chicago taxi passengers during COVID-19. *Journal of Economic Psychology, 89*, Article 102475.

Fong, S. F. (2005). *The socio-economic motives underlying tipping behaviour*. Masters thesis, University of Saskatchewan.

Gourlay, K., & Brewster, Z. W. (2023). Seeing red: Color effects on restaurant tipping may not be as significant as thought. *Journal of Foodservice Business Research*, 1–18.

Harris, M. B. (1995). Waiters, customers, and service: Some tips about tipping. *Journal of Applied Social Psychology, 25*(8), 725–744.

Jahan, N. (2018). *Determinants of Tipping Behavior: Evidence from US Restaurants*. Electronic Theses and Dissertations. 26–33. https://openprarie.sdstate.edu/etd/2633.

Jahan, N., Leschewski, A., & Davis, D. E. (2020). Restaurant tipping discrimination: Evidence from a representative sample of US households. *Journal of Agricultural & Food Industrial Organization, 21*(2), 117–127.

Jahan, N., Leschewski, A., & Davis, D. E. (2023). Restaurant tipping discrimination: Evidence from a representative sample of US households. *Journal of Agricultural & Food Industrial Organization, 21*(2), 117–127.

Jewell, C. N. (2008). Factors influencing tipping behavior in a restaurant. *Psi Chi Journal of Undergraduate Research, 13*(1).

Künzli, N., Mazzoletti, P., Adam, M., Götschi, T., Mathys, P., Monn, C., & Brändli, O. (2003). Smoke-free cafe in an unregulated European city: Highly welcomed and economically successful. *Tobacco Control, 12*(3), 282–288.

Kvasnička, M., & Szalaiová, M. (2015). Determinants of gratuity size in the Czech Republic: Evidence from four inexpensive restaurants in Brno. *Review of Economic Perspectives, 15*(2), 121–135.

Lynn, M., & McCall, M. (2000*). Beyond gratitude and gratuity: A meta-analytic review of the predictors of restaurant tipping*. Unpublished manuscript, Cornell University.

Lynn, M. (2023b). How did the Covid-19 pandemic affect restaurant tipping? *Journal of Foodservice Business Research*, 1–20.

Lynn, M. (2003). Restaurant tips and service quality: A weak relationship or just weak measurement. *International Journal of Hospitality Management, 22*(3), 321–325. https://doi.10.1016/S0278-4319(03)00048-3

Lynn, M. (2004). Black-white differences in tipping of various service providers. *Journal of Applied Social Psychology, 34*(11), 2261–2271.

Lynn, M. (2006a). Geodemographic differences in knowledge about the restaurant tipping norm. *Journal of Applied Social Psychology, 36*(3), 740–750.

Lynn, M. (2006b). Race differences in restaurant tipping: A literature review and discussion of practical implications. *Journal of Foodservice Business Research, 9*(4), 99–113.

Lynn, M. (2008). Personality effects on tipping attitudes, self-reported behaviors and customs: A multi-level inquiry. *Personality and Individual Differences, 44*(4), 989–999. https://doi.10.1016/j.paid.2007.10.025

Lynn, M., Sturman, M., Ganley, C., Adams, E., Douglas, M., & McNeil, J. (2008). Consumer racial discrimination in tipping: A replication and extension. *Journal of Applied Social Psychology, 38*(4), 1045–1060. https://doi.10.1111/jasp.2008.38.issue-4 10.1111/j.1559-1816.2008.00338.x

Lynn, M. (2009). Individual differences in self-attributed motives for tipping: Antecedents, consequences, and implications. *International Journal of Hospitality Management, 28*(3), 432–438.

Lynn, M. (2011). Race differences in tipping: Testing the role of norm familiarity. *Cornell Hospitality Quarterly, 52*(1), 73–80.

Lynn, M. (2013). A comparison of Asians', Hispanics', and Whites' restaurant tipping. *Journal of Applied Social Psychology, 43*(4), 834–839.

Lynn, M. (2014). The contribution of norm familiarity to race differences in tipping: A replication and extension. *Journal of Hospitality & Tourism Research, 38*(3), 414–425.

Lynn, M. (2015a). Explanations of service gratuities and tipping: Evidence from individual differences in tipping motivations and tendencies. *Journal of Behavioral and Experimental Economics, 55*, 65–71.

Lynn, M. (2015b). Negative perceptions of Christian tippers: How widespread are they? *Journal of Foodservice Business Research, 18*(2), 163–170.

Lynn, M. (2021a). Effects of the Big Five personality traits on tipping attitudes, motives, and behaviors. *International Journal of Hospitality Management, 92*, Article 102722.

Lynn, M. (2021b). The effects of occupational characteristics on the motives underlying tipping of different occupations. *Journal of Behavioral and Experimental Economics, 95*, Article 101783.

Lynn, M., & Brewster, Z. W. (2015). Racial and ethnic differences in tipping: The role of perceived descriptive and injunctive tipping norms. *Cornell Hospitality Quarterly, 56*(1), 68–79.

Lynn, M., Giebelhausen, M., Garcia, S., Li, Y., & Patumanon, I. (2016). Clothing color and tipping: An attempted replication and extension. *Journal of Hospitality & Tourism Research, 40*(4), 516–524.

Lynn, M., Jabbour, P., & Kim, W. G. (2012a). Who uses tips as a reward for service and when? An examination of potential moderators of the service–tipping relationship. *Journal of Economic Psychology, 33*(1), 90–103.

Lynn, M., & Katz, B. (2013). Are Christian/religious people poor tippers? *Journal of Applied Social Psychology, 43*(5), 928–935.

Lynn, M., Pugh, C. C., & Williams, J. (2012b). Black–white differences in tipping: The moderating effects of socioeconomic status. *Cornell Hospitality Quarterly, 53*(4), 286–294.

Lynn, M., & Thomas-Haysbert, C. (2003). Ethnic differences in tipping: Evidence, explanations, and implications. *Journal of Applied Social Psychology, 33*(8), 1747–1772.

Maynard, L. J., & Mupandawana, M. (2009). Tipping behavior in Canadian restaurants. *International Journal of Hospitality Management, 28*(4), 597–603.

McCall, M., & Lynn, A. (2009). Restaurant servers' perceptions of customer tipping intentions. *International Journal of Hospitality Management, 28*(4), 594–596.

Mok, C., & Hansen, S. (1999). A study of factors affecting tip size in restaurants. *Journal of Restaurant & Foodservice Marketing, 3*(3–4), 49–64.

Parrett, M. (2006). An analysis of the determinants of tipping behavior: A laboratory experiment and evidence from restaurant tipping. *Southern Economic Journal, 73*(2), 489–514.

Pew Center. (2022, September 13). Modeling the future of religion in America. https://www.pewresearch.org. Accessed February 19, 2024.

Sánchez, A. (2002). The effect of alcohol consumption and patronage frequency on restaurant tipping. *Journal of Foodservice Business Research, 5*(3), 19–36.

Schwer, K. R., & Daneshvary, R. (2000). Tipping participation and expenditures in beauty salons. *Applied Economics, 32*(15), 2023–2031.

Shrestha, J. (2014). *Tipping differences of domestic and foreign customers in casual dining restaurants: An investigation of customers' and servers' perception.* Oklahoma State University.

Square. (2014, October 19). Which customers tip the most? https://squareup.com. Accessed February 21, 2024.

Thomas-Haysbert, C. D. (2002). The effects of race, education, and income on tipping behavior. *Journal of Foodservice Business Research, 5*(2), 47–60. https://doi.10.1300/J369v05n02_04

Van Dessel, P., Ratliff, K., Brannon, S. M., Gawronski, B., & De Houwer, J. (2021). Illusory-correlation effects on implicit and explicit evaluation. *Personality and Social Psychology Bulletin, 47*(10), 1480–1494.

Young, D. (2018, August 2). Intentionally bad tippers are trash people you should never trust, and there are no exceptions to this rule. https://www.theroot.com. Accessed March 2, 2024.

4

A Time for Tipping (When Do People Tip More? … or Less?)

Ecclesiastes 3:1 tells us that "There is a time for everything and a season for every activity under Heaven." The obvious time for tipping is after services have been delivered. It is that timing that separates tips from bribes, which are paid upfront in order to get service. The after-service timing of tips facilitates their use as a reward for a job well done, a form of insurance against mistreatment by service workers, and a way to display generosity and wealth.

While most tips are given after service, recent growth in online payments for delivery services and of digital screens asking for tips in retail settings have led many businesses to start asking for pre-service tips in these contexts. However, they may want to reconsider that practice because customers find such pre-service tip requests to be manipulative and unfair (Park et al., 2024; Warren et al., 2021). Furthermore, consumers leave smaller tips and report lower word-of-mouth and return intentions (as well as lower online ratings) when tip requests come before rather than after service has been delivered (Warren et al., 2021). At the very least, businesses intent on asking for pre-service tips need to come up with ways to mitigate these negative effects. There is some evidence that providing a reason to tip is helpful in this regard (Fan et al., 2025), but much more thought and research needs to be devoted to this issue before pre-service tip requests can be regarded as safe for businesses.

Aside from the effects of pre-service vs post-service tip requests, are there other temporal effects on tipping? Do people tip more at some times— such as hours of the day, days of the week, or months of the year—than others? The answers to these questions might help service workers forecast their earning potential for any given time period and, thus, allow them to better exercise any influence they have over their work hours. The answers might also allow managers to more equitably assign workers to workdays and shifts and to know when servers are likely to reduce their service efforts in response to lower expected tips. Finally, the answers may help consumers to anticipate workers' tip expectations for a given time period as well as help consumers assess the level of the workers' tip compensation from other customers (hence, need for more) during that time period. Given these potential benefits, we examine temporal effects on tipping in this chapter. We start with time-of-day effects, move on to consider day-of-week effects, then monthly/seasonal effects, and end with holiday effects.

Time-of-Day Effects

Our planet spins on its axis in a roughly 24 hour period creating daily cycles of light and dark, so we have evolved corresponding Circadian rhythms in bodily processes and behaviors. For example, physiological arousal increases at a marginally decreasing rate from early morning until late afternoon and then starts to decline (Wilson, 1990). In addition, we experience increasing functional connectivity between regions of our brains as our waking day unfolds (Orban et al., 2020). Accompanying (and perhaps resulting from) these physiological and neurological effects are effects on our decision making, moods, and behaviors. For example, our sensitivity to losses declines, while our moods and variety-seeking behavior increase, as the day progresses from morning to early evening (Bedder et al., 2023; Gullo et al., 2019).

It is easy to imagine that at least some of these time-of-day effects might impact consumers' tipping. For example, increased moods and reduced sensitivity to losses may both lead people to give larger tips later in the day. However, any such effects could be counteracted by other situational factors that also vary from morning to night. For example, restaurant bill sizes tend to be larger at dinner than at breakfast or lunch and this could depress tip percentages in the evenings. Furthermore, time-of-day affects service providers' moods and energy levels as well as those of consumers, so it might affect service levels, which would further complicate potential time-of-day effects on tipping. Ultimately, what effects (if any) time-of-day has on tipping is an empirical issue to be settled by research. Such research is scant, but a few studies of these effects on tipping in restaurant and taxicab settings do exist and their findings are briefly described below.

Restaurant Tips

The best data about time-of-day effects on restaurant tipping that I know of come from a study involving three years of credit card transactions at 1202 restaurants operating in 41 states. That study found higher tip percentages at breakfast and late-night than at other times—tip percentages were about 2/3rds of a point higher at breakfast and over 2 points higher at late-night than at lunch or dinner (Ali et al., 2023). These time-of-day effects were observed after controlling for bill size, group size, restaurant busyness, and meal duration, which suggests that they are not due to differences in these factors across the different dayparts. Perhaps they compensate for the extremity of the work-hour itself, but this idea needs to be tested to know for sure.

My own unpublished analyses of data (given to me by Upserve) on credit card transactions at nine California restaurants for the entire year of 2013 found similar time-of-day effects on restaurant tip percentages—they were slightly higher at early morning and late-night hours than at other times.[1] However, the hour-of-day effects differed across different restaurants (see Fig. 4.1), so there is no universally optimal hour for getting large restaurant tip percentages. Furthermore, dollar tips tend to be larger at dinner and smaller at breakfast than at lunch (because of differences in bill size), so high tip percentage dayparts are not necessarily the most lucrative dayparts for servers to work.[2]

Taxicab Tips

NYC taxicab data indicates that taxicab riders give more generous tips during morning and afternoon (6 a.m.–6 p.m.) hours, less generous tips during the evening (6 p.m.–12 a.m.), and the least generous tips in the very early morning (12–6 a.m.) (Hu and Du, 2024). These differences in percent tip are statistically reliable but of relatively small size—with just a little over 1% point separating the highest and lowest tipped hours (Kozikowski, 2014). Other factors such as demand for and supply of cabs seem likely to have even

---

[1] Hour-of-day was recoded into dummies for breakfast (6–11), lunch (12–16), dinner (17–21), and late-night (22–24). A regression of percent tips on restaurant, breakfast, dinner, and late-night dummies produced a significant positive coefficient for breakfast ($B = 0.37$, SE = 0.05, $p < 0.001$) and late-night ($B = 0.38$, SE = 0.10, $p < 0.001$), but not dinner ($B = 0.03$, SE = 0.03, n.s.).

[2] A regression of dollar tips on restaurant, breakfast, dinner, and late-night dummies produced a significant negative coefficient for breakfast ($B = -0.49$, SE = 0.06, $p < 0.001$) and a positive coefficient for dinner ($B = 3.56$, SE = 0.07, $p < 0.001$) and for late-night ($B = 0.73$, SE = 0.10, $p < 0.001$).

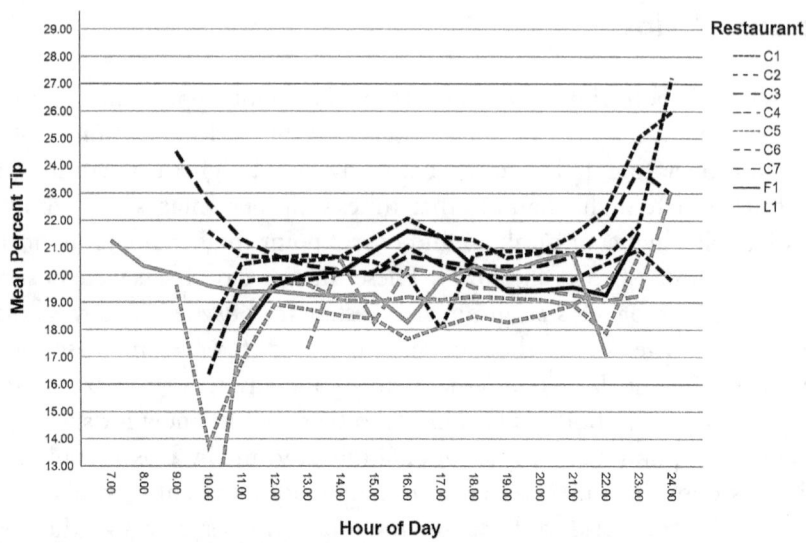

Fig. 4.1 Average percentage tip amounts in nine California restaurants by hour of day. *Note* C1–C7 are casual-dining restaurants; F1 is a fine-dining restaurant; L1 is a limited-service restaurant. Source of Data: Upserve

larger effects on dollar tip income, so time-of-day effects on tip percentages should probably not dominate taxi drivers' decisions about when to work.

Day-of-Week Effects

Modern life is built around a seven-day week, with most people working Monday through Friday and pursuing more leisure activities on the weekend. For example, people visit more business, finance, government, and health-related websites during weekdays and more food and drink, entertainment, gambling, and lifestyle-related websites on weekends (Bussiere, 2016). They also drink more alcohol (Liang & Chikritzhs, 2015), dine-out away from home more (Hiemstra & Kim, 1995), and have larger restaurant dining party and bill sizes (Ali et al., 2024b) on weekends than on weekdays. As a result, people may have a more utilitarian mindset on weekdays and a more hedonic mindset on weekends (Bussiere, 2011), which may help explain why they generally report being in better moods on the weekends (Tsai, 2019).

It is possible that better moods and less utilitarian thinking decrease cost-consciousness and, thus, increase average tip percentages on weekends. On the other hand, increased recreational activities on weekends may mean that a larger proportion of those customers are non-regulars, and more hedonic mindsets may mean that weekend customers run up larger service bill sizes, and these factors may decrease average tip percentages on weekends. The countervailing nature of these potential effects makes it difficult to generate strong, a-priori expectations about day-of-week differences in tipping. Fortunately, modern point-of-sales systems provide data that can resolve the uncertainty.

Restaurant Tips

The data on credit card transactions at 1202 restaurants from across the U.S. that produced the time-of-day effects described above was also used to test for day-of-week effects. That analysis found that percentage tips tend be about half a point lower, on weekends than on weekdays (Ali et al., 2025). The analysis controlled for bill size, group size, restaurant busyness, meal duration, and other factors, so the effect is not attributable to day-of-week effects on these aspects of the dining experience. Here too, I was able to replicate the effect using the Upserve data described previously.[3] However, the day-of-week effects varied across restaurants (see Fig. 4.2), so there is no universally optimal day of the week for getting large tip percentages.

The weekend effect on tip percentages say little about the overall desirability of working various day-of-week shifts, because in restaurants (and perhaps elsewhere) they are offset by larger numbers of customers as well as larger bill sizes and dollar and cent tip amounts on weekends (Ali et al., 2024b; Hiemstra & Kim, 1995). In the Upserve data described above, for example, servers got about \$1.25 more in tips per dining party on weekends than on weekdays.[4] Nevertheless, lower weekend tip percentages may be large enough to affect workers' tip expectations and attitudes toward customers. We saw something like this in Chap. 3, where we discussed the fact that many restaurant servers perceive Christians as poor tippers—probably because they misattribute lower than typical tip percentages on Sundays to this religious group. There is some evidence that servers give better service when they expect better tips (Barkan & Israeli, 2004; Brewster, 2013, 2015;

---

[3] Percent tips were regressed on restaurant dummies, business day-of-week (DOW), and residual DOW squared (w/linear effects of DOW partialed out). The analysis produced a negative linear DOW effect ($B = -0.02$, $SE = 0.004$, $p < 0.001$) and a negative quadratic DOW effect ($B = -0.05$, $SE = 0.003$, $p < 0.001$). In other analyses, Friday, Saturday, and Sunday were coded as weekends and the other days as weekdays. A regression of percent tips on restaurant and weekend dummies produced a significant negative coefficient for weekend ($B = -0.34$, $SE = 0.02$, $p < 0.001$).

[4] A regression of dollar and cent tip amounts on restaurant and weekend dummies produced a significant positive coefficient for weekend ($B = 1.29$, $SE = 0.04$, $p < 0.001$).

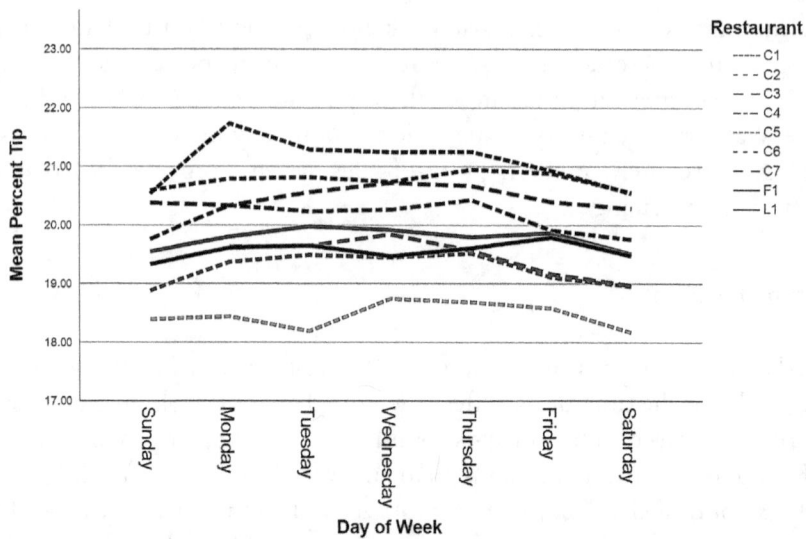

Fig. 4.2 Average percentage tip amounts in nine California restaurants by day of week. *Note* C1–C7 are casual-dining restaurants; F2 is a fine-dining restaurant; L1 is a limited-service restaurant. Source of data: Upserve

Lynn, 2017), so it is plausible that servers may reduce their service levels when working on days of the week associated with lower tip percentages. Managers may want to take extra steps to prevent that from happening by monitoring service levels more closely on weekends.

Taxi Tips

Like restaurant tips, NYC taxicab tip percentages are higher during the week than they are during the weekend (Devaraj & Patel, 2017; Elliott et al., 2017; Hu and Du, 2024; Kozikowski, 2014). Whether this effect is due to weekday taxi trips being more likely than weekend trips to be covered by business expenses, to weekday passengers being more frequent taxi riders (and therefore more familiar with taxi tipping norms) than are weekend passengers, or to some other causal process is unclear. However, the effects are small with less than half a percentage point difference in average tip between the best- and worst-tipped day of week.

Seasonal Effects

The earth circles the sun every 365.24 days resulting in seasonal variation in sunlight, temperature, and other meteorological conditions. These seasons have been shown to affect our moods, aggressiveness, sexual activity, food consumption, and pro-social behavior among other things (Hohm et al., 2024). Thus, it is possible that they also affect our tipping behavior.

However, as with time-of-day and day-of-week effects, the potential impacts on tipping are too numerous and conflicting to make strong a-priori predictions. Accordingly, we have to look to data to tell us what those effects are.

Effect on Tipping Likelihood

Daily point-of-sale data on tipping likelihood and tip size for several different types of services (provided to me by the payment company Square) are graphed by month in Fig. 4.3.[5] The share of tippable transactions with a tip tended to be slightly lower in the winter months—though only the effects for beauty salons and full-service restaurants were statistically reliable (meaning, unlikely to be due to chance).[6] The negative winter effects in bars, beauty salons, and full-service restaurants were equally strong in northern and southern states. Since seasonal differences in meteorological conditions are greater in northern states than in southern ones, this latter finding suggests that the causal processes underlying the seasonal effects on tipping are independent of meteorological conditions.[7] However, the winter effect in quick-service restaurants was stronger in more northern latitudes,

---

[5] Square provided me daily, state-level data from 2019 on the share of tippable transactions with a tip and the average tip percentage when a tip was left for each of several different types of business.

[6] Share of tipped transactions was regressed on month and residual month squared (w/linear effects of month partialed out) for each of the businesses displayed in Fig. 4.3. Error terms were clustered within state. The coefficients for the linear trends in month were not significant and those for quadratic trends in month were as follows—for bar/club/lounge ($B_{quadratic} = -0.01$, SE = 0.01, n.s.), for beauty salons ($B_{quadratic} = -0.03$, SE = 0.01, $p < 0.05$), for FSR ($B_{quadratic} = -0.03$, SE = 0.01, $p < 0.008$), and for QSR ($B_{quadratic} = -0.003$, SE = 0.01, n.s.). In other analyses, December thru February were coded as winter months and share of tippable transactions was regressed on a dummy variable for winter. Again, error terms were clustered within state. The coefficients for winter were as follows—for bar/club/lounge ($B = -0.42$, SE = 0.29, n.s.), for beauty salons ($B = -0.53$, SE = 0.25, $p < 0.05$), for FSR ($B = -0.36$, SE = 0.18, $p < 0.06$), and for QSR ($B = -0.06$, SE = 0.12, n.s.).

[7] I regressed share of tippable transactions on latitude, winter, and their product (using errors clustered with state) and found the following coefficients for the product or interaction term—for bar/club/lounge ($B = 0.003$, SE = 0.11, n.s.), for beauty salons ($B = -0.04$, SE = 0.08, n.s.), for FSR ($B = 0.01$, SE = 0.05, n.s.), and for QSR ($B = -0.06$, SE = 0.02, $p < 0.006$).

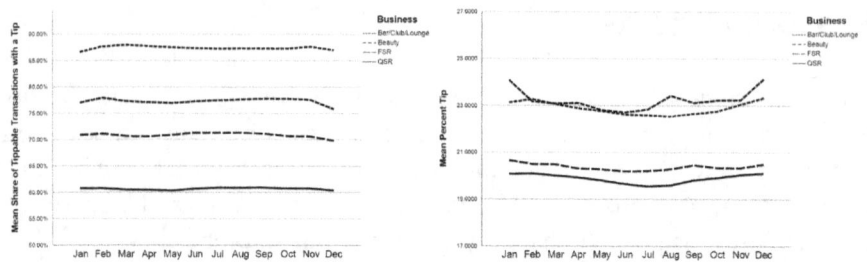

Fig. 4.3 Tipping likelihood goes down and tip size goes up during winter months. Source of Data: Square

so it may be attributable to seasonal variations in meteorological conditions. Generating and testing other explanations for these effects is something I leave for future researchers.

Effect on Tip Size

Interestingly, the average tip percentage (when a tip was left) showed a monthly pattern opposite to that for tipping likelihood—with slightly larger tip percentages in the winter months.[8] This pattern of monthly effects was reliable (unlikely to be due to chance) for bars/clubs/lounges, beauty salons, full-service restaurants, and quick-service restaurants and it replicates a similar pattern of monthly effects on taxicab tip percentages reported by Kozikowski (2014). Again, many of the effects—those involving bars, beauty salons, and full-service restaurants—were equally strong in northern and southern states, which suggests that they are not attributable to seasonal variations in meteorological conditions.[9]

---

[8] Percent tipped was regressed on month and residual month squared (w/linear effects of month partialed out) for each of the businesses displayed in Fig. 4.3. Error terms were clustered within state. The coefficients for the linear trends in month were not significant and those for quadratic trends in month were as follows—for bar/club/lounge ($B_{quadratic} = 0.02$, SE = 0.003, $p < 0.001$), for beauty salons ($B_{quadratic} = 0.03$, SE = 0.005, $p < 0.001$), for FSR ($B_{quadratic} = 0.01$, SE = 0.002, $p < 0.001$), and for QSR ($B_{quadratic} = 0.02$, SE = 0.001, $p < 0.001$). In other analyses, December thru February were coded as winter months and percent tip was regressed on a dummy variable for winter. Again, error terms were clustered within state. The coefficients for winter were as follows—for bar/club/lounge ($B = 0.47$, SE = 0.07, $p < 0.001$), for beauty salons ($B = 0.76$, SE = 0.11, $p < 0.001$), for FSR ($B = 0.23$, SE = 0.06, $p < 0.001$), and for QSR ($B = 0.29$, SE = 0.02, $p < 0.0001$).

[9] I regressed percent tip on latitude, winter, and their product (using errors clustered with state). These analyses produced the following coefficients for the product or interaction term—for bar/club/lounge ($B = -0.01$, SE = 0.01, n.s.), for beauty salons ($B = 0.02$, SE = 0.02, n.s.), for FSR ($B = 0.01$, SE = 0.01, n.s.), and for QSR ($B = 0.01$, SE = 0.003, $p < 0.004$).

The seasonal effect on tip percentages conceptually replicates other research finding that charitable giving is greater in December and January than other months (Ekström, 2018). Ekström (2018) attributed his seasonal effect on charitable giving to a spirit of altruism that grows as Christmas Day approaches and then fades as that date recedes into the past. If correct, that could also explain the winter effect on tip percentages across various service contexts, but I find it unlikely that Christmas has such long-lasting effects on behavior. In my opinion, other explanations need to be identified and tested.

Holiday Effects

As shown in Fig. 4.3, seasonal effects on tipping tend to be small, but what about the effects of specific days such as holidays? Holidays are typically times of celebration and fun that are communally shared. Might an elevated mood or sense of social connectedness during holidays (aka, holiday spirits) increase tips substantially on these days?

The first published study to address this question examined tipping at a college-town restaurant and found that tips were about three percentage points higher in the two weeks surrounding Christmas than at other times (Greenberg, 2014). This is an interesting finding, which I will call the Christmas effect, but its generalizability is questionable. College students typically go home during Christmas break, so Greenberg's Christmas effect may have had more to do with a shifting customer base than with a holiday or Christmas spirit effect on individual tippers.

Fortunately, a more recently published analysis of the large, national, multi-restaurant, point-of-sale dataset described previously provides some evidence for the generalizability of Greenberg's (2014) Christmas effect. It found that restaurant tips are larger at Christmas and other religious and family-oriented holidays (such as Easter, Thanksgiving, and Mother's Day) than at other times (Ali et al., 2024a). However, the Christmas bump in this study was only about one percentage point, which was much smaller than that reported by Greenberg, and the other holiday effects were even smaller (around half a percentage point). Interestingly, this study found that tips were lower than normal on more secular and less family-oriented holidays (such as New Year's Day, Memorial Day, Labor Day, and St. Patrick's Day). Although these holiday effects seem to be too small to have many practical implications, they are interesting and may help shed light on the psychological processes underlying tipping.

The authors argue that religious and family-oriented holidays (but not other holidays) increase tips because the family gatherings on these holidays evoke feelings of empathy, belonging, and togetherness, which foster pro-social behavior. They speculate that the negative effects of other holidays on tipping may reflect heightened cost-consciousness given the extra celebratory spending on those days. Testing these speculations, as well as the generalizability of the various holiday effects to other service contexts, would be a worthwhile pursuit for future research.

Conclusions

In summary, tippers do appear to leave more and/or larger tip percentages at some times than at others, but these temporal differences tend to be modest in size and to vary across service industries and even across businesses within industries. The modest size of temporal effects on tip percentages means that the most lucrative shifts for tipped workers are often defined more by how many customers there are and how large those customers' bills are than by how large their tip percentages are. Tipped employees (and their managers) should keep this in mind when requesting (or scheduling) work shifts. However, this seems obvious and many readers may be frustrated that more novel practical insights failed to emerge from this chapter on temporal differences in tipping. I know that this paucity of practical insights frustrated me when writing the chapter. The only consolation I have to offer readers (and myself) is that we needed to check to be sure we were not overlooking something important. Having checked, we now know to focus our attention elsewhere in the pursuit of practically useful insights about tipping. So, read on—I promise that the remaining chapters of this book will prove to be more fruitful.

References

Ali, F., Olson, C. C., Pantzalis, C., Park, J. C., Robinson, D. & Wang, P. (2025). Why are Tipping Rates Lower on Weekends? *International Journal of Contemporary Hospitality Management.* Unpublished manuscript, University of South Florida. https://doi.org/10.1108/IJCHM-05-2024-0691

Ali, F., Olson, C. C., Pantzalis, C., Park, J. C., & Park, J. C. (2024a). Holiday effects on tipping rates in full-service restaurants. *International Journal of Hospitality Management, 122,* Article 103826.

Ali, F., Olson, C. C., Pantzalis, C., Park, J. C. & Robinson, D. & Wang, P. (2024b). Why are Tipping Rates Lower on Weekends? Unpublished manuscript, University of South Florida.

Ali, F., Olson, C. C., Pantzalis, C., Park, J. C., & Park, J. C. (2023). Large sample evidence on tipping rates in the restaurant industry: A comprehensive study. *International Journal of Hospitality Management, 111*, 103458.

Barkan, R., & Israeli, A. (2004). Testing servers' roles as experts and managers of tipping behaviour. *The Service Industries Journal, 24*(6), 91–108.

Bedder, R. L., Vaghi, M. M., Dolan, R. J., & Rutledge, R. B. (2023). Risk taking for potential losses but not gains increases with time of day. *Scientific Reports, 13*(1), 5534.

Brewster, Z. W. (2013). The effects of restaurant servers' perceptions of customers' tipping behaviors on service discrimination. *International Journal of Hospitality Management, 32*, 228–236.

Brewster, Z. W. (2015). Perceptions of intergroup tipping differences, discriminatory service, and tip earnings among restaurant servers. *International Journal of Hospitality Management, 46*, 15–25.

Bussière, D. (2016). Understanding of the day of the week effect in online consumer behaviour. In *Proceedings International Marketing Trends, presented at the International Marketing Trends*. Available at: www.marketing-trends-congress.com/archives/2016/pages/PDF/BUSSIERE.pdf. Accessed 12 June 2017.

Bussière, D. (2011). The day of the week effect in consumer behavior: Analyzing utilitarian and hedonistic consumer modes. *Journal of Promotion Management, 17*(4), 418–425.

Devaraj, S., & Patel, P. C. (2017). Taxicab Tipping and Sunlight. *Plos One, 12*(6), e0179193.

Ekström, M. (2018). Seasonal altruism: How Christmas shapes unsolicited charitable giving. *Journal of Economic Behavior & Organization, 153*, 177–193.

Elliott, D., Tomasini, M., Oliveira, M., & Menezes, R. (2017, Aug). Tippers and stiffers: An analysis of tipping behavior in taxi trips. In *2017 IEEE SmartWorld, Ubiquitous Intelligence & Computing, Advanced & Trusted Computed, Scalable Computing & Communications, Cloud & Big Data Computing, Internet of People and Smart City Innovation (SmartWorld/SCALCOM/UIC/ATC/CBDCom/IOP/SCI)* (pp. 1–8). IEEE.

Fan, A., Wu, L., Ma, C., & Wang, P. (2025). The manipulative effects in the technology-facilitated preservice tipping experience. *Cornell Hospitality Quarterly, 66*(1), 56–70.

Greenberg, A. E. (2014). On the complementarity of prosocial norms: The case of restaurant tipping during the holidays. *Journal of Economic Behavior & Organization, 97*, 103–112.

Gullo, K., Berger, J., Etkin, J., & Bollinger, B. (2019). Does time of day affect variety-seeking? *Journal of Consumer Research, 46*(1), 20–35.

Hiemstra, S. J., & Kim, W. G. (1995). Factors affecting expenditures for food away from home in commercial establishments by type of eating place and meal occasion. *Hospitality Research Journal, 19*(3), 15–31.

Hohm, I., Wormley, A. S., Schaller, M., & Varnum, M. E. (2024). Homo temporus: Seasonal cycles as a fundamental source of variation in human psychology. *Perspectives on Psychological Science, 19*(1), 151–172.

Hu, Y., & Du, R. Y. (2024). *Passenger group size and tipping: an empirical study of 50 million NYC yellow taxi rides.* Available at SSRN 4705908.

Kozikowski, D. (2014). *Analysis of NYC taxi tip data: 44% of passengers hit the 20% button.* https://tumblr.com/dfkoz/106719206826/analysis-of-nyc-taxi-tip-data-44-of-passengers. Accessed 16 May 2024.

Liang, W., & Chikritzhs, T. (2015). Weekly and daily cycle of alcohol use among the US general population. *Injury, 46*(5), 898–901.

Lynn, M. (2017). Should US restaurants abandon tipping? A review of the issues and evidence. *Psychosociological Issues in Human Resource Management, 5*(1), 120–159.

Orban, C., Kong, R., Li, J., Chee, M. W., & Yeo, B. T. (2020). Time of day is associated with paradoxical reductions in global signal fluctuation and functional connectivity. *PLoS Biology, 18*(2), e3000602.

Park, S., Kim, H., Kim, S. and Gim, J. (2024). Tipping dilemma in restaurant's age of automation: Exploring the role of social obligations, explicit requests, and their timing. *International Journal of Hospitality and Tourism Administration,* 1–22.

Tsai, M. C. (2019). The good, the bad, and the ordinary: The day-of-the-week effect on mood across the globe. *Journal of Happiness Studies, 20*(7), 2101–2124.

Warren, N., Hanson, S., & Yuan, H. (2021). Feeling manipulated: How tip request sequence impacts customers and service providers? *Journal of Service Research, 24*(1), 66–83.

Wilson, G. D. (1990). Personality, time of day and arousal. *Personality and Individual Differences, 11*(2), 153–168.

5

A Place for Tipping (How and Why Does Tipping Vary Across Geographic Areas?)

The old adage that "geography is destiny" almost certainly goes too far, but geography does matter in human affairs. Research in geographical psychology has found that the residents of different urban/rural, state, regional, and national areas share behavioral tendencies, personality traits, and outlooks on life that differ from those of other areas (Rentfrow, 2020). Some of this spatial clustering of psychological traits is due to selective migration with different environments attracting different types of people, some of it is due to social influence with different cultures, histories, and other population characteristics affecting the residents of different areas, and some is due to ecological influence with different climates and landscapes affecting the residents of different areas.

To invoke a theatrical metaphor, geography is stage. Previous chapters have mentioned some of the ways that this stage influences tipping. For example, we have seen that restaurant tips are higher in states with lower minimum wages for tipped workers and that the number of customarily tipped occupations is smaller in more egalitarian countries. This chapter provides a broader examination of such geographical differences in tipping. It begins with urban/rural differences, moves on to state differences, and ends with national differences.

Urban/Rural Differences

Rural areas are often thought to be populated by poorer, less educated, White, Christian, and conservative people with a community orientation while urban areas are thought to contain wealthier, more educated, more racially and religiously diverse, and more liberal populations with an individualistic orientation (c.f., RuralFinds, 2023). While data indicates that these urban/rural differences are smaller than commonly believed (c.f., Parker et al., 2018), there is some truth to many of these stereotypes. How do these real urban/rural differences affect tipping?

Research suggests that urban consumers are more generous tippers in many (but not all) respects than are rural consumers. For example, restaurant tips are bigger in larger metropolitan areas than in smaller metropolitan areas and larger there than in non-metropolitan or rural areas (McCrohan & Pearl, 1991; Sienkiewiez, 2016). In addition, the residents of metropolitan areas are more likely than those of non-metro areas to tip bartenders, haircutters, taxi/limo drivers, food-deliverers, porters, and masseuses (see Table 5.1). These small to moderate differences are found even after controlling for the tippers' educations and incomes, so they are not completely explained by the greater wealth and education in larger urban areas. Nor does awareness of tipping norms appear to explain the difference in urban and rural tipping, because awareness of the restaurant tipping norm is comparable across these groups of consumers once education, income and other variables are controlled for (Lynn, 2006). Unfortunately, it is unclear what other differentiating characteristics (i.e., attitudes, values, life-styles, etc.…) help explain them. Whatever those responsible characteristics are, they do not appear to affect the sizes of tips given to service workers outside of restaurants, because observed urban/rural differences in non-zero tip sizes to such service workers tend to be small and could easily be due to chance (see Table 5.1 again). A similar pattern of urban/rural differences in tipping likelihood but not in tip size has been documented in Slovenia too (Raspor & Divjak, 2017), so it is not just a U.S. phenomenon. Hopefully, future research will be undertaken to explain why those patterns exist.

State Differences

The popular media often reports on state differences in tipping (c.f., Conlisk, 2023; Michaels & Kiersz, 2018; Rawson et al., 2024; Risen, 2016). Typically, these reports describe the average likelihood of tipping and/or the average

Table 5.1 People in metropolitan areas are more likely to say they would leave a tip for many service providers, but their claimed tip sizes are significantly larger only for waiters/waitresses

Service	Percentage of people leaving a tip (for good service)		Average tip size (when left)	
	Metro area (%)	Non-metro area (%)	Metro area	Non-metro area
Waiter/waitress	99*	96	16.6%*	15.5%
Bartender	82*	71	$1.57[a]	$1.52[a]
Barber/stylist	85*	71	$3.73	$3.30
Taxi/limo driver	85*	76	$6.94	$6.71
Food-delivery	89*	81	$2.72	$2.60
Hotel maid	72	70	$6.94[b]	$6.71[b]
Skycap/bellhop	92*	85	$3.36[c]	$3.46[c]
Masseuse	68*	59		
Usher	23	22		

Data from a national telephone survey conducted by TNS Intersearch in 2000 or 2001—see Lynn (2004) for details; probabilities and means control for respondent's age, sex, education, income, and region of country
*Metro versus Non-Metro difference is larger than would be expected by chance ($p < 0.01$)
[a]for 1 drink
[b]for 2 night stay
[c]for 2 bags

tip size in each state in an effort to identify where people are more and less generous. Although some of this data is indeed meaningful, it cannot all be taken at face value for reasons that vary with the source and nature of the data.

Cautions About Public Media Reports of State Differences in Tipping

Some public media reports about state differences in tipping are based on consumer surveys of general tipping habits (e.g., Rawson et al., 2024). Such surveys are subject to biases in memory as well as self-presentational concerns. In addition, they sometimes ask about tipping without specifying the service context. Since different people may have different contexts in mind when answering the question and since tipping varies across service contexts, this could bias state differences in self-reported tipping. Finally, surveys typically ask people what percentage of the bill they tip. However, many people tip flat amounts rather than a percentage of the bill, so the percentage responses of those flat-tippers are of questionable validity and this too could bias state differences in average self-reported tipping percentages. These considerations mean that state differences in self-reported tipping habits may reflect real differences in tipping behaviors, differences in self-presentational concerns, differences in question meaningfulness/validity, or some combination of these things.

Most public media reports of state differences in tipping are based on point-of-sale records from transactions involving digital or credit card payments. These data reflect real tipping behaviors and, thus, avoid the self-presentational and question meaningfulness problems with survey data. However, they have another set of problems that undermine interpretation of the state differences they reveal. First, the companies (like Square or Toast) that provide the data often calculate state averages across their many different clients. Tipping differs across businesses, so the state differences reported could reflect differences across states in the composition of the point-of-sale companies' client bases rather than differences across states in tipping for the same services. This problem is mitigated to some degree by reporting of tipping behavior by specific categories of businesses, such as full-service restaurants, quick-service restaurants, coffee shops, and beauty salons. At least state differences in clients' broad business categories do not contaminate such state tipping averages. However, the composition of clients within these categories still varies across states and can bias the reported state differences in tipping.

A second problem with point-of-sale records as sources of data about state differences in tipping is that they typically average across all the transactions of the clients. For example, the dine-in, carryout, and delivery transactions are usually all included in the average tip size for full-service restaurants. Tipping likelihood and tip sizes can both vary across different types of transactions, so the state differences derived from point-of-sale data could reflect differences across states in the proportions of different types of transactions as well as differences across states in tipping for the same types of transactions. This issue seems particularly problematic in the restaurant industry where off-premise dining has become a much larger proportion of transactions since the COVID-19 pandemic.

A final problem with point-of-sale records as sources of data about state differences in tipping is that only credit card, or other digitally paid, tips are recorded. Many people paying the bill with credit or other digital means nevertheless tip in cash. This is problematic because those customers appear as non-tippers in point-of-sale data. State differences in the share or proportion of charge customers leaving a charge tip could reflect state differences in stiffing (or not tipping), state differences in the proportion of charge customers leaving a cash tip, or some combination of the two. Of course, this biases not only state differences in tipping likelihood but also state differences in average tip size when those averages include tips of zero. State differences in average non-zero charge tips are not affected by this problem, so they should be the preferred measures of state tipping generosity. However, even this preferred measure has potential problems because it excludes a group of people—charge customers who tip in cash—whose prevalence may differ across states and whose tips may differ from those of charge customers who tip with credit.

These problems with interpreting various measures of state differences in tipping should cause consumers of public media to be skeptical of claimed state differences in tipping. However, those claims do often contain some meaningful information. To extract that meaning, we can average measures with different biases in the hope that the biases at least partially cancel one another out, so that the index provides a more valid indication of state differences in tipping generosity than do its individual component measures.[1] We can also try to obtain raw data that minimizes the above biases by providing state averages in tipping for similar transactions and services. Such a relatively bias-free measure could not only tell us what those specific state differences are, but could be compared with other measures of state differences in tipping to get an idea of how biased or valid those other measures are as well.

With regard to the later point, the best measure of state differences in tipping that I am aware of comes from records provided to me by NCR Corporation of credit card transactions during April 2013 at 4 large, multi-state, full-service restaurant brands. The point-of-sale data avoids problems with self-presentation and question meaningfulness that plague survey data. The use of only 4 restaurant brands whose state tip averages were highly correlated with one another minimizes problems with the comparability of businesses underlying those averages. The 2013 data come from a time when off-premise dining was much rarer than it is today and most full-service restaurant transactions were for dine-in service, so biases from mixing different types of transactions are also minimized. Finally, less than one-tenth of one percent of the transactions involved charge tips of zero, so problems stemming from cash tipping on credit transactions are also minimized. This data set is not completely free of bias, but using it can give us a pretty good picture of state differences in tipping for similar full-service restaurant transactions and services in 2013. It can also be used to gauge how biased other,

---

[1] When different measures have different biases (or uncorrelated errors), then some state tip averages are under-estimated by one measure and over-estimated by another, so the average of the measures comes closer to the true value than do either of the separate measures alone.

and more recent, state tip averages are likely to be. Specifically, the more those other measures are correlated with the NCR measures, the less systematic bias they are likely to contain.

Which States Are the Best and Worst Tippers?

So, what does the NCR data tell us about actual state differences in tipping and about the accuracy and/or meaning of public media portrayals of those differences? Using this data, Table 5.2 presents the average across the four full-service restaurant chains of the median, charge tip percentage by state as well as the proportions of tips that were normative, sub-normative, and super-normative.[2] The data indicate that state differences in tipping do exist. However, with only about 3 percentage points separating the two states with the smallest and largest median tip percentages, those differences are only small to moderate in size.

Figure 5.1 shows the relationship between the 2013 NCR measure of state differences in tipping and four other measures of those differences from public media—(i) one based on charge restaurant tips in 2015 from the point-of-sale system by Lavu (reported by Wells, 2016), (ii) a second based on self-reported generic tip percentages from a 2018 survey commissioned by TSheets, a time-tracking software company now called QuickBooks (reported by TSheets.com, 2018), (iii) a third based on charge restaurant tips in 2023 from the point-of-sale system by Toast (reported in Toast's Q2, Q3 and Q4 2023 Restaurant Trends Reports), and (iv) a final measure averaging the previous three. All four measures were more positively related to the NCR measure than would be expected by chance alone, so all appear to reflect some true and stable differences in states' restaurant tipping percentages. The index averaging the other measures was the most strongly correlated with the NCR measure as would be expected since some of the errors in the individual measures should cancel one another out when the measures are averaged together (see Footnote 1). However, none of the individual measures by themselves shared more than half of their variance with the NCR measure, so those publicly reported state differences appear to be more misleading than valid indicators of tipping generosity.

---

[2] To avoid bias from extreme cases, only observations with both a bill size between $5 and $500 and a tip amount between $0.01 and $500 were used to calculate these proportions.

Table 5.2 Best (in my opinion) measures of state differences in tipping currently available for public use

	Median tip %	Proportion of normative tips (≥ 15% and ≤ 20%)	Proportion of sub-normative tips (< 15%)	Proportion of super-normative tips (> 20%)
Alabama	17.96	0.40	0.28	0.32
Alaska	na.	na.	na.	na.
Arizona	18.43	0.43	0.25	0.33
Arkansas	17.84	0.38	0.30	0.31
California	16.93	0.42	0.34	0.25
Colorado	18.91	0.43	0.21	0.36
Connecticut	18.87	0.45	0.20	0.35
Delaware	19.47	0.43	0.16	0.41
Florida	18.73	0.43	0.22	0.35
Georgia	18.50	0.41	0.25	0.34
Hawaii	17.93	0.46	0.26	0.28
Idaho	18.02	0.39	0.29	0.32
Illinois	18.60	0.46	0.21	0.33
Indiana	18.33	0.41	0.26	0.33
Iowa	17.63	0.40	0.30	0.29
Kansas	18.17	0.42	0.26	0.32
Kentucky	18.51	0.41	0.25	0.35
Louisiana	18.05	0.41	0.27	0.32
Maine	19.33	0.41	0.18	0.42
Maryland	19.13	0.43	0.19	0.38
Massachusetts	19.39	0.44	0.16	0.40
Michigan	18.90	0.44	0.21	0.35
Minnesota	18.26	0.45	0.25	0.31
Mississippi	17.35	0.36	0.33	0.31
Missouri	18.58	0.43	0.24	0.34
Montana	17.69	0.38	0.30	0.32
Nebraska	17.74	0.41	0.30	0.29
Nevada	18.10	0.43	0.26	0.31
New Hampshire	19.71	0.42	0.13	0.45
New Jersey	19.01	0.46	0.18	0.36
New Mexico	18.35	0.42	0.25	0.33
New York	18.36	0.46	0.21	0.33
North Carolina	18.34	0.42	0.26	0.33
North Dakota	16.63	0.36	0.37	0.27
Ohio	18.70	0.43	0.23	0.34
Oklahoma	17.55	0.38	0.32	0.30
Oregon	17.88	0.43	0.27	0.29
Pennsylvania	19.09	0.45	0.19	0.37

(continued)

Table 5.2 (continued)

	Median tip %	Proportion of normative tips (≥ 15% and ≤ 20%)	Proportion of sub-normative tips (< 15%)	Proportion of super-normative tips (> 20%)
Rhode Island	19.54	0.43	0.15	0.42
South Carolina	18.34	0.41	0.25	0.33
South Dakota	17.00	0.37	0.35	0.28
Tennessee	18.25	0.42	0.26	0.33
Texas	17.91	0.40	0.29	0.31
Utah	18.21	0.42	0.26	0.32
Vermont	19.19	0.44	0.17	0.39
Virginia	18.84	0.41	0.23	0.36
Washington	17.62	0.44	0.29	0.27
West Virginia	18.11	0.35	0.29	0.35
Wisconsin	18.52	0.45	0.23	0.33
Wyoming	18.19	0.36	0.28	0.36

Source: 2013 NCR data used and reported by Lynn (2022)

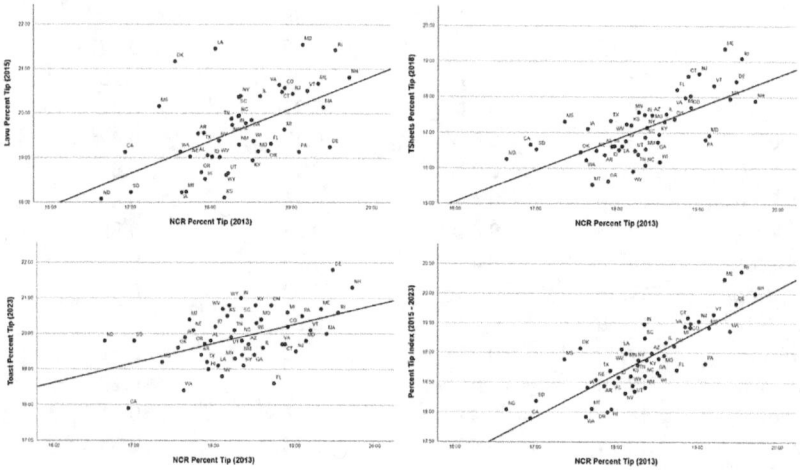

Fig. 5.1 Different publicly reported measures of state differences in tipping are positively, but only modestly, correlated with what I believe to be the truest measure of those differences, so treat public reports of state differences in tipping with some skepticism

Context Specificity of State Differences in Tipping

Further complicating the identification of more and less generous tipping states is the fact those state differences may not be the same across different service contexts. That is, the states that tip restaurant servers the most are not necessarily the states that tip counter-workers, haircutters, or taxi drivers the most. Indeed, a study I did in 2020 found that states tipping more in restaurants tipped less in coffee shops and vice versa (Lynn, 2020). In more recent, unpublished explorations of this issue, I compared average state restaurant tip percentages from the 2013 NCR data, average state bar, beauty salon and taxicab tip percentages from Square data reported by Risen (2016), and state ride-share tip likelihoods from Lyft data reported by Conlisk (2023).[3] I found that state average restaurant and beauty salon tips are positively correlated with one another as are state differences in average coffee shop, taxicab, and ride-share tips. However, the states with higher average restaurant and beauty salon tips have significantly LOWER average coffee shop, taxicab, and ride-share tips.[4] State average tip percentages in bars were unrelated to any of the other state tipping measures. These findings suggest that there is not just one set of genuine and meaningful state differences in tipping but many.

Causes and Consequences of State Differences in Tipping

Our discussion thus far has focused on public consumption and interpretation of media reports about the best and worst tipping states, but state differences in tipping offer more than just the entertainment value provided by these reports. They can also be used to test ideas about the causes of tipping and, in doing so, can expand our understanding of the phenomenon and can sometimes inform company and/or government policies regarding it. Three examples of these points are discussed next.

Tip Credit Effects on State Tip Averages. In Chap. 2, we presented data showing that state average restaurant tip percentages were positively related to the size of the tip credit (i.e., underpayment of tipped workers) in those states. Complimenting this effect are other, previously unpublished findings that state tip credits in 2016 were positively related to 2016 state tip averages given to bartenders (another worker commonly paid the tipped minimum wage) but not to the state tip averages given to beauticians, baristas, and cab drivers (who are typically paid the regular minimum wage or more). State

---

[3] Risen (2016) did not report exact tip percentages for every state, but did map the tipping categories each state fell into. Similarly, Conlisk (2023) did not report the exact tipping likelihood by state but did graph the data. I was able to use their maps and graphs to get reasonably good measures of the respective state differences in tipping.
[4] The correlation between state average restaurant and beauty salon tips was $r = 0.63$ ($n = 49$, $p < 0.001$). The correlations between state average coffee shop, taxicab, and ride-share tips ranged from $r = 0.32$ to $r = 0.38$ (n's $= 50$, p's < 0.03). The correlations between these two sets of state tip averages ranged from $r = -0.51$ to $r = -0.28$ (n's $= 49$ or 50, p's < 0.05).

average tips to the later groups of workers, though unrelated to the tip credit, were related to the regular minimum wages in those states. Those workers got larger tips in states with lower regular minimum wages.[5] Together, these findings provide reasonably compelling (though not definitive) support for the idea that tipping is motivated in part by a desire to help underpaid workers make a living. They also suggest that decreasing the tip credit, as some people are calling for (c.f., Onefairwage.org), may not help restaurant workers as much as expected because the increased wages will be accompanied by lower tip percentages. As we will see in Chap. 10, the net impact on total income of these opposing effects appears to be positive, but more research on state differences in dollar tip amounts per hour would increase our confidence in this conclusion.

Population Kindness Effects on State Tip Averages. Chap. 2 also introduced data showing that coffee shop tip averages were higher in states whose populations scored higher on kindness. The measure of state kindness used in that analysis captured willingness to help others at some cost to the self, so its relationship with state average coffee shop tips supports the impact of altruistic motives on at least some tips. This measure of state kindness was also associated with larger state average tips in taxicabs and ride-share vehicles, but not in bars, beauty salons, or restaurants.[6] Perhaps very strong tipping norms and social pressures to tip in these later service settings drive out altruistic motivations for tipping. This would be consistent with evidence from one of my other studies indicating that self-reported altruistic motives for tipping increased the individuals' likelihood of tipping occupations with moderate tipping norms more than it did the likelihood of tipping occupations with weaker and stronger tipping norms (Lynn, 2016a).

More research is needed to fully test the idea that high levels of social pressure drive out altruistic motivations for tipping, but the existing evidence supporting that idea suggests that businesses and workers in services with strong tipping norms might be better off reducing (rather than increasing) social pressures on their customers to tip. This is true because altruistic

---

[5] All of these state tipping averages are based on Square data reported by Risen (2016). The correlation between bar tips and tip credits was $r = 0.35$ ($n = 50$, $p < 0.02$). The correlations between coffee shop and taxicab tips and tip credits were $r = -0.25$ and 0.07, respectively (n's $= 50$, p's > 0.08). The correlations between coffee shop and taxicab tips and the regular minimum wage were $r = -0.40$ and -0.35, respectively (n's $= 50$, p's < 0.02).

[6] State kindness correlated with average taxicab, ride-share, bar, beauty salon, and restaurant tips at $r = 0.37$ ($p < 0.01$), 0.31 ($p < 0.03$), 0.04 ($p > 0.79$), -0.19 ($p > 0.19$), and -0.18 ($n = 49$, $p > 0.21$), respectively—using the previously described tip data from NCR, Risen (2016), and Conlisk (2023).

motives tend to increase tip sizes more than do social obligation or pressure motives (see Lynn, 2015a). If very high social pressures to tip do drive out altruistic motives for tipping, then increasing those social pressures may reduce (not increase) tip sizes.

Partisanship Effects on State Tipping. Not long ago, *Business Insider* looked at data from Square and reported that Red (or Republican) states had higher average tips than Blue (or Democrat) states (Michaels & Kiersz, 2018). Unfortunately, that analysis examined state tipping averages across all of Square's clients and, as we have already discussed, this can bias the measure of state tipping as well as hide differences in state tipping across different service contexts. Therefore, I took the Cook Partisanship Index used by Michaels and Kiersz (2018) and examined its relationships with state average taxicab, ride-share, bar, beauty salon, and restaurant tips. That analysis indicated that Red states did indeed tip more than Blue states in coffee shops, taxicabs, and ride-share vehicles, but they tipped less than Blue states in full-service restaurants and beauty salons.[7] These findings reinforce my previous caution against generalizing state tipping differences across service contexts. However, I mention these findings primarily to help make an important new point—that the predictors of tipping can differ at different levels of analysis.

Many people might conclude from the state level relationships just described that Republicans are better tippers than Democrats in coffee shops, taxicabs, and ride-share vehicles, while the reverse is true in restaurants and beauty salons. However, that conclusion assumes relationships at the state level result from (and therefore reflect) similar relationships at the individual consumer level. This could, but need not, be true! Red states differ from Blue ones in more ways than just the proportion of Republican to Democrat voters. For example, Red states tend to have lower costs of living, lower minimum wages, and higher tip credits than do Blue states. These and other state characteristics could produce Red vs Blue state differences in tipping even if individual Republicans tipped no differently from Democrats in the same states.[8] More generally, relationships between variables can, and often do, differ at different levels of analysis, so not only should reported

---

[7] State partisanship (tendency to vote Republican over Democrat) correlated with average taxicab, ride-share, bar, beauty salon, and restaurant tips at $r = 0.60$ ($p < 0.001$), 0.26 ($p < 0.07$), 0.07 ($p > 0.61$), $- 0.34$ ($p < 0.02$), and $- 0.44$ ($n = 49$, $p < 0.001$), respectively—using the previously described tip data from NCR, Risen (2016), and Conlisk (2023).

[8] In fact, while some of my studies have found that Democrats (or liberals) do tip restaurant servers more than Republicans (or conservatives) do (Lynn et al., 2012; Lynn, 2021), others have found no reliable differences and one national survey found the exact opposite (Spector, 2017). These mixed findings lead me to believe that the effects of political ideology on individual consumers' tipping are too small and inconsistent to be the principal cause of Red vs Blue state differences in tipping.

state differences in tipping be viewed with a critical eye, but so should interpretations of their relationships with other variables.

Summary about State Differences

The key takeaways from these analyses and considerations are that real and meaningful state differences in tipping do exist and can be used to gain insight into the psychology and economics of tipping. However, you should be cautious about taking publicly reported state differences in tipping at face value, because WHAT is being measured is less straightforward than many people (including some of the data providers themselves) know. In addition, you should not assume that state differences in tipping some service providers generalize to all service providers or that the predictors of state differences in tipping generalize across all service contexts, because the data tell us that they often differ. Finally, you should not assume that relationships between state differences in tipping and other state characteristics necessarily inform us about the relationships between those variables at the individual level of analysis, because states differ in ways that individuals do not and some of those state-only differences can affect not only tipping but also relationships with other variables. Correctly identifying and interpreting state differences in tipping, as well as their causes and consequences, is difficult, but I believe that this a potentially fruitful area of inquiry that deserves more research attention than it has received to date.

National Differences

Anyone who travels internationally soon learns that tipping norms vary widely around the globe. Knowing the tipping customs of their destinations is of obvious value to those international travelers. That is why international tipping guides exist and why travel guides to specific locations typically describe local tipping customs. These guides are helpful, but travelers may want to consult more than one because academic researchers have found only moderate consistency across tipping guides in the reported customary size of both restaurant and taxicab tips. Correlations among different guides' restaurant tips range from 0.22 to 0.80 while those for taxicab tips range from 0.45 to 0.93 (Lynn & Lynn, 2004; Mansfield, 2016; Starbuck, 2009). To give you a sense of what these correlations mean, I have plotted the customary restaurant tip percentages (when service charges are not added to the bill) from two international travel guides whose 0.57 correlation is near the middle of the range described above (see Fig. 5.2). As you can see, the guides do agree somewhat on which countries tip more and which tip less, but not enough to confidently follow either one's tip recommendations for a specific country. Some guides agree with one another more than do these two, but some agree less than do these two. One way to address the uncertainty raised by such inconsistencies in tipping guides is to consult three different guides and accept any recommendation shared by two or more of the guides. If no two of the guides agree, then go with the middle one.

Awareness of national differences in tipping customs is of obvious benefit to international travelers. Although less obvious, there are also benefits of knowing WHY national tipping customs vary the way they do. To travelers, such understanding would enrich the cultural experience of travel abroad. To hospitality businesses, some understanding of why national tipping customs differ would allow them to make more informed decisions about the tipping policies at their establishments. Although tipping is guided by social norms, businesses do not have to passively accept local norms. In fact, many hospitality firms have adopted counter-normative tipping policies as a way to differentiate their offerings from the competition (see Lynn & Starbuck, 2015). Understanding why national tipping norms differ as they do would help managers to better anticipate, avoid, and/or address customer reactions to such counter-normative policies (Lynn, 2000). So, what do we know about the predictors and causes of national differences in tipping?

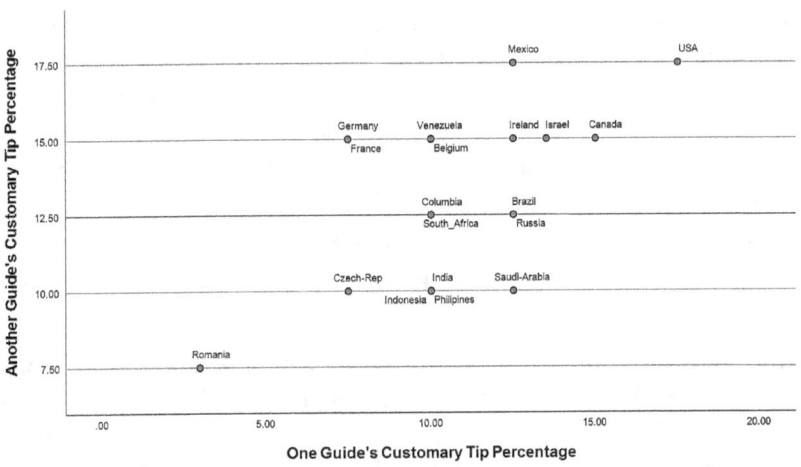

Fig. 5.2 Two international travel guides display only modest consistency in their reports of the customary restaurant tip percentages (when no service charges are added to the bill) of different nations ($r = 0.57$, $n = 19$, $p < 0.02$)

Tipping Customs Reflect Consumers' Values

I have long believed that national tipping customs reflect the value that consumers place on the effects or consequences of tipping (c.f., Lynn, 2006, 2015b). There is no "God of Tipping" who imposes tipping norms from above. Rather, tipping norms emerge from the behaviors of individuals—with those behaviors that are widely adopted or copied eventually becoming seen as socially expected. Thus, I believe it is widely shared goals or motivations for and against tipping that primarily drive national tipping customs and norms. Supporting this idea, national values and traits consistent with those motivations for and against tipping are related to the prevalence of tipping and/or the customary sizes of tips across countries. Some of these relationships are briefly described and discussed below.

National Values/Traits Connected to Reciprocity and Reward. A study—known as the World Values Survey—has asked large numbers of people in many countries around the world about their values and beliefs (Ingelhart et al., 1998). Two of the questions from this survey seem particularly relevant to reciprocity and reward motivations for tipping. One question asked how important an opportunity to "repay for something, give something back" was as a reason for their voluntary work. The other asked how fair it was for a more efficient secretary to earn more pay than a less efficient secretary. When I examined the relationships of average national scores on these questions to various measures of national tipping propensities, I found that answers to those questions were positively related to how common tipping was in a country and/or how much it was customary to tip restaurant servers in the country (see Table 5.3 and Fig. 5.3). Consistent with the idea that widely shared reciprocity and reward motivations for tipping underlie tipping customs, the more people in a country care about giving-back and think pay should be tied to performance, the more often and/or the larger amounts it is customary to tip in that country. Further supporting this idea is a study by Mansfield (2016) finding that customary restaurant tip percentages are lower in countries where service is already paid for because service charges are added to restaurant bills.

National Values/Traits Connected to Incentives. Several questions from the aforementioned World Values Survey seem relevant to incentive-based motivations for tipping. One question asked how much respondents agreed that "There should be greater incentives for individual effort." This was expected to be positively related to tipping customs on the grounds that people who believe more incentives are needed should especially value the incentives

Table 5.3 Correlations of national, motivation-related measures from the World Values Survey with the customary prevalence and size of tips

Value	Tipping prevalence (as measured by Lynn & Starbuck, 2015)	Tipping prevalence (as measured by Starbuck, 2009)	Customary restaurant tip percentage (as measured by Lynn & Starbuck, 2015)	Customary restaurant tip percentage (as measured by Starbuck, 2009)
Reciprocity/reward-related measures				
I volunteer to give back	0.29 (n = 24)	0.29 (n = 29)	0.70* (n = 27)	0.52** (n = 30)
Efficient worker should be paid more	0.57** (n = 29)	0.37* (n = 36)	0.35* (n = 33)	0.32† (n = 36)
Incentive-related measures				
More incentives needed	−0.05 (n = 29)	0.10 (n = 37)	0.24 (n = 34)	0.30† (n = 37)
Good pay important aspect of job	0.28 (n = 29)	0.42** (n = 36)	0.41* (n = 33)	0.40* (n = 36)
I do more when paid more	0.26 (n = 27)	0.09 (n = 35)	0.21 (n = 33)	0.24 (n = 36)
I do my best at work	−0.36† (n = 25)	−0.30† (n = 33)	−0.24 (n = 32)	−0.30† (n = 34)
Most people can be trusted	−0.62** (n = 30)	−0.41** (n = 38)	−0.18 (n = 35)	−0.26 (n = 38)
Altruism-related measures				
I volunteer out of compassion	0.44* (n = 24)	0.39* (n = 29)	0.52** (n = 27)	0.49** (n = 30)
Children should learn unselfishness	−0.39* (n = 29)	−0.21 (n = 37)	0.08 (n = 34)	−0.17 (n = 37)
Impression management-related measures				

(continued)

Table 5.3 (continued)

Value	Tipping prevalence (as measured by Lynn & Starbuck, 2015)	Tipping prevalence (as measured by Starbuck, 2009)	Customary restaurant tip percentage (as measured by Lynn & Starbuck, 2015)	Customary restaurant tip percentage (as measured by Starbuck, 2009)
Respect important aspect of job	0.31 (n = 28)	0.35* (n = 35)	− 0.10 (n = 33)	0.05 (n = 35)
Duty-related measures				
I volunteer out of a sense of duty	**0.69** (n = 24)**	0.53* (n = 29)	0.43* (n = 27)	0.42* (n = 32)
Cost-consciousness-related measures				
Children should learn thrift	− 0.20 (n = 30)	− 0.15 (n = 37)	− 0.14 (n = 34)	**− 0.33* (n = 37)**

‡ p < 0.10; *p < 0.05; **p < 0.01

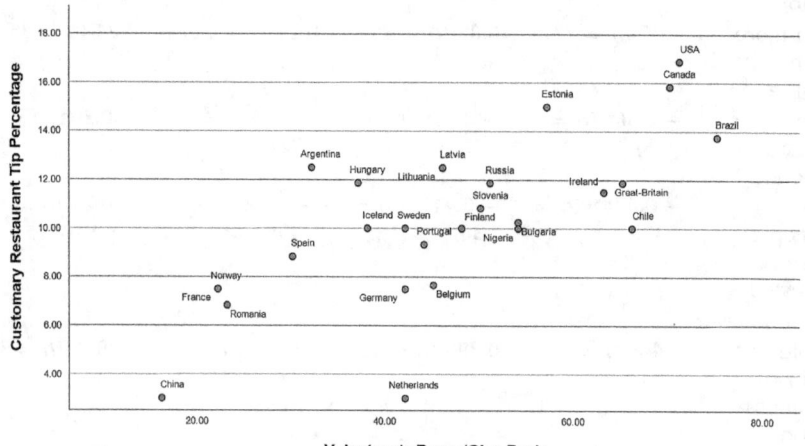

Fig. 5.3 Customary tip percentages are larger in nations with a larger percentage of the population rating giving-back as a "very important" reason for their volunteer work

provided by tipping. A second question asked how important "good pay" is in a job. This was also expected to be positively related to tipping customs on the grounds that people who consider pay a more important part of jobs should find tips to be especially effective incentives to do a good job. A third question asked if respondents viewed work as a business transaction in which they did more when paid more. Assuming people project their own motivations on others, then this was expected to be positively related to tipping customs on the grounds that people with a transactional approach to work should see tips as more effective incentives. A fourth question asked if respondents always do their best at work regardless of pay. Again, assuming people project their own motivations on others, then this was expected to be negatively related to tipping customs on the grounds that the people who do their best at work regardless of pay should see tipping as less necessary to get good service. A fifth question asked whether respondents thought that most people can be trusted. This too was expected to be negatively related to tipping customs on the grounds that the people who distrust others should see greater need for extrinsic incentives such as tips to ensure that others treat and serve them well.

When I tested these expected relationships using several different measures of tipping customs, I found that the relationships were generally in the expected direction and that almost half of them were strong enough to say that they were probably due to something other than just chance (see Table 5.3). Consistent with the idea that widely shared incentive-based motivations for tipping underlie tipping customs, the more people in a country care about monetary pay and the less confident they are that others are intrinsically motivated to work hard and treat them well, the more often and the larger amounts it is customary to tip in that country. Also supporting this idea is other research finding that tipping is more prevalent in countries where (i) bribery (another form of monetary incentive) is more common (Starbuck, 2009; Torfason et al., 2012) and (ii) high levels of neuroticism (aka, anxiety) and uncertainty avoidance are likely to make people more concerned about how service workers will treat them (Lynn et al., 1993; Lynn, 2000).

National Values/Traits Connected to Altruism. Two questions from the World Values Survey seem relevant to altruism-based motivations for tipping. One question asked how important "compassion for those in need" was as a reason for their voluntary work. The other asked if children should be encouraged to learn "unselfishness." Answers to the first question (but not the second) were positively related to both how common tipping was in a country and how much it was customary to tip restaurant servers in the country (see Table 5.3). Consistent with the idea that widely shared altruistic motivations for tipping underlie tipping customs, the more people in a country who say compassion is a "very important" reason for their volunteer work, the more often and the larger amounts it is customary to tip in that country (see Fig. 5.4). Also consistent with this idea is other research finding that tipping is more prevalent and tip sizes are larger in countries whose populations score lower on the anti-social personality trait of psychoticism (Lynn, 2000, 2008).

National Values/Traits Connected to Impression Management. One question from the World Values Survey was relevant to impression management concerns. It asked how important respondents thought respect was as an aspect of a job. Responses to that question were not significantly related to tipping customs (see Table 5.3), but other published research has found that national values and traits related to impression management do predict national differences in tipping customs. One of those findings was presented in Chap. 2, where we saw that the number of tipped occupations was greater in nations whose populations valued "recognition" more. In addition, research has found that the number of customarily tipped occupations is greater in countries whose populations have a self-enhancing tendency called "monumentalism" (Minkov, 2008) and have a greater tendency to manage social impressions by lying in self-enhancing ways on personality tests (Lynn & Starbuck, 2015). Consistent with the idea that widely shared impression management motivations for tipping underlie tipping customs,

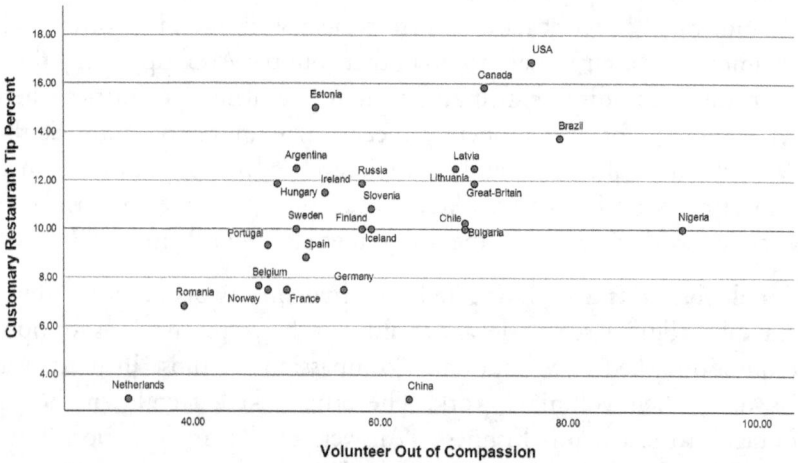

Fig. 5.4 Customary tip percentages are larger in nations with a larger percentage of the population rating compassion as a "very important" reason for their volunteer work

the more people in a country value recognition and self-enhancement, the more occupations it is customary to tip in that country.

National Values/Traits Connected to Duty. One question from the World Values Survey asked how important "a sense of duty" was as a reason for their voluntary work. Answers to this question were positively related to both how common tipping was in a country and how much it was customary to tip restaurant servers in the country (see Table 5.3 and Lynn & Starbuck, 2015). Consistent with the idea that widely shared duty motivations for tipping underlie tipping customs, the more people in a country who say duty is a "very important" reason for their volunteer work, the more often and the larger amounts it is customary to tip in that country.

National Values/Traits Connected to Thrift. One question from the World Values Survey asked if children should be encouraged to learn "thrift." Answers to this question were negatively related to both how common tipping was in a country and how much it was customary to tip restaurant servers in the country—though only one of those relationships was strong enough to be confident it was not due to chance (see Table 5.3). Consistent with the idea that widely shared cost considerations impact tipping customs, the more people in a country who say thrift is an important attribute for children to learn, the smaller amounts it is customary to tip in that country.

National Values/Traits Connected to Egalitarianism. Chap. 2 mentioned that it is customary to tip a fewer number of occupations in countries that are less tolerant of status and power differences between people. Other research has found that both the prevalence of tipping and customary restaurant tip sizes increase with the level of economic inequality in a country (Fergusson et al., 2017, 2018). These findings are consistent with, and thus support, the idea that tipping customs are constrained by national egalitarianism.

Caveats and Conclusions about National Differences

All of the research on national differences in tipping is correlational, so we cannot be sure the predictors of national tipping customs described above cause the observed relationships. Furthermore, small samples of nations mean that statistical power is low, which limits our abilities to find significant relationships and to use statistical controls to rule out alternative explanations for those significant relationships we do find. Finally, measurement and sample inconsistencies across analyses contribute to inconsistent findings. These considerations make interpretation of any observed relationship (or lack thereof) between specific national characteristics and tipping customs inherently ambiguous.

Nevertheless, the significant individual relationships described above are consistent with, and therefore provide at least prime facie, provisional support for, the specific motivational processes mentioned. Together, the number and diversity of those significant relationships provide stronger support for the more general idea that national tipping customs and norms are the product of culturally shared motivations for and against tipping. This conclusion and the research supporting it have important implications for international travelers and for the managers of hospitality businesses.

The predictors of national differences in tipping described above mean that travelers to foreign countries can view tipping guides for those countries not just as rulebooks to be followed, but also as windows into the cultural motivations and values of the countries. Of course, there are many motivations for tipping and it will not be automatically clear which ones are responsible for a given country's tipping norms, but the curious traveler can look at other customs and societal traits to formulate hypotheses about what specific tipping and/or anti-tipping motivations seem to be dominate in a particular travel destination. For example, visitors to countries with little to no tipping, low economic inequality, and explicitly egalitarian values can reasonably infer that one of the key reasons the residents of those countries tip so rarely is that they share a dislike of tipping's status and power implications. Even if such inferences are only educated guesses, the processes of observation, inference, and integration involved in developing them can only enrich the cultural experience of traveling abroad.

In addition, the predictors of national differences in tipping described above mean that managers should be careful about adopting tipping policies that are counter to the tipping norms in their location—as some resorts, private clubs, hotels, and restaurants in the United States and elsewhere have done (see Lynn & Starbuck, 2015). Those norms reflect the net value that locals place on the consequences of tipping, so counter-normative tipping policies effectively reduce benefits and/or increase costs to those consumers. Managers contemplating counter-normative tipping policies should try to determine how much their target market differs from the local population on values and beliefs similar to those shown in the preceding paragraphs to predict tipping customs. If the differences are numerous and large, then counter-normative tipping policies may be called for. If not, then managers might be better off either forgoing such counter-normative policies or finding alternative ways to provide the benefits lost, or make up for the costs imposed, by the counter-normative policies they do adopt.

Summary

We have seen that geography matters when it comes to tipping. People tip differently depending on whether they live in urban or rural areas, one state of the U.S. or another, and one country or another. Awareness of these differences can help consumers know what tips are expected of them in different locations and public media (such as tipping guides, press articles, and various websites) often provide this information to them. However, much of that information is more inconsistent and error prone than most people realize. Wise consumers of this information will remember that it is generally better to look at the agreements between, and/or the average of, several different sources than to rely upon any one source alone.

Explanations for the observed geographic differences in tipping also have practical value, but are hard to nail down. Urban vs rural differences in tipping are particularly puzzling because the obvious explanatory candidates—namely differences in age, education, income, and awareness of tipping norms—have been ruled out. More insight than is available to me at this time will be needed to explain this geographic difference in tipping.

In contrast, plausible explanations for state and national differences in tipping are readily available even if unproven. First, state differences in tipping appear to reflect (in part) state differences in workers' need for tips, because tips for workers earning the tipped minimum wage (but not those of workers earning the regular minimum wage) go up as the difference between the two minimum wages goes up and tips for workers earning the regular minimum wage go up as that minimum wage goes down. Second, national differences in tipping appear to reflect (in part) the value that consumers place on the effects or consequences of tipping, because the customary prevalence and/or size of tips varies with national values and traits plausibly related to desires to reward and help workers, ensure good treatment from workers, gain social esteem, do one's duty, and treat others as equals.

Unfortunately, measurement problems, small sample sizes, and reliance upon correlational data prohibit definitive conclusions about these potential causes of state and national differences in tipping. In addition, even if valid, these are unlikely to be the only explanations for those geographical differences. Thus, I feel compelled to repeat a refrain you have read in this book before and one you will read again—i.e., this topic deserves more research. If nothing else, this should make clear to you how I could spend an entire career studying tipping—I found that the more I learned about this rich and complex topic, the more aware I became of what I didn't know and still needed to learn. Hopefully, the same thing is happening to you as you read this book.

References

Conlisk, S. (2023). *The United States of Tipping: When and Where Riders Tip Most*. https://www.lyft.com/blog/posts/the-united-states-of-tipping-when-and-where-riders-tip-most,accessed5/16/24.

Ferguson, G., Megehee, C. M., & Woodside, A. G. (2017). Culture, religiosity, and economic configural models explaining tipping-behavior prevalence across nations. *Tourism Management, 62*, 218–233.

Ferguson, G., Megehee, C. M., & Woodside, A. G. (2018). Applying asymmetric, case-based, forecasting modeling in service research: Cultures' consequences on customers' service gratuities. *Australasian Marketing Journal, 26*(4), 369–381.

Inglehart, R. F., Basanez, M., & Moreno, A. (1998). *Human values and beliefs: A cross-cultural sourcebook*. University of Michigan Press.

Lynn, M. (2000). National character and tipping customs: The needs for achievement, affiliation and power as predictors of the prevalence of tipping. *International Journal of Hospitality Management, 19*(2), 205–210.

Lynn, M. (2004). Black-white differences in tipping of various service providers 1. *Journal of Applied Social Psychology, 34*(11), 2261–2271.

Lynn, M. (2006). Geodemographic differences in knowledge about the restaurant tipping norm. *Journal of Applied Social Psychology, 36*(3), 740–750.

Lynn, M. (2008). Personality effects on tipping attitudes, self-reported behaviors and customs: A multi-level inquiry. *Personality and Individual Differences, 44*(4), 989–999.

Lynn, M. (2015a). Explanations of service gratuities and tipping: Evidence from individual differences in tipping motivations and tendencies. *Journal of Behavioral and Experimental Economics, 55*, 65–71.

Lynn, M. (2015b). Service gratuities and tipping: A motivational framework. *Journal of Economic Psychology, 46*, 74–88. https://doi.org/10.1016/j.joep.2014.12.002

Lynn, M. (2016a). Motivations for tipping: How they differ across more and less frequently tipped services. *Journal of Behavioral and Experimental Economics, 65*, 38–48.

Lynn, M., & Lynn, A. (2004). National values and tipping customs: A replication and extension. *Journal of Hospitality & Tourism Research, 28*(3), 356–364.

Lynn, M., & Starbuck, M. M. (2015). Tipping customs: The effects of national differences in attitudes toward tipping and sensitivities to duty and social pressure. *Journal of Behavioral and Experimental Economics, 57*, 158–166.

Lynn, M. (2020). The effects of minimum wages on tipping: a state-level analysis. *Compensation & Benefits Review, 52*(3), 98–108.

Lynn, M. (2022). State Differences in Tipping Attitudes and Behavior: Attributable to State Differences in Tipping Motivations?. *Review of Regional Studies, 52*(3), 367–386. https://doi.org/10.52324/001c.66200

Mansfield, E. D. (2016). The political economy of the itching palm: An analysis of tipping norms. *International studies quarterly, 60*(3), 375–386. https://doi.org/10.1093/isq/sqw015

McCrohan, K. F., & Pearl, R. B. (1991). An application of commercial panel data for public policy research: Estimates of tip earnings. *Journal of Economic and Social Measurement, 17*(3–4), 217–231.

Michaels, M., & Kiersz, A. (2018, Apr 9). *How much people tip on average across the US—and there is a big difference between red and blue states*. https://www.businessinsider.com/how-much-americans-tip-every-state-ranked-2018-3. Accessed 2 July 2024.

Minkov, M. (2008). Self-enhancement and self-stability predict school achievement at the national level. *Cross-Cultural Research, 42*(2), 172–196.

Parker, K., Horowitz, J.M., Brown, A., Fry, R., Cohn, D., & Ingielnik, R. (2018, May 22). What unites and divides urban, suburban and rural communities. https://www.pewresearch.org/social-trends/2018/05/22/what-unites-and-divides-urban-suburban-and-rural-communities/. Accessed 18 July 2024.

Raspor, A., & Divjak, M. (2017). What is tipping in post-communist countries? A case study from Slovenia. *Teorija in Praksa, 6*.

Rawson, C., Flanagan, G. L., & Frankel, R. S. (2024, Apr 5). *Tipping point: Best and worst states for tips*. https://www.usatoday.com/money/blueprint/credit-cards/states-with-the-best-and-worst-tippers/. Accessed 2 July 2024.

Rentfrow, P. J. (2020). Geographical psychology. *Current Opinion in Psychology, 32*, 165–170.

Risen, T. (2016, June 22). Where Americans tip the most. https://www.usnews.com/news/articles/2016-06-22/where-americans-tip-the-most. Accessed 2 July 2024.

Ruralfinds (2023, Nov 10). *Understanding the distinct worlds: Rural vs. urban areas*. https://www.ruralfinds.net/articles/understanding-the-distinct-worlds-rural-vs-urban-areas/. Accessed 18 July 2023.

Sienkiewicz, J. H. (2016). *Waiting on you: A study of tipped minimum wages' effects on job tenure among white restaurant servers* (Master's Thesis, Loyola University Chicago).

Spector, N. (2017, July 12). *Hey, big spender! Republicans, boomers leave the fattest tips, poll finds*. https://www.nbcnews.com/business/consumer/hey-big-spender-republicans-boomers-leave-fattest-tips-poll-finds-n782221. Accessed 16 July 2024.

Starbuck, M. (2009). *A comparative study of tipping practices and attitudes*. Doctoral Dissertation, Department of Sociology, Green Templeton College, Oxford University.

Torfason, M. T., Flynn, F. J., & Kupor, D. (2013). Here is a tip: Prosocial gratuities are linked to corruption. Social Psychological and Personality Science, 4(3), 348–354. https://doi.org/10.1177/1948550612454888

Wells, J. (2016). *America's Best (and Worst) Tippers*. https://lavu.com/blog/americas-best-and-worst-tippers/#.XZT19_IKiUk

6

Perk of the Job (Why Do We Tip Some Service Occupations and not Others?)

Around the world, many service occupations, such as bartenders, doormen, hotel maids, parking valets, and restaurant servers, commonly receive tips. However, many other service occupations, such as accountants, bank tellers, copy machine operators, doctors, and lawyers, are rarely if ever tipped. What differentiates these sets of services? Why are some occupations more likely to be tipped than others?

The answers to these questions are of more than just academic and/or idle interest. They can inform efforts to mold occupational tipping norms. Before the COVID-19 pandemic, some businesses had tried to encourage more tipping of their employees. For example, Marriott put envelopes in guests' rooms encouraging them to tip its maids (Harpaz, 2014) and Frontier airlines added an option to tip its stewardesses to its onboard, digital billing tablets (Berger, 2019). In the aftermath of the pandemic, this practice has become even more common—with contract home repairers, convenience store workers, and even self-service kiosks now asking for tips (Taylor, 2024). Understanding why some occupations are tipped and others are not tipped could enhance our ability to predict and influence the success of such efforts.

There is unlikely to be a single answer to these questions. Tipping involves at least three parties—the tipper, the tip recipient, and the firm employing the tip recipient—any one of which can affect the likelihood of a tip being given. Thus, stable occupational differences in likelihood of receiving tips could stem from characteristics of the occupations that affect one or more of these parties. In line with this reasoning, theorists have speculated that we are more likely to tip occupations (i) for which tipping is a more efficient way to motivate good service, (ii) whose workers are otherwise more likely to envy and harm us, (iii) whose handling of bill payments facilitates tipping, (iv) whose characteristics enhance the extrinsic (social-esteem and future-service) rewards we get from tipping, (v) whose characteristics strengthen the intrinsic, personal satisfaction we get from helping and rewarding service workers with tips, and (vi) whose characteristics diminish our concerns that tips may not be welcome. This chapter will elaborate on each of these ideas and describe the results of efforts to empirically test them.

More Efficient Incentives

Economists argue that tipping exists because it is the most efficient way to incentivize good service from service workers (Bodvarsson and Gibson, 1994; Jacob and Page, 1980). The intangible and customized nature of many services make it difficult for firms and their managers to evaluate and reward service workers' efforts. For example, restaurant managers cannot tell if a server who rarely visits a table of customers is delivering inattentive and bad service or is respecting the customers' desires for private and uninterrupted conversation. Customers, on the other hand, can easily evaluate their satisfaction with service, so it is more efficient and effective for them rather than managers to monitor and reward service workers' efforts on their behalf. Therefore, firms allow and/or encourage customers to perform this monitoring/reward function via tipping in order to enhance the firm's economic efficiency.

Since tipping is supposed to be a mechanism for enhancing economic efficiency, Azar (2005) argued that we are more likely to tip occupations whose customers have a larger advantage over managers in monitoring and evaluating service. This occupational characteristic will be referred to as "customer monitoring advantage." In a test of his theory, Azar (2005) found no relationship between judges' ratings of the extent to which customers had an advantage over managers in evaluating the service provided by each of 37 occupations and how common or important tipping was a source of income for those occupations. However, subsequent research with slightly different measures and a much larger sample of service occupations has found that customer monitoring advantage is positively and significantly related to the likelihood of an occupation being tipped—see Fig. 6.1. Furthermore, this relationship remains positive and significant even after controlling for a variety of other occupational characteristics (Lynn, 2016). Thus, although alternative explanations for this relationship are possible (as will be discussed

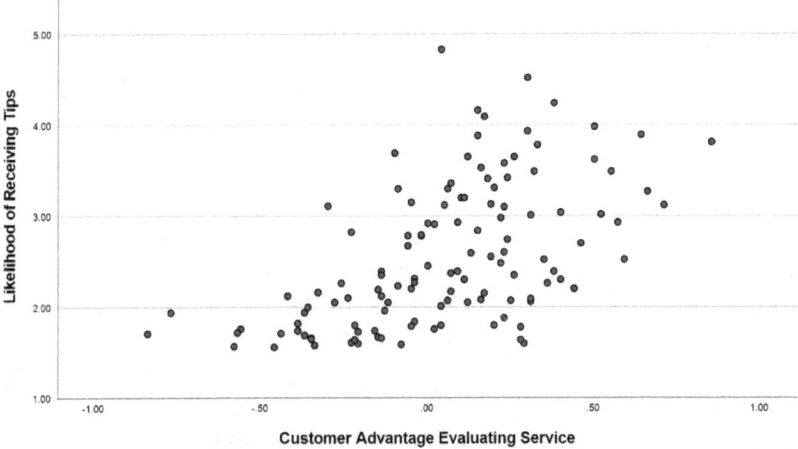

Fig. 6.1 Likelihood that a service occupation is tipped increases with its customer monitoring advantage. Each dot is one of 122 service occupations. Graph of relationship reported in Lynn (2016)

later), Azar's "customer monitoring advantage" theory does have some empirical support.

Greater Concerns About Envy/Harm

The anthropologist George Foster (1972) theorized that tipping in eating and drinking places is an attempt by consumers to symbolically share their food and drink with the service worker who might otherwise envy them. Restaurant and bar tips, he argued, are given to buy off the envy of waiters and bartenders. Although Foster explicitly declined to offer a formal explanation of why we tip other service providers as well, he did claim that tipping is a "payment, pure and simple, for protection" and he noted that most tipped workers have "considerable power over the tipper or his possessions" (Foster, 1972, pg. 181). Thus, he implied that we are more likely to tip service workers with stronger motivation to harm their customers. Reasoning that greater hedonic disparity between service workers and their customers would elicit more worker envy and motivation to harm customers, I tested this implication by examining the relationship of tipping likelihood and hedonic disparity among 122 occupations (Lynn, 2016b). I found that we are more likely to tip service occupations whose workers are less happy at the time of service than are their customers—see Fig. 6.2. This relationship also remains

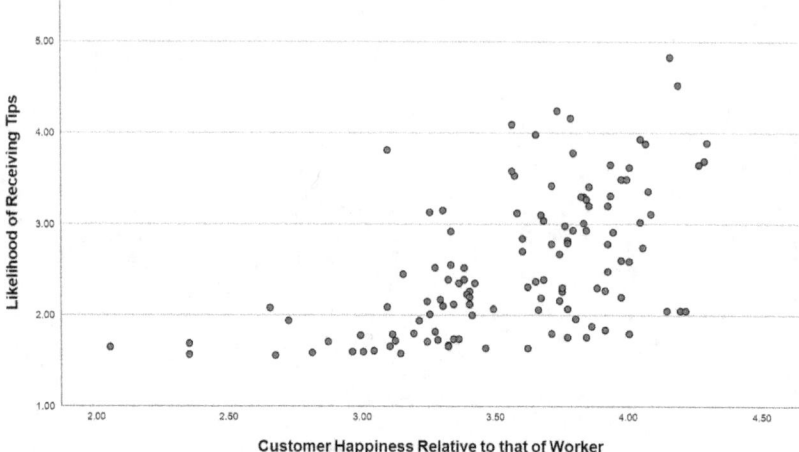

Fig. 6.2 Likelihood that a service occupation is tipped increases with the disparity between customer and worker happiness during the service encounter. Each dot is one of 122 service occupations. Graph of relationship reported in Lynn (2016)

positive and significant even after controlling for a variety of other occupational characteristics. Thus, there is reasonably good evidence that we are more likely to tip those service providers who might otherwise envy and want to harm us.

More Convenient Tipping

I have argued that tipping should be easier and, therefore, more common for occupations in which the tipped worker handles customers' payment of the bill, because money is "already being exchanged between customers and servers" and customers can "more easily get any needed change for an appropriate tip" (Lynn, 2019; pg. 224). To test this hypotheses, I asked one sample of US consumers to rate how likely they would be to tip each of 108 service occupations (assuming good service) and another sample to rate how likely the workers in each of those occupations are to handle bill payment (Lynn, 2019). Consistent with my expectations, I found that occupations were more likely to be tipped the more likely their workers were to handle bill payments and that this relationship remained significant even after controlling for several other occupational characteristics (see Fig. 6.3). Thus, occupational differences in receipt of tips do appear to reflect differences in how easy and convenient tipping is.

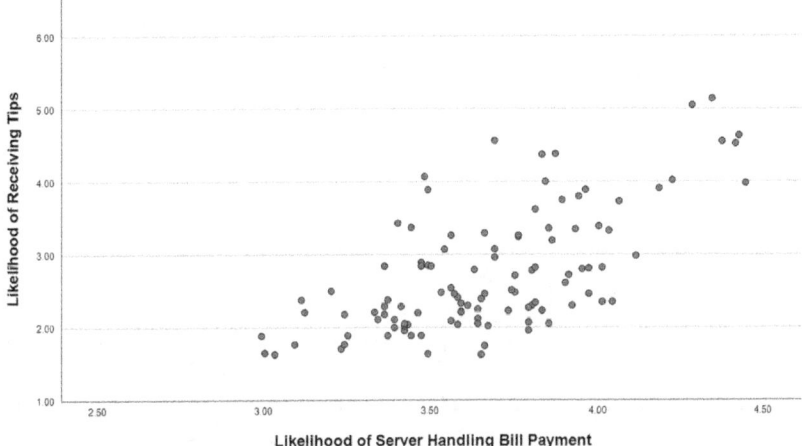

Fig. 6.3 Likelihood that a service occupation is tipped increases with the likelihood that potential tip recipients handle customer payment of the bill. Each dot is one of 108 service occupations. Graph of relationship reported in Lynn (2019)

Enhanced Extrinsic Tipping Motives

Assuming that tipping is motivated in part by desires for enhanced social status and future service, several scholars have argued that we should be more likely to tip occupations to the extent that their characteristics, such as patronage frequency and likelihood of encountering the same server when returning, enhance these extrinsic rewards from tipping (Gambetta, 2015; Lynn, 2016, 2019; Starbuck, 2009). However, empirical tests of this idea have provided only mixed and limited support for it.

Consistent with this enhanced extrinsic rewards theory, we are more likely to tip occupations whose services we use frequently than those less frequently used. However, this relationship could be driven by a tendency to use low status workers' services more frequently than high status workers' services and to tip for the former more than the latter, because it disappears once occupational status is controlled for.

Evidence against the enhanced extrinsic rewards theory comes from the findings that our likelihood of tipping an occupation goes down, not up, with the likelihood of encountering the same server on future visits and with the amount of time servers and customers interact face-to-face. Unlike the effects of usage frequency, these relationships remain significant after controlling for other occupational characteristics (Lynn, 2016) and they suggest occupational differences in the extrinsic rewards provided by tipped workers have little effect on occupational tipping likelihood.

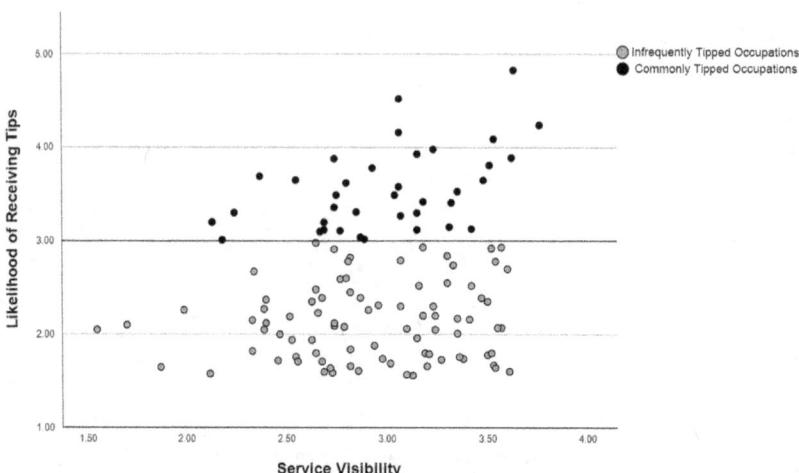

Fig. 6.4 Likelihood that a service occupation is tipped increases with the visibility of the service encounter to third parties. This effect is stronger among more commonly tipped occupations (those on/above the neutral reference line). Each dot is one of 122 service occupations. Graph of relationship reported in Lynn (2016)

Extrinsic rewards provided by other consumers, however, may have an effect on occupational tipping likelihood, because research indicates that we are more likely to tip occupations whose services are visible to others (Lynn, 2016b, 2019). Furthermore, this relationship is stronger among more commonly tipped occupations (see Fig. 6.4) and the effect among those occupations remains significant after controlling for other occupational characteristics (Lynn, 2016b, 2019). These findings suggest that occupational differences in public disapproval following non-compliance with tipping norms may partially drive occupational differences in tipping likelihood.

Stronger Intrinsic Tipping Motives

Given that tipping is largely motivated by intrinsic desires to help service workers and to reward them for a good job, theorists have also argued that we should be more likely to tip those occupations whose characteristics more strongly enhance one or both of these motivations for tipping (Azar, 2005; Gambetta, 2015; Lynn, 2015). Consistent with this theory, research has found that altruistic and/or reciprocity motivations for tipping are stronger among occupations with lower worker income, greater server unhappiness relative to the customer, greater service customization, and greater customer ability to evaluate server performance (Lynn, 2021) and that the likelihood an occupation receives tips also increases with these occupational characteristics (Lynn, 2016, 2019)[1] The relationships of service customization and customer monitoring advantage with tipping likelihood have been discussed and graphed previously (see Figs. 2.2 and 6.1). For a depiction of the relationship between tipping likelihood and occupational income, see Fig. 6.5.

Noting that we are more likely to help people we know and are close to than those we do not know personally, several researchers have assumed that altruistic motivations for tipping and, therefore, tipping likelihood would be higher for occupations involving more personal relationships and more frequent, prolonged, and intimate contact between worker and customer (Azar, 2005; Lynn, 2016, 2019; Starbuck, 2009). Two early studies found support for this expectation (Azar, 2005; Starbuck, 2009), but I have been unable to replicate those findings in two studies involving much larger samples of occupations (Lynn, 2016b, 2019). My studies have found that

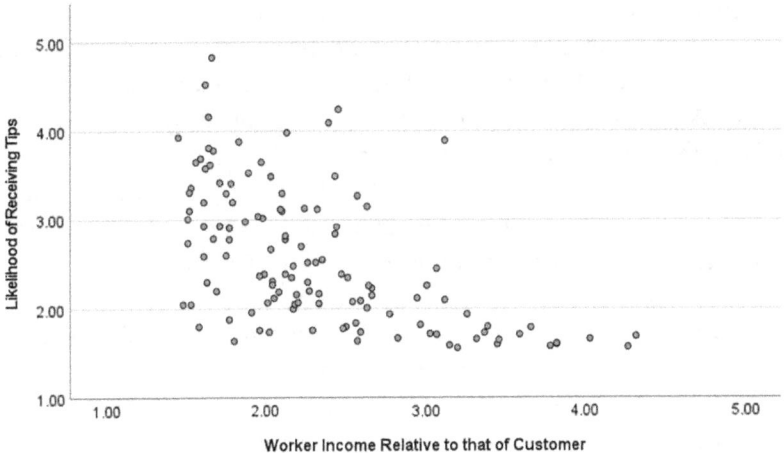

Fig. 6.5 Likelihood that a service occupation is tipped decreases with the income of the typical worker in that occupation (relative to their customers' incomes). Each dot is one of 122 service occupations. Data from Lynn (2016)

---

[1] Occupational income/status and hedonic disparity between workers and their customers increased both altruistic and reciprocity motives for tipping while service customization and customer monitoring advantage increased reciprocity (but not altruistic) motives for tipping. Motive strength was measured as predictive power. Self-reported altruistic and/or reciprocity motivations for tipping predicted individual consumers' claimed likelihood of tipping more strongly when the tip recipient worked in an occupation with these characteristics (Lynn, 2021). The effects of occupational income/status, hedonic disparity, and customer monitoring advantage on tipping likelihood were observed in both bi-variate and multi-variate analyses while the effects of service customization on tipping likelihood were observed only in multivariate analyses controlling for occupational income and other occupational characteristics (Lynn, 2016, 2019).

the likelihood of an occupation receiving tips is unrelated to the likelihood of the worker touching his or her customers and that it goes down (not up) with the amount of face-to-face contact time between worker and customer and with the tendency to encounter the same worker again when re-patronizing a service business. The conflict between my findings and those of previous researchers suggest that some other occupational characteristic moderates (or alters) the relationships of occupational tipping likelihood with server-customer closeness and associated variables. In attempts to identify that moderator, I have determined that is not occupational income/status, worker happiness on the job, or even tipping likelihood itself, but I have been unable to identify what it is. This is yet another question waiting to be answered by some future researcher with more insight and data than I have at this time.

Greater Offense at Being Offered Tips

A few scholars have suggested that we are less likely to tip occupations whose workers would be offended by and would reject offers of tips (Gambetta, 2006; Lynn, 2016). In a clumsy effort to test this idea, I asked people to rate how likely various occupations are to be offended by offers of tips and how likely those occupations are to actually be tipped and I found that these ratings were strongly negatively related (see Fig. 6.6).[2] This seems to support the theory under consideration, but there is a bigger than typical problem determining what causes what in this relationship. Occupational tipping likelihood is unlikely to affect the other occupational characteristics discussed previously in this chapter, but it almost certainly affects peoples' perceptions of occupational willingness to accept tips. Thus, it is possible that the relationship depicted in Fig. 6.6 is entirely due to tipping likelihood affecting fear of giving offense with tips rather than the reverse.

Fortunately, the previously discussed effects of other occupational characteristics on the likelihood that an occupation receives tips provide some evidence regarding the validity of the "greater offence" theory. Unpublished analyses of data reported in Lynn (2016) indicate that we are more likely to think an occupation will be offended by offers of tips when the occupation has high income/status, its customers are more likely to encounter the same worker on future visits, its worker-customer contact time is greater, its workers are happier (relative to customer happiness), and its services are more

---

[2] The correlation was $r = -0.82$ ($p < 0.001$) from unpublished analysis of data on 122 service occupations reported in Lynn (2016).

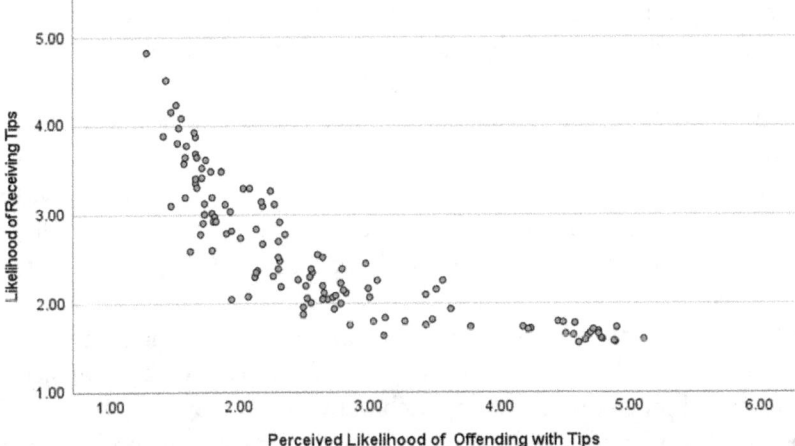

Fig. 6.6 Likelihood that a service occupation is tipped decreases with the likelihood tips will be seen as offensive by the recipient. Each dot is one of 122 service occupations. Data described in Lynn (2016)

customized. Importantly, these relationships remain significant after controlling for occupational tipping likelihood, so they cannot be attributed to the effects of occupational tipping likelihood on perceptions of occupational offense at being offered a tip.[3] All of these offense enhancing occupational characteristics, except service customization, are also negatively related to occupational tipping likelihood, so occupations whose characteristics enhance the perceived offensiveness of tips are less likely to receive them.

Summary and Conclusion

The world is complex and research findings about it are often messy and inconsistent. Research on occupational differences in receipt of tips is no different. Nevertheless, that research generally indicates that we are more likely to tip occupations with the following characteristics:

- Customers can monitor and evaluate service more easily than can managers,

---

[3] The partial correlations between rated occupational characteristic and offense at being offered a tip (after controlling for occupational tipping likelihood) were: occupation income/status (pr = 0.72), same worker (pr = 0.52), contact time (pr = 0.37), workers happier (pr = 0.51), and service customization (pr = 0.59)—all p's < 0.001. From unpublished analyses of data on 122 service occupations reported in Lynn (2016).

- Customers are happier than workers during the service encounter,
- Service providers also handle customer payment of the bill,
- Workers have low income and status,
- Workers provide more customized services (after controlling for occupational status),
- Customers are less likely to encounter the same worker on future visits,
- Customers spend less time in face-to-face contact with workers, and
- Service encounters are visible to third parties.

All of these relationships are correlational and more than one plausible explanation is available for many of them, so we cannot be sure what the specific causal processes underlying each of them are. However, these relationships are consistent with and, therefore, should enhance our confidence in the ideas that occupational differences in tipping are due to differences across occupations in tipping's (i) enhancement of firm efficiency in monitoring and rewarding workers, (ii) reduction in consumer fear of mistreatment by service workers, (iii) convenience and easiness, (iv) avoidance of the public disapproval that failure to comply with tipping norms would bring, (v) enhancement of personal satisfaction from helping and rewarding service workers, and (vi) offensiveness to the dignity of service workers.

As mentioned in the introduction of this chapter, these findings and their explanations are of more than just academic and/or idle interest. They can enhance our ability to predict and influence the success of efforts to reshape occupational tipping norms. Specifically, they suggest that efforts to increase tipping of a particular occupation will be easier and more successful the more tip-enhancing characteristics—described above—that occupation has. For this reason, any such efforts to encourage greater tipping of a particular occupation should call attention to those characteristics of the occupational that research shows enhance occupational tipping likelihood and should deflect attention away from those occupational characteristics that research shows inhibit occupational tipping likelihood. For example, low customer monitoring advantage, regular wages, and standardized service may explain why only 26% of consumers say they usually tip for restaurant takeout despite widespread requests for such tips by restaurants (Kelton, 2024). Given these occupational characteristics, the percentage of customers who tip for restaurant carryout will probably never get much larger than it currently is, but that percentage may be marginally increased by tweaking the service encounter to make the service seem more customized and public. For example, taking specialized orders and letting customers know that tips are shared with the cooking staff who prepared those orders and having carryout picked up in full view of the dining room might increase carryout tipping at least a little.

The reverse is also true for efforts to discourage the tipping of service occupations whose workers usually receive tips—as some US hotels and restaurants have tried to do in recent years. The ease and success of such efforts are likely to decline with the number and strength of tip-enhancing characteristics possessed by the service occupation in question. For example, the high customer monitoring advantage and potential for service customization of ride-share services and the low perceived income and status of ride-share drivers may have contributed to the ultimate failure of Ubers' anti-tipping policy (Reuters, 2017). For this reason, any such efforts to discourage tipping of a particular occupation should probably be accompanied by messages calling attention to those characteristics of the occupational that research shows inhibit occupational tipping likelihood and deflecting attention away from those occupational characteristics that research shows encourage occupational tipping likelihood. Going back to the Uber example, it might have diminished pressures to add tipping functions to its app had it more successfully portrayed its "driver-partners" as highly satisfied, independent, businessmen making more per hour than do taxicab drivers.

In summary, occupational tipping norms are not arbitrary, but largely reflect the effects of occupational characteristics on consumers' motivation to tip. Of course, firms and workers can discourage tipping, but the critical role of consumers' motivation means that occupational tipping norms are not easily molded by workers', managers', or policymakers' to fit their desires. Ultimately, whom we extend this perk of the job to is mostly up to us tippers.

References

Azar, O. H. (2005). Who do we tip and why? An Empirical Investigation. *Applied Economics, 37*(16), 1871–1879.
Berger, S. (2019, Jan 11). *This airline is asking passengers to tip their flight attendants.* www.cnbc.com. Accessed 12 Aug 2021.
Foster, G. (1972). The anatomy of envy: A study of symbolic behavior. Current Anthropology, 13, 165–186.
Gambetta, D. (2006). What makes people tip: Motivations and predictions. Aegis le Libellio d', 2 (3), 2–10.
Gambetta, D. (2015). What makes people tip. *Rationality, democracy and justice: The legacy of Jon Elster,* 97–114.

Harpaz, B.J. (2014, Sept 15). *Marriott starts envelope program to encourage tips for maids.* www.huffingtonpost.com. Accessed 28 Nov 2015.

Jacob, N. & Page, A. (1980). Production, information costs, and economic organization: The buyer monitoring case. American Economic Review, 70 (3), 476–478.

Kelton, K. (2024, June 5). *Survey: More than 1 in 3 Americans think tipping culture has gotten out of control.* www.bankrate.com. Accessed 22 Aug 2024

Lynn, M. (2015). Service gratuities and tipping: A motivational framework. *Journal of Economic Psychology,* 46, 74–88.

Lynn, M. (2016b). Why are we more likely to tip some service occupations than others? Theory, evidence, and implications. *Journal of Economic Psychology,* 54, 134–150.

Lynn, M. (2019). Predictors of occupational differences in tipping. *International Journal of Hospitality Management,* 81, 221–228.

Lynn, M. (2021). The effects of occupational characteristics on the motives underlying tipping of different occupations. *Journal of Behavioral and Experimental Economics,* 95, 101783.

Michael, Lynn (2016) Why are we more likely to tip some service occupations than others? Theory evidence and implications Journal of Economic Psychology 54 134–150 https://doi.org/10.1016/j.joep.2016.04.001

Örn B., Bodvarsson William A., Gibson (1994) Gratuities and customer appraisal of service: Evidence from Minesota restaurants. The Journal of Socio-Economics 23(3) 287–302 https://doi.org/10.1016/1053-5357(94)90005-1

Reuters, H. S. (2017, June 20). Uber reverses course, will allow tipping for drivers via app. www.reviewjournal.com. Accessed 22 Aug 2024.

Starbuck, M. (2009). *A comparative study of tipping practices and attitudes.* Doctoral Dissertation, Department of Sociology, Green Templeton College, Oxford University.

Taylor, C. (2024, July 2). *Tipped off: American consumers grapple with tip creep.* www.reuters.com. Accessed 22 Aug 2024.

7

Unequal Pay (Who Gets the Best Tips and Who Gets the Worst?)

Service workers differ widely in age, gender, race, appearance, personality, and work experience. Unsurprisingly, they also differ in the sizes of tips they receive. A national survey in 2006 found that approximately 1 in 3 restaurant servers reported getting average tips of 15% or less while 1 in 4 reported getting average tips of 20% or more.[1] While some of these differences in tip size are attributable to the different restaurants and geographic regions the surveyed workers came from, other data reveals meaningful differences in the tip percentages received by different servers at the same restaurant. For example, sales-transaction records from several casual-dining restaurants in California during 2017 indicate that approximately 15 out of 100 servers got average tips of 18% or less while another 3 in 100 got average tips of 22% or more (see Fig. 7.1). These differences are important because they can have a substantial impact on tip income when accumulated over the many dining parties served in a year (or even month). For example, with $10,000 a month in sales, a server earning average tips of 18% will make approximately $1800 a month (or $21,600 a year) while a server earning average tips of 22% will make approximately $2200 a month (or $26,400 a year).

Knowing who gets the biggest (and smallest) tips would benefit workers, businesses, and consumers alike. It would help potential service workers decide whether (or not) to work in a tipped job. After all, it is easier and more rewarding to work in a job where one's physical and/or psychological traits

---

[1] These are unpublished findings from the Study 2 survey reported in Kwortnik et al. (2009).

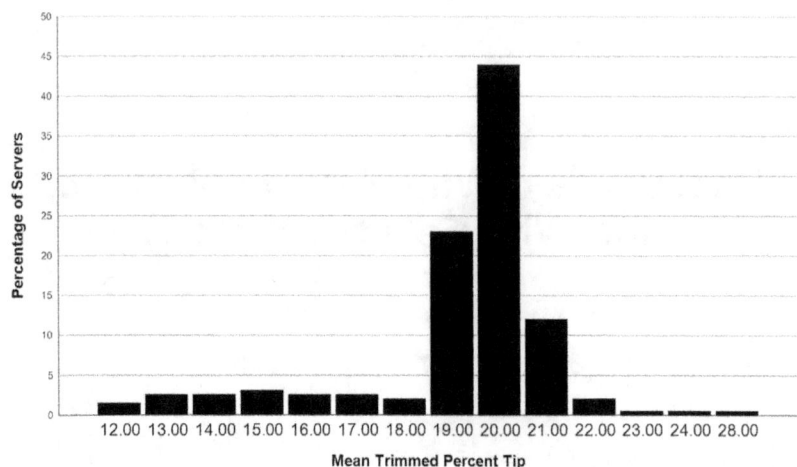

Fig. 7.1 Although the vast majority of servers get close to average tip percentages, sizeable minorities get substantially more or less than that [*This analysis of data from Upserve examines the average charge tips of 191 servers working in casual-dining restaurants in California during 2017 who received at least 20 tips counting only tips between 6 and 50% of the bill size to avoid biases from unusual tips and controlling for restaurant differences so that only server differences are displayed*]

contribute to success than to work in a job where those characteristics are an impediment to success. Such knowledge might also help existing service workers receive more equitable pay. In Griggs vs. Duke Power, the Supreme Court ruled that the Civil Rights Act of 1964 prohibits business policies and practices that have a disproportionate and negative impact on protected classes of workers (such as women, the elderly, and racial minorities) even if those policies and practices appear to be neutral and are not intended to discriminate. If protected classes of workers get smaller than typical tips, then businesses' reliance on tipping as part of employee compensation is one of those apparently neutral business practices that may be unlawful under the Civil Rights Act of 1964 (Lynn et al., 2008). Knowledge about the existence and extent of such disparate impacts on workers' incomes would give those workers a moral and legal basis for demanding more equitable compensation.

Such knowledge about who gets the biggest and smallest tips could help managers identify and hire those job applicants with the greatest tip earning potential and, therefore, likelihood of being retained. Of course, some classes of applicants with lower tip earning potential may be protected against discrimination in hiring, but hiring based on other characteristics that predict tip income remains legal. In addition, knowing if protected classes, such as older, female, or ethnic minority employees, get smaller tips than others could also help businesses avoid expensive lawsuits (Lynn et al., 2008). Specifically, it would inform them if they need to address any inequities in order to forestall potential class action discrimination lawsuits.

Finally, knowledge about who gets the best and who gets the worst tips would help altruistically minded tippers assess how much the servers they encounter need a generous tip from them. Arguably, those workers who routinely get smaller tips need more financial help than those who routinely get larger tips. To help achieve these varied benefits, the current chapter reviews research on who gets larger (and smaller) tip percentages. Specifically, we will look at how average tip percentages co-vary with the recipients' sexes, ages, races, physical appearances, work-experiences, work attitudes, and personalities.

Do Men Get Larger (or Smaller) Tips Than Women?

In 2022, U.S. women were paid 82 cents for every dollar a U.S. man was paid (Kochar, 2023). Does this gender pay gap generalize to tip sizes? Opinions of restaurant workers about this issue seem to differ, as reflected in the following comments found online at Quora.com:

> I've been a server for over 20 years and we all know waiters get tipped more than women. R.M.
> As a server, I can tell you women always make more money than men. S.S.
> I waited tables, and tips were very rarely gender specific. T.D.

Interestingly, empirical research on the issue is as divided as servers' opinions—some studies found that waiters got larger average tip percentages than waitresses (Brewster, 2015; Lynn, 2017; Lynn & McCall, 2009), others that waitresses got larger average tip percentages than waiters (Banks et al., 2018; Rodrigue, 1999), and still others (the vast majority of studies) that waiters and waitresses got comparable average tip percentages (Chi et al., 2011; Kim et al., 2017; Parrett, 2015). Despite their inconsistency with one another, each of these results has been found often enough to be taken seriously. What the data suggests is that server-sex affects tip sizes through a variety of processes whose combined or net effect depends on the circumstances. To better understand those processes and effects, we need to dig deeper into the data.

Why and When Waiters Get Larger Tips

Most of the studies finding that waiters earned larger tips than waitresses involved national samples of servers working at different restaurants (Brewster, 2015; Lynn, 2017; Lynn & McCall, 2009). One possible reason waiters may get larger tip percentages than waitresses in these studies is that societal and managerial biases lead waiters to work different shifts and at different types of restaurants than do waitresses and these employment differences lead to differences in tip percentages. In fact, surveys of U.S. restaurant servers that I conducted in 2006 and 2013 found that waiters are more likely than waitresses to work PM shifts and to work at expensive, fine-dining, and urban restaurants while waitresses are more likely than waiters to work AM shifts and to work at casual-dining and suburban restaurants. Furthermore, servers working PM shifts and those working at expensive, fine-dining, and urban restaurants report getting larger average tip percentages while servers working AM shifts and those working at suburban restaurants report getting smaller average tip percentages. Thus, it is possible that the observed gender gaps in tip percentages favoring waiters reflect employment differences among servers rather than sex-biases among tippers.

The only evidence I've seen that waiters get larger tips than waitresses working at comparable restaurants comes from an unpublished data set of charge sales records at a multi-state, Italian restaurant chain that I obtained about 20 years ago. Analyzing that data, I found that waiters got larger tip percentages than did waitresses even though both worked at the same chain and (judging from bill sizes) worked the same shifts. However, the tendency for waiters to get larger tip percentages than waitresses in that data was significantly more pronounced among older customers (see Fig. 7.2). This finding, combined with the absence of similar waiter vs. waitress effects on tipping that are more recent and robust, suggests to me that, although consumers may have once been biased against waitresses when tipping in restaurants, such a bias has probably declined over succeeding generations and is likely to have little effect among the vast majority of todays' restaurant customers. If waiters today earn larger tips than waitresses, it is probably only because they work better shifts and at more upscale and urban restaurants than do the waitresses against whom their tips are compared.

Why and When Waitresses Get Larger Tips

One potential reason waitresses sometimes get larger tips than waiters may be found in the idea that people often want to impress and please members of

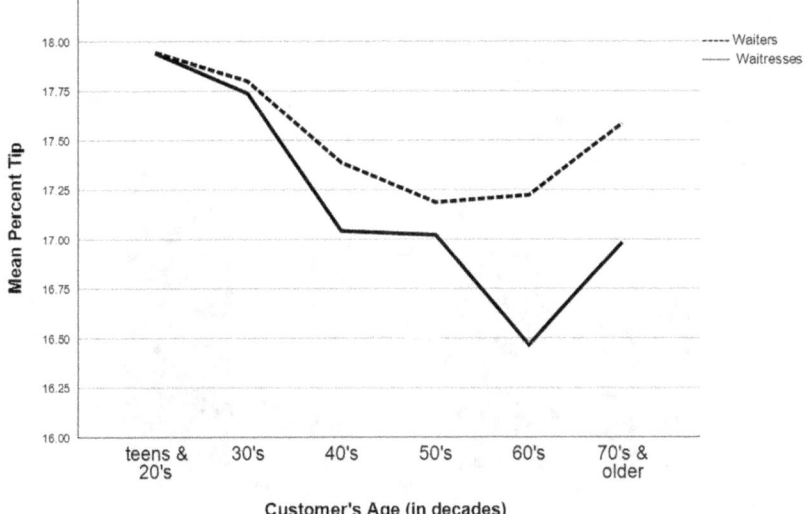

Fig. 7.2 Tendency for waiters to get larger tip percentages than waitresses at comparable restaurants was significantly more pronounced among older customers in an unpublished data set I obtained in 2001 [*The data, provided to me by a point-of-sale technology company called Gazelle, are over 25,000 anonymized charge sales records from among the top customers of a large, Italian restaurant chain along with demographic information about those anonymous customers*]

the opposite sex more than members of their own sex. In other words, people may tend to tip opposite-sex servers more than same-sex servers. Consistent with this possibility, studies have provided evidence that men (but not women) tip waitresses better than waiters (see Fig. 7.3) as well as evidence that women (but not men) tip waiters better than waitresses (Lynn et al., 2016; Conlin et al., 2003). Not all studies find these effects and those that do tend to find one effect or the other—no one has reported significant, opposite-sex-of-server effects on the tip sizes given by both male and female customers in a single study. However, the failures to find such effects for one or both sexes of customers may simply reflect insufficient sample sizes and/or differences in the relative attractiveness of the waiters and waitresses in those studies. People do not always tip opposite-sex servers more than same-sex servers, but the evidence suggests that they do so at least sometimes. Such an opposite-sex bias would obviously benefit waitresses more than waiters when a restaurant has more male than female customers paying the bill.

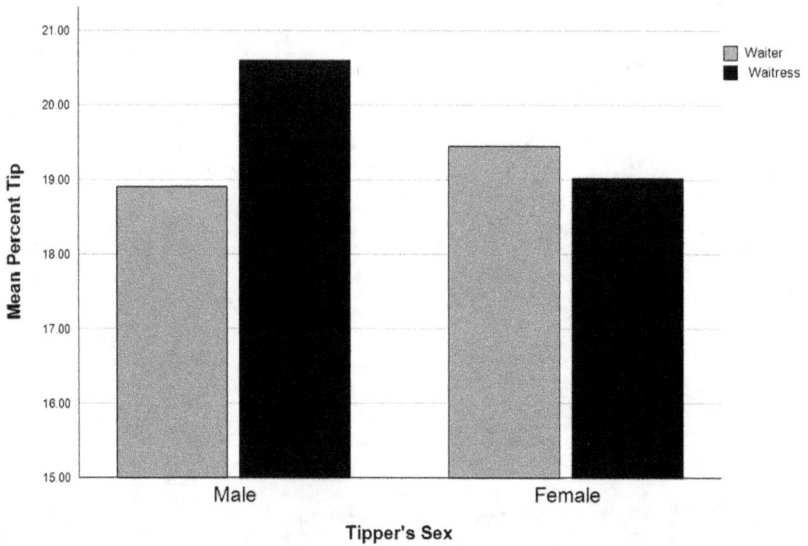

Fig. 7.3 Waitresses sometimes get larger tips than waiters when the tipper is male, but not when the tipper is female [*Data come from over 1000 consumers from across the U.S responding to a hypothetical scenario experiment in 2013* (Lynn et al., 2016)]

Conclusions About Server Sex Effects

In summary, there is some evidence that, as a group, waiters earn bigger tips than do waitresses, but that is largely because waiters tend to work better shifts and at more upscale and urban restaurants than do waitresses. There is also some evidence that, as a group, waitresses sometimes earn bigger tips than waiters working at the same restaurants. This may be attributable to a tendency for consumers to tip opposite-sex servers more than same-sex servers combined with a greater number of male than female restaurant customers who pay the bill at those restaurants. Most recent studies have found no significant differences in the overall tip percentages received by waiters and waitresses. Thus, there is little direct evidence of a broad or general tendency for both male and female consumers to tip waiters more than comparably employed waitresses or vice versa.[2]

---

[2] Some indirect and, to me, unpersuasive evidence of consumer discrimination in tipping that favors female service workers over male service workers can be found in a paper by Compton and Compton (2024). They report that (i) women are disproportionately represented in restaurant and bar service jobs (vs. comparable, non-tipped jobs), (ii) this imbalance is greater the larger the gap between the tipped and regular minimum wages, and (iii) this imbalance is greater for higher quality (e.g., more educated) workers. Assuming that most people seek the highest paying jobs available to them, these facts seem to suggest that women get larger tips than do men. However, it is more correct to say that the findings indicate women believe that tipped jobs pay more than comparable non-tipped

Of course, the evidence reviewed above does not rule out the possibility that women may get larger tips than men (or vice versa) in other service occupations. In fact, Chandar et al. (2019) report that both men and women tip female Uber drivers more than male Uber drivers. Whether other service occupations have worker-sex effects on tipping that resemble those for waiters/waitresses or those for ride-share drivers remains to be seen and would be a worthwhile topic for future research.

Does a Worker's Age Affect His or Her Tip Sizes?

The myriad motivations underlying tipping mean that there are good reasons to believe both that young workers will get larger tips than older ones and the reverse. Consumers may be inclined to tip young workers more generously than older ones because our society tends to view youth as more attractive and desirable than age (Chopik & Giasson, 2017), so consumers may care about the social approval and welfare of young workers more than that of older ones. On the other hand, consumers may be inclined to tip older workers more generously than younger ones because older workers are more likely to be fully supporting themselves and/or a family, so may have a greater perceived need for tip income. Given traditional sex roles in this country, one might expect that the former effect is stronger for waitresses while the latter effect is stronger for waiters. In that case, age may decrease the tips of female workers, but increase the tips of male workers. However, all of this is just speculation. Ultimately, the question of how worker age affects tip percentages is an empirical one.

Several published studies have addressed this empirical question by examining the relationship between restaurant servers' ages and the average tip sizes they receive. The results of those studies have been mixed—with some finding that younger restaurant servers get larger tips than older ones (Brewster, 2015; Lynn & McCall, 2009), some finding that older servers get larger tips than younger ones (Lynn, 2017; Lynn et al., 2011), others finding no reliable differences in the tip sizes received by restaurant servers of different ages (Medler-Liraz, 2020; Medler-Liraz & Seger-Guttmann, 2021), and one finding that waitresses in their thirties get larger tips than younger or older waitresses (Lynn, 2009). All of these studies involved surveys of current and/

---

jobs to a greater degree than do men. Since women are generally paid less than men for comparable work, they could be better off doing tipped work even if men earn the same or larger tips than women do. Tipped jobs may simply represent the lesser of two evils in this regard. Moreover, these findings could reflect sex differences in beliefs about compensation rather than sex differences in actual compensation.

or former restaurant servers, so their conflicting findings are unlikely to be methodologically based.

One thing the studies have in common is finding that server-sex effects on tip sizes (if any) are small. For example, Lynn and McCall's (2009) negative effect of server age on tipping accounted for only about half a percent of the variance in servers' average tips. Similarly, Lynn's (2017) positive effect of server age accounted for only about 1% of the variance in servers' average tips. Using other metrics, average tip percentages in the later study increased only 0.3% of the bill with every 10 years of server age (see Fig. 7.4). If one age group gets better restaurant tips than the other, the difference is too small to be of consequence.

How well this conclusion applies to other tipped occupations remains to be seen, but a recent unpublished study of the tips given to Uber drivers suggests that it may generalize. That study found that tips declined with driver age (especially for female drivers), but the difference in average tip between the best- and worst-tipped age categories was only 2 cents for male drivers and only 5 cents for female drivers (Chandar et al., 2019). Again, age differences in workers' tips were small and of little consequence.

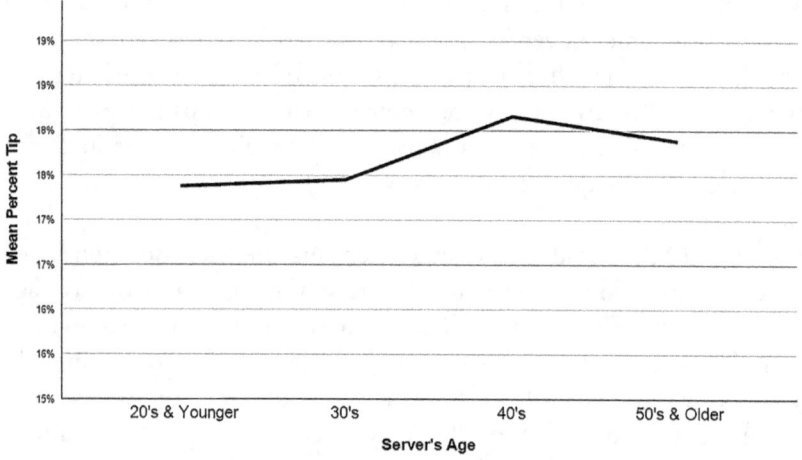

Fig. 7.4 Servers' average tip percentages increase only about 0.3% of the bill with every 10 years of server age [*Data are from* Lynn's (2017)*survey of almost 700 current restaurant servers from across the U.S.*]

Do Ethnic Minorities Get Smaller Tips?

Psychologists have documented widespread racial biases favoring Whites in the US population with 29% of people consciously espousing a pro-White bias and 65% demonstrating an automatic and unintended (implicit) bias favoring Whites over Blacks (Morehouse & Banaji, 2024). Even racial/ethnic minorities in America are highly likely to show an implicit bias favoring Whites over their own racial group. Since people tend to tip more when experiencing positive affect (Frank & Lynn, 2020), it is reasonable to expect that these racial biases would lead people to tip White service workers more than ethnic minority service workers. In fact, there is some evidence supporting this expectation.

A study of taxicab drivers in New Haven, CT, found that White drivers got substantially larger tips (20% vs. 13%) than other drivers (Ayres et al., 2004). Similarly, an unpublished study of Uber drivers from across the U.S found that drivers who resided in predominately White neighborhoods got larger tips than those who resided in more Black or Hispanic neighborhoods (Chandar et al., 2019). Finally, two surveys of restaurant diners who had just completed their meals (in Mississippi and Michigan) found that both Black and White diners reported tipping White servers more than Black servers (Brewster & Lynn, 2014; Lynn et al., 2008).[3]

This evidence of consumer racial discrimination in tipping notwithstanding, other research findings indicate no such bias. For example, two surveys of restaurant consumers about recently completed dining experiences found that respondents with White servers reported tipping no more or less than those with Non-White servers (Cho, 2014; Parrett, 2015). In addition, Brewster et al. (2022) conducted three hypothetical scenario studies all of which found that people said they would tip the same amount regardless of the server's apparent race, which was manipulated via server names (e.g., Tamika and Jamal vs. Emily and Brad) or via photographs of the server. It is tempting to dismiss these consumer-based findings as reflecting impression management demands rather than real tipping tendencies, but several surveys

---

[3] The paper by Compton and Compton (2024) previously discussed in footnote 2 also reported that (i) Whites are disproportionately represented in restaurant and bar service jobs (vs comparable, non-tipped jobs), (ii) this imbalance is greater the larger the gap between the tipped and regular minimum wages, and (iii) this imbalance is greater for higher quality (e.g., more educated) workers. Assuming that most people seek the highest paying jobs available to them, these facts seem to suggest that Whites get larger tips than do Non-Whites. However, it is more correct to say that the findings indicate that Whites are more likely than Non-Whites to believe that tipped jobs pay more than comparable non-tipped jobs. This could simply reflect a tendency for ethnic minorities to expect more discrimination in tipping than in wages. Thus, these findings could reflect race/ethnic differences in beliefs about discrimination in tipping rather than in actual discrimination in tipping.

of restaurant servers have found that White and Black servers report receiving similar average tip percentages (Brewster, 2015; Lynn, 2017; Lynn & McCall, 2009). Again, there is too much data both supporting and not supporting racial discrimination in tipping to ignore or discount either. This suggests that such discrimination does occur on some occasions, but not on others.

Identifying those boundary conditions for racial discrimination in tipping is an important task still to be accomplished. Some of my colleagues and I have made a start on this task (Lynn et al., 2008)—we found the Black servers got lower tips than White servers only when service was rated excellent (as opposed to moderately good). White servers delivering excellent service got an average tip of 23%, while Black servers delivering excellent service and both White and Black servers delivering moderately good service got an average tip of about 17%. We also found that the magnitude of the server race effect on tipping increased with the size of the dining party. However, these interactions need to be replicated before we should put much faith in them and other boundary conditions no doubt exist and are waiting to be found. Numerous restaurant chains and HR firms have data that would be helpful in studying this issue, but I have been unable to find one willing to make the data available for analysis. I suspect that they are afraid of the public relations and legal problems that might stem from public evidence of consumer racial discrimination in tipping. Hopefully, some enlightened company will eventually find the bravery to let their data speak about this important issue.

Do Physically Attractive Workers Get Larger Tips?

Lots of research indicates that we have a strong tendency to favor physically attractive people over less attractive ones. Attractive people are perceived as more intelligent and socially competent (Eagly et al., 1991) and as more desirable co-workers, dates, and marriage partners (Feingold, 1990; Stroebe et al., 1971) than are less attractive people. Furthermore, attractive employees receive better performance evaluations, promotions, and salaries than do less attractive employees (Toledano, 2013). It would be surprising if this bias did not also affect tipping and tests of this expectation in France, the Netherlands, and the United States have strongly supported it. Researchers have found that (i) restaurant diners who rate their server as more attractive leave larger tips (Parrett, 2003; Rønhovde, 2012), (ii) waitresses rated as more attractive by independent judges get larger tips (Lynn & Simons, 2000; May, 1978), and

(iii) waitresses with conventionally attractive features, such as made-up faces, large breasts, low body mass, and blond hair get larger average tips (Jacob et al., 2010; Lynn, 2009). Most of this research focused on waitresses, and one suggests that it may be limited to them (Lynn & Simons, 2000), but at least two studies have found that attractive waiters also get larger tips (Parrett, 2015; Xu et al., 2020).

Importantly, the effects of server attractiveness are large enough to be meaningful. May (1978) found that attractive waitresses (those rated 8–10 out of 10) were tipped about 3% of the bill more than their less attractive co-workers) while Parrett (2003) found that customers rating their server's attractiveness a 4 or 5 out of 5 tipped about 77 cents more than customers rating their servers a 3 out of 5. Using different metrics, Lynn and Simons (2000) found that ratings of server attractiveness accounted for 16% of the variability in waitresses' average tips (though none of the variability in waiters' average tips). These findings suggest that physically attractive people are likely to be happier in tipped jobs and to stay in them longer than less attractive people, something that both prospective tipped workers and the managers hiring them may want to keep in mind when making employment decisions.

Do Workers with Certain Personalities Get Larger Tips?

Psychologists are in general agreement that there are five major dimensions of personality—openness, conscientiousness, extraversion, agreeableness, and neuroticism. Openness is characterized by flexibility in thinking and acceptance of change. Conscientiousness is a tendency toward self-control and rule-following. Extraversion is tendency to be social, outgoing, and focused on rewards. Agreeableness is a tendency get along with and care for others. Neuroticism is a tendency toward emotional volatility and negative affect. These big five personality traits are related to a variety of different behaviors including employee performance and it seems likely that they may also affect tip income. In particular, to the extent that tipping is a reward for attentive, friendly, and good service, then outgoing, agreeable, and hard-working service employees might be expected to receive larger tips than others. Surprisingly, however, a study of 259 restaurant servers in Israel found no reliable relationships between the servers' tip averages and any of their big five personality traits—whether those traits were assessed by the servers themselves or by their customers (Zeigler-Hill et al., 2015).[4] It would appear that role demands and the incentives provided by tips overcome servers' personalities in driving their verbal and non-verbal behaviors toward customers.

Do More Experienced Servers Get Larger Tips?

The old adage that "practice makes perfect" suggests another potential explanation for differences in the average tips received by different workers. Perhaps job experience is responsible. Experienced servers may be the ones getting larger tips because practice has taught them how to do the job better—both how to deliver better service and how to establish better rapport with customers. Consistent with this possibility, researchers have found that restaurant servers with more tenure in the occupation report getting larger average tips than do servers with shorter tenures (Brewster, 2015; Lynn & McCall, 2009; Lynn et al., 2011).[5] However, this relationship may have nothing to do with the effects of experience or tenure on tipping. It could reflect the opposite, namely a tendency for servers who get good tips to stay in the occupation longer than those who get poor tips.

Consistent with the alternative "tips cause tenure" possibility are results from an analysis I did of the charge tips of restaurant servers over time (Lynn, 2023). I found that servers' tip percentages did not reliably increase with a running count of their workdays (i.e., growing experience) when controlling for total number of workdays eventually accumulated (i.e., job tenure), but did increase with job tenure when controlling for the effects of growing experience. These findings suggest that growing job experience has no causal effect on servers' tips, which lends credence to the idea that the tenure-tipping relationship may reflect a tendency for those who get better tips to stay in the job or occupation longer. This study looked at job rather than occupational tenure, so more research is needed to see if similar results would be obtained with occupational tenure. However, if experience on the job does not increase tips it is hard to see why experience in the occupation would. Thus, I doubt that differences in work experience account for differences in the tips received by different workers.

---

[4] Other tests involving single personality traits have replicated some of these null results. Chi et al. (2011) found that extraverted servers got the same size tips as more introverted servers ($N = 60$ servers) and Midler-Liraz (2020) found that agreeable servers got the same size tips as more disagreeable servers ($N = 502$ servers).
[5] The data is less consistent about the relationship of tip averages with tenure in a specific job. One study found a positive relationship (Lynn, 2023), but two others did not (Kim, Nemeschansky and Brandt, 2017; Medler-Liraz, 2020).

Do Service Workers with a Better Work Attitude Get Larger Tips?

If work experience does not explain why some tipped employees get larger tips than others, what about work attitude? Do more service-oriented workers who like their jobs get better tips than less service-oriented and contented co-workers? The answer to this question is "perhaps." Researchers have found that workers with more positive service attitudes and greater job satisfaction do get larger tips (Kim et al., 2017; Lynn, 2017; Lynn et al., 2011). However, causality could go the other direction here as well—getting larger tips may make workers happier with their work and job. Even if positive work attitudes do increase tips, their effects are modest at best. Job satisfaction accounts for less than 6% of the variability in servers' average tip percentages.

Summary and Conclusions

In summary, tipping compensates some workers substantially more than others even when the services they provide are comparable. Under at least some conditions, men and ethnic minorities in the U.S. are tipped less than women and Whites. This raises the very real possibility that, as a business practice that adversely affects protected classes of workers, the use of tipping as form of regular compensation violates the Civil Rights Act of 1964. This is not a court tested interpretation of the law, but it is a reasonable interpretation that has been seriously considered in several law review articles (Bartlett & Gulati, 2016; Feltham, 2017; Kline, 2016; Wang, 2014). Unfortunately for workers and for social justice broadly, it is unclear how pervasive the adverse impact of tipping is. Major restaurant chains should allow use of their data to identify the extent (or boundary conditions) of tipping's adverse impact on protected workers. Doing so would provide them with forewarning about potential legal problems that they could then take action to ward off. Providing such data to academic researchers could be made contingent on a non-disclosure agreement ensuring that the data source remains anonymous. Furthermore, withholding such data from the public seems unlikely to prevent lawsuits. Even without more public data, there is probably enough evidence of adverse impact to initiate a class action lawsuit, which would entail mandatory disclosure of relevant tip compensation data. Again, I would encourage restaurant chains to get ahead of the problem rather than wait to be blindsided by such a potential lawsuit.

There is also evidence that physically attractive workers (especially women) get larger tips than their less attractive co-workers. While not surprising, this supports the decisions of some less attractive people to pursue non-tipped rather than tipped employment as well as the no doubt common practice of managers to hire more physically attractive job applicants. Note that while hiring based on looks may be politically incorrect, it is not unlawful unless it is used to discriminate against protected classes like the elderly or people of color. Since less physically attractive people get smaller tips and are not protected against such wage discrimination under law, compassionate consumers may want to go against the common practice and tip those workers more than they otherwise would. Conversely, consumers who tip mostly to make up for poor server wages may want to give smaller tips to physically attractive workers because those workers get larger tips from their other customers.

The effects of other server characteristics—server age, personality, work experience, and work attitude—appear to have little if any effect on the servers' average tip percentages. In fact, all of the server characteristics discussed in this chapter together explain only a small fraction of the variance in servers average tip percentages. For this book, I reanalyzed a dataset from Lynn (2017) involving almost 700 current servers at sit down restaurants from across the country to see what the joint effect of server sex, age, race (White vs. Non-White), big five personality traits, work experience, job satisfaction, and service-orientation on the servers' tip averages was. Unfortunately, the data did not include a measure of server attractiveness, but all of the other server characteristics combined accounted for only 7% of the variance in servers' average tip percentages. What this suggests is that no server characteristic is really critical to getting good tips. Instead, servers' average tip percentages are determined by the unique combination of many traits that each server brings to the table.

References

Ayres, I., Vars, F. & Zakariya, N. (2004). To insure prejudice: Racial disparities in taxicab tipping. Yale Law Journal, 114, 1613–1674.

Banks, G. C., Woznyj, H. M., Kepes, S., Batchelor, J. H., & McDaniel, M. A. (2018). A meta-analytic review of tipping compensation practices: An agency theory perspective. *Personnel Psychology, 71*(3), 457–478.

Bartlett, K. T., & Gulati, M. (2016). Discrimination by customers. *Iowa Law Review, 102*, 223.

Brewster, Z. W. (2015). Perceptions of intergroup tipping differences, discriminatory service, and tip earnings among restaurant servers. *International Journal of Hospitality Management, 46*, 15–25.

Brewster, Z. W., Gourlay, K., & Nowak, G. R., III. (2022). Are black restaurant servers tipped less than white servers? Three experimental tests of server race effects on customers' tipping behaviors. *Cornell Hospitality Quarterly, 63*(4), 433–447.

Brewster, Z. W., & Lynn, M. (2014). Black–white earnings gap among restaurant servers: A replication, extension, and exploration of consumer racial discrimination in tipping. *Sociological Inquiry, 84*(4), 545–569.

Chandar, B., Gneezy, U., List, J. A., & Muir, I. (2019). *The drivers of social preferences: Evidence from a nationwide tipping field experiment* (No. w26380). National Bureau of Economic Research.

Cho, S. B. (2014). Factors affecting restaurant consumers' tipping behavior. *Journal of the Korean Society for Quality Management, 42*(1), 15–32.

Compton, J., & Compton, R. A. (2024). Disentangling customer and employer discrimination using state variation in the tipped minimum wage. *Journal of Economics, Race, and Policy, 7*(2), 65–81.

Conlin, M., Lynn, M. & O'Donoghue, T. (2003). The norm of restaurant tipping. Journal of Economic Behavior & Organization, 52 (3), 297–321.

Eagly, A. H., Ashmore, R. D., Makhijani, M. G., & Longo, L. C. (1991). What is beautiful is good, but…: A meta-analytic review of research on the physical attractiveness stereotype. *Psychological Bulletin, 110*(1), 109.

Feingold, A. (1990). Gender differences in effects of physical attractiveness on romantic attraction: A comparison across five research paradigms. *Journal of Personality and Social Psychology, 59*(5), 981.

Feltham, J. (2017). The limits of the law: Tipping, employment discrimination, and legal theories for plaintiffs under Title VII. *Wisconsin Journal of Law, Gender & Society, 32*, 65.

Frank, D. G., & Lynn, M. (2020). Shattering the illusion of the self-earned tip: The effect of a restaurant magician on co-workers' tips. *Journal of Behavioral and Experimental Economics, 87*, Article 101560.

Hana, Medler-Liraz Tali, Seger-Guttmann (2021) The joint effect of flirting and emotional labor on customer service-related outcomes Journal of Retailing and Consumer Services 60: 102497. https://doi.org/10.1016/j.jretconser.2021.102497

Jacob, C., Guéguen, N., Boulbry, G., & Ardiccioni, R. (2010). Waitresses' facial cosmetics and tipping: A field experiment. *International Journal of Hospitality Management, 29*(1), 188–190.

Kim, P. B., Nemeschansky, B., & Brandt, L. (2017). An exploratory study of determinants for restaurant servers' actual tip earnings: Individual characteristics and work conditions. *Journal of Foodservice Business Research, 20*(1), 15–33.

Kline, J. (2016). Fifteen percent or less: A Title VII analysis of racial discrimination in restaurant tipping. *Iowa Law Review, 101*, 1651.

Kochar, R. (2023, March 1). The enduring grip of the gender pay gap. Available at: www.pewresearch.orh. Accessed August 30, 2024.

Kwortnik Jr., R.J., Lynn, M. & Ross, W.T. (2009). Buyer monitoring: A means to insure personalized service. *Journal of Marketing Research*, 46 (5), 573–583.

Lynn, M. (2009). Determinants and consequences of female attractiveness and sexiness: Realistic tests with restaurant waitresses. *Archives of Sexual Behavior*, 38, 737–745.

Lynn, M. (2017). Does tipping help to attract and retain better service workers? *Journal of Foodservice Business Research*, 20(1), 82–89.

Lynn, M. (2023). Do tip percentages affect server job tenure, or vice versa?: Evidence from a panel dataset. *Compensation & Benefits Review*, 55(2), 76–84.

Lynn, M., Giebelhausen, M., Garcia, S., Li, Y., & Patumanon, I. (2016). Clothing color and tipping: An attempted replication and extension. *Journal of Hospitality & Tourism Research*, 40(4), 516–524.

Lynn, M., Kwortnik, R. J., Jr., & Sturman, M. C. (2011). Voluntary tipping and the selective attraction and retention of service workers in the USA: An application of the ASA model. *The International Journal of Human Resource Management*, 22(9), 1887–1901.

Lynn, M., & McCall, M. (2009). Techniques for increasing servers' tips: How generalizable are they? *Cornell Hospitality Quarterly*, 50(2), 198–208.

Lynn, M., & Simons, T. (2000). Predictors of male and female servers' average tip earnings 1. *Journal of Applied Social Psychology*, 30(2), 241–252.

Lynn, M., Sturman, M., Ganley, C., Adams, E., Douglas, M., & McNeil, J. (2008). Consumer racial discrimination in tipping: A replication and extension. *Journal of Applied Social Psychology*, 38(4), 1045–1060.

May, J. M. (1978). *Tip or treat: A study of factors affecting tipping behavior*. Masters Thesis, Loyola University of Chicago.

Medler-Liraz, H. (2020). Customer incivility, rapport and tipping: The moderating role of agreeableness. *Journal of Services Marketing*, 34(7), 955–966.

Morehouse, K. N., & Banaji, M. R. (2024). The science of implicit race bias: Evidence from the Implicit Association Test. *Dædalus*, 153(1), 21–50.

Nai-Wen, Chi Alicia A., Grandey Jennifer A., Diamond Kathleen Royer, Krimmel (2011) Want a tip? Service performance as a function of emotion regulation and extraversion. Journal of Applied Psychology 96(6) 1337–1346 https://doi.org/10.1037/a0022884

Parrett, M. (2003). *The give and take of restaurant tipping*. Dissertation, Dept. of Economics, Virginia Polytechnic Institute and State University.

Parrett, M. (2015). Beauty and the feast: Examining the effect of beauty on earnings using restaurant tipping data. *Journal of Economic Psychology*, 49, 34–46.

Rodrigue, K. (1999). Tipping tips: The effects of personalization on restaurant gratuity. Masters Thesis, Division of Psychology and Special Education, Emporia State University.

Rønhovde, A. S. (2012). *Relationship between service quality and tipping in Norway: Do perceived service quality and other factors have a relationship with tip size in Norwegian restaurants?* Master's thesis, University of Stavanger.

Stroebe, W., Insko, C. A., Thompson, V. D., & Layton, B. D. (1971). Effects of physical attractiveness, attitude similarity, and sex on various aspects of interpersonal attraction. *Journal of Personality and Social Psychology, 18*(1), 79.

Toledano, E. (2013). May the best (looking) man win: The unconscious role of attractiveness in employment decisions. *Cornell HR Review.* https://hdl.handle.net/1813/73005

Wang, L. I. (2014). At the tipping point: Race and gender discrimination in a common economic transaction. *Virginia Journal of Social Policy & the Law, 21*, 101.

William J., Chopik Hannah L., Giasson (2017) (2017) (2017) Age Differences in Explicit and Implicit Age Attitudes Across the Life Span The Gerontologist 57(suppl_2) S169–S177 https://doi.org/10.1093/geront/gnx058

Xu, S., Martinez, L., & Smith, N. A. (2020). The effects of attractiveness, gender and self-esteem in service jobs. *International Journal of Contemporary Hospitality Management, 32*(1), 249–266.

Zeigler-Hill, V., Besser, A., Vrabel, J., & Noser, A. E. (2015). Would you like fries with that? The roles of servers' personality traits and job performance in the tipping behavior of customers. *Journal of Research in Personality, 57*, 110–118.

8

Mega Tips (How Can Servers Get Larger Tips?)

Approximately 4 million workers in the United States receive at least a portion of their compensation in the form of tips (Tedeschi, 2024). According to data from the online compensation company Payscale (2015), tips represent up to 10% of income for counter attendants, dog groomers, hotel housekeepers, tattoo artists, and tow truck drivers; 11–29% for baristas, doormen, haircutters, massage therapists, parking attendants, taxi drivers, and tour guides; 30–49% for baggage porters (or bell hops), busboys/girls, pizza delivery drivers, and sommeliers; and 50% or more for bartenders, casino/gaming dealers, and waiters/waitresses (Lynn, 2024). All of these workers would benefit to some degree from learning strategies and tactics that increase the tips their consumers leave. Managers and executives in tipped industries also stand to benefit from learning how to increase their employees' tips, because better compensated workers tend to be happier, more productive, and less prone to quit (Lynn, 2005). Even consumers might benefit from learning about the techniques that tipped workers use to extract more money out of their wallets.

Given its utility, researchers have devoted a fair amount of effort studying this issue. Most of the research has been done in restaurants, but not all. Furthermore, many of the techniques for increasing restaurant tips should work in other service contexts as well, so service workers in a variety of occupations should find them of interest. This chapter will summarize what that body of research has taught us.[1] It begins with the broader strategies of maximizing sales and delivering better service and then moves on to more specific, tactical behaviors that have been experimentally proven to increase tips. Many of the later tactics are not obvious, and they increase tips by 20% or more, so read on if you are a service worker wanting to increase your own tip income, a service manager wanting to increase your employee's tip incomes, and/or a consumer wanting to identify (and perhaps resist) the formers' techniques for parting you from your money.

Maximizing Sales

It is customary to tip restaurant servers, as well as some other service providers, a percentage of the bill. For these workers, tip income can be increased by increasing sales. Waiters and waitresses can increase their sales and, therefore, tip income by working at more expensive restaurants, working busier shifts (e.g., on weekend and/or dinner shifts over weekday and/or breakfast shifts), turning tables quickly, and/or engaging in suggestive selling. Most servers already know this, but what they may not know is how important this strategy is and how much to prioritize it.

In an average U.S. restaurant, bill size accounts for 70% of the variance in tips that different dining parties leave (Lynn & McCall, 2000). This means ***bill size is twice as powerful as everything else combined*** in determining dollar and cent tip amounts! Thus, increasing their sales should be one of the highest priorities of servers seeking to earn more tip income. Aside from changing work shifts or places of employment, this means using suggestive selling—recommending appetizers, liquor, wine, expensive entrée selections, and desserts. Research has demonstrated that suggestive selling is an effective way to increase restaurant bills by as much as 23% (Butler & Snizek, 1976). Suggesting more expensive options is usually a good idea, but suggestive selling of appetizers and desserts may be counter-productive during a busy shift because those add-on items will increase the customer's meal duration and slow down table turnover. Since entrées are more expensive than appetizers and desserts, servers should probably avoid suggestive selling of appetizers and desserts in favor of turning tables quickly as long as new customers are waiting to be seated. When turning tables is not possible, then sell more appetizers and desserts too.

---

[1] Portions of this chapter are drawn from my 2011 Cornell Center for Hospitality Research paper titled "MegaTips 2: Twenty Tested Techniques to Increase Your Tips" (Lynn, 2011), available online at https://ecommons.cornell.edu/items/aaa79631-eff5-43eb-96ac-473e4ffea561.

Delivering Better Service

Tips are supposed to be an incentive/reward for good service and (as discussed in Chap. 2) consumers do tip more for better service. Tips have been found to increase with the number of items waiters and waitresses bring to a table (Bodvarsson & Gibson, 1994), the number of in-room service activities performed by hotel bellmen (Lynn & Gregor, 2001), the speed of restaurant delivery services (Kerr & Domazlicky, 2009), the safer driving behaviors of Uber drivers (Chandar et al., 2019), and the length and timeliness of answers to questions provided by online researchers working at Google Answers (Regner, 2014). Thus, tipped workers should always strive to provide good service.

I have argued elsewhere that service is a weak determinant of restaurant tips because the average correlation between percent tip and the best measures of service (i.e., indices averaging customers' ratings of multiple dimensions of service) is only 0.22 (Lynn & McCall, 2000). This means that customers' perceptions of service explain only about 5% of the variance (or differences) in tips left by different dining parties. The average correlation is even smaller (about $r = 0.11$) when single item and/or other measures of service quality are used (Lynn & McCall, 2000). However, correlations (or variance accounted for) may not be the descriptor of the service-tipping relationship most relevant to tipped workers. What these workers want to know is how much their tips will go up for a given improvement in service. To answer this question, I obtained 12 estimates of the slope of the tip-service relationship from various academic publications and data sets in my possession. All involved surveys of restaurant customers asking them to rate the service and indicate what their bill and tip sizes were on specific dining occasions. On average, a 1-point increase in service on a 5-point scale was associated with a 1.5-point increase in percent tip in this limited sample. Thus, improving service from middling (3/5) to excellent (5/5) can reasonably be expected to increase tips by 3% of the bill on average.

Unfortunately, improving service is a vague goal which most service workers are unlikely to achieve. Specifically, what about current service a server should try to improve and how they can do so are not obvious. Furthermore, for the average service worker, substantial improvements in service are unlikely because their baseline of current service is already high. Conlin et al. (2003) interviewed over 1300 customers leaving numerous restaurants in Texas and found that they rated their server an average of 4.4 out of 5 on appearance, 4.5 on knowledge, 4.6 on friendliness, 4.4 on speed, and 4.3 on attentiveness. This case is not atypical. Eleven other studies with customer ratings of restaurant service during a specific dining experience have found average service ratings that varied from 3.7 to 4.6 with a grand mean of 4.2 on a 5-point scale. When servers are already delivering service this good, it is unlikely that they could consistently and substantially improve their service further.

Mega Tips for Workers

The strategies of selling more and improving service are important, but arguably tipped workers would benefit more from tactical advice about specific behaviors they can easily perform that increase tips. Fortunately for them, there is a body of experiments and quasi-experiments in applied social psychology, communications, and hospitality management identifying such behaviors.[2] This research is summarized in Table 8.1 and discussed briefly in the sections that follow. The table and discussion are organized around key reasons likely to explain the behaviors' effectiveness in increasing tips. To be clear and transparent, all of the tactics or "mega tips" to be discussed have been empirically shown to increase tips in actual service settings (no hypothetical scenario studies here). However, the explanations I offer for their effectiveness, though plausible and consistent with research in other domains, are conjectural and in need of testing.

Rapport Building Tactics

The largest set of behavioral tactics that increase tips also increase interpersonal attraction, closeness, and/or liking. We are more likely to help people and to care about others' opinions of us when we feel connected with them (Kelley & Byrne, 1976; Millar, 2002), so these behaviors are likely to increase tips because they increase altruistic and/or impression-management motivations for tipping. The specific rapport building behaviors that have been shown to increase tips are smiling, touching customers, standing close to

---

[2] Experiments and quasi-experiments involve experimenter manipulation of some variable to examine its impact on another variable. The difference between experiments and quasi-experiments is that the manipulation is done randomly in experiments and non-randomly in quasi-experiments. Random assignment to experimental conditions means that the experimental and control groups differ only by chance, so any post-manipulation differences in the outcome variable that is bigger than expected by chance must be caused by the manipulation. Unfortunately, random assignment is not always possible, so manipulations are sometimes done non-randomly. Such quasi-experiments permit causal inferences that are weaker than those from true experiments with random assignment, but even non-random experimental manipulation allows stronger causal inferences that can be drawn from purely observational or correlational research.

Table 8.1 Description of experiments and quasi-experiments on concrete ways servers can increase their tips

Author (year)/Country	Experimental treatment	Average tip in control condition	Average tip in treatment condition	Percentage increase in tip	Comments
Rapport building tactics					
#1 Smile at customers					
Tidd and Lockard (1978)/USA	Cocktail waitress gave customers big smile (versus small smile)	$4.70	$11.60	147%	Big smile increased tips from men and women
Rind and Bordia (1996)/USA	Restaurant servers drew a smiley face on check (versus not)	27.8%	33.0%	19%	Results are for waitress only; drawing a smiley face non-significantly decreased waiter's tips
#2 Touch customers					
Crusco and Wetzel (1984)/USA	Waitresses touched customer on hand or shoulder (versus not)	12.2%	15.6%	28%	Slightly better results with touching customer on hand
Stephen and Zweigenhaft (1986)/USA	Waitress touched customers from two-tops (versus not)	11%	14%	27%	

(continued)

Table 8.1 (continued)

Author (year)/Country	Experimental treatment	Average tip in control condition	Average tip in treatment condition	Percentage increase in tip	Comments
Hornik (1992)/unknown country	Restaurant servers touched customers (versus not)	14.5%	17.7%	22%	Effect was stronger for female customers; Effect was especially strong when attractive waitresses touched female customers
Lynn et al. (1998)/USA	Waiter touched customer (versus no touch)	11.5%	14.8%	29%	Brief and prolonged touch produced same effect on tipping
Gueguen and Jacob (2005)/France	Bar waitress touched customer (versus not)	10.8% tipped 0.24 Euro	24.6% tipped 0.28 Euro	Tipping likelihood: 128% Size of tip: < 2%	
Hubbard et al. (2003)/USA	Restaurant servers touched customers (versus not)	10.5% in restaurant 15.8% in bar	15.8% in restaurant 28.8% in bar	50% in restaurant 82% in bar	Effect in restaurant was similar across server and customer sex; Effect in bar was stronger when male and female customers were touched by opposite sex server

Author (year)/Country	Experimental treatment	Average tip in control condition	Average tip in treatment condition	Percentage increase in tip	Comments
Jewell (2008)/USA	Waitresses touched customers (versus not)	$4.68	$4.71	< 1%	Effect was not significant
#3 Stand close to customers					
Jacob and Gueguen (2012)/France	Waitresses stood 0.5 ft away from table (versus normal 1.5 ft away)	31.1% tipped 1.17 Euros	42.9% tipped 1.41 Euros	Tipping likelihood: 38% Size of tip: 21%	Standing 2.5 ft away decreased tipping slightly (versus 1.5 ft away)
#4 Squat next to the table					
Lynn and Mynier (1993 S1)/USA	Waiter squatted next to table (versus stood)	$5.18 (14.9%)	$6.40 (17.5%)	24%	
Lynn and Mynier (1993 S2)/USA	Waitress squatted next to table (versus stood)	$2.56 (12%)	$3.28 (15%)	28%	
Davis et al. (1998)/USA	Restaurant servers squatted next to table (versus not)	13.9%	15.8%	14%	
Leodoro and Lynn (2007)/USA	Restaurant waitress sat down at table (versus stood)	White customers: 18.3% Black customers: 13.0%	White customers: 20.5% Black customers: 11.6%	White customers: 12% Black customers: −11%	Effect for whites was significant, but not effect for blacks; race × posture interaction was significant
#5 Introduce yourself by name					

(continued)

Table 8.1 (continued)

Author (year)/Country	Experimental treatment	Average tip in control condition	Average tip in treatment condition	Percentage increase in tip	Comments
Garrity and Degelman (1990)/USA	Waitress introduced herself by name (versus not)	$3.49	$5.44	56%	
Shih et al. (2019)/USA	Room contained a signed greeting card with picture of maid (versus an unsigned card with no picture of maid)	4% tipped $6.10 (when given)	6% tipped $6.10 (when given)	Tipping likelihood: 50% Size of tip: 0%	Effect on tip size when given was not statistically significant
Shih et al. (2019)/USA	Room contained a handwritten greeting card for guests (versus a printed card)	4% tipped $6.47 (when given)	6% tipped $5.76 (when given)	Tipping likelihood: 50% Size of tip: -11%	Effect on tip size when given was not statistically significant
Shih et al. (2019)/USA	Room contained a greeting card for guests (versus no card)	4% tipped $4.64 (when given)	5% tipped $7.92 (when given)	Tipping likelihood: 15% n.s Size of tip: 71%	Effect on tipping likelihood was not statistically significant
#6 Call customers by name					
Adams and Pettijohn (2016)/USA	Restaurant servers added customer's title and last name to "Thank You" written on check (versus not)	15.6%	18.6%	19%	Adding customer's first name (instead of last name) did not increase tips

Author (year)/ Country	Experimental treatment	Average tip in control condition	Average tip in treatment condition	Percentage increase in tip	Comments
Rodrigue (1999 S!)/ USA	Restaurant servers called credit card customers by name (versus not)	14.0%	15.4%	10%	Effect was similar at lunch and dinner and for waiters and waitresses
Seiter et al. (2016)/ USA	Waitresses invited mutual introductions and used customers names (versus not)	17.3%	23.6%	36%	
Seiter and Weger (2013)/USA	Restaurant servers thanked customers with customers' first or last name (versus no name)	16%	18.9%	18%	Calling younger customers by first name increased tips more than using their title and last name, while the reverse was true for older customers

#7 Mimic customers

Van Baaren et al. (2003 S!)/ Netherlands	Waitress repeated customer's order verbatim when taking order (versus not)	61% tipped 1.76 Dutch Guilders	81% tipped 2.97 Dutch Guilders	Tipping likelihood: 33% Size of tip:69%	

(continued)

Table 8.1 (continued)

Author (year)/Country	Experimental treatment	Average tip in control condition	Average tip in treatment condition	Percentage increase in tip	Comments
Van Baaren et al. (2003 S2)/Netherlands	Waitress repeated customer's order verbatim when taking order (versus not)	52% tipped 1.36 Dutch Guilders	78% tipped 2.73 Dutch Guilders	Tipping likelihood: 50% Size of tip: 100%	
Jacob and Gueguen (2013)/France	Waitress repeated customer's order verbatim when taking order (versus no mimicry)	31.1% tipped 1.27 Euros	46.6% tipped 1.65 Euros	Tipping likelihood: 50% Size of tip: 30%	
#8 Thank customers					
Rind and Bordia (1995)/USA	Waitress wrote "Thank You" on check (versus not)	16.3%	18.1%	11%	Server signing thank-you did not improve tips further; Alferovicova (2016) failed to replicate this effect in Czechoslovakia

Author (year)/ Country	Experimental treatment	Average tip in control condition	Average tip in treatment condition	Percentage increase in tip	Comments
#9 Highlight common social identities					
Seiter and Gass (2005)/USA	Waitresses wrote "United We Stand" on checks (versus "Have a Nice Day")	15.9%	19.9%	25%	Writing "God Bless America" on the check resulted in a tip average of 17.9%. This study was conducted shortly after the 9/11 attacks
#10 Display charitableness					
Jacob et al. (2013)/ France	Waitresses wrote "A good turn never goes amiss" on the check (versus no note)	38.8% tipped 0.24 Euros	47.0% tipped 0.56 Euros	Tipping likelihood: 21% Size of tip: 133%	Writing "He who writes reads twice" had no effect on tipping; Alferovicova (2016) failed to replicate this effect in Czechoslovakia
Khadjavi (2017)/ Germany	Hairdressers collected donations for a children's charity (versus not)	2.21 Euros	2.83 Euros	28%	Tips did not increase further when the hairdressers pledged to personally donate 1 Euro per customer

(continued)

Table 8.1 (continued)

Author (year)/Country	Experimental treatment	Average tip in control condition	Average tip in treatment condition	Percentage increase in tip	Comments
Appearance enhancing tactics					
#11 Go blond					
Gueguen (2012)/France	Waitress wore blond wig (versus other color wigs)	38.6% tipped 0.93 Euros	56.2% tipped 1.24 Euros	Tipping likelihood: 24% Size of tip: 33%	Results are for male customers only; wig color did not affect female customers' tipping; Lynn (2009) also found a positive correlation between blond hair and waitresses tips
Jiang and Galm (2014)/USA	Waitresses dyed hair blond (versus Natural color)	17.2%	18.6%	8%	Significance test was not reported
#12 Wear make-up					
Jacob et al. (2009)/France	Waitresses wore make-up (versus not)	34.4% tipped 1.11 Euros	51.2% tipped 1.40 Euros	Tipping likelihood: 49% Size of tip: 26%	Results are for male customers only; wearing make-up did not affect female customers' tipping

Author (year)/ Country	Experimental treatment	Average tip in control condition	Average tip in treatment condition	Percentage increase in tip	Comments
Gueguen and Jacob (2011)/France	Waitress wore make-up (versus not)	32.2% tipped 1.12 Euros	55.2% tipped 1.61 Euros	Tipping likelihood: 71% Size of tip: 44%	Results are for male customers only; wearing make-up did not affect female customers' tipping
Gueguen and Jacob (2012)/France	Restaurant waitresses wore red lipstick (versus none)	30.3% tipped 1.04 Euros	50.6% tipped 1.53 Euros	Tipping likelihood: 67% Size of tip: 47%	Results are for male customers only; wearing red lipstick did not affect female customers' tipping; wearing pink or brown lipstick had weaker effects on the tips of male patrons
#13 Ornament your hair					
Stillman and Hensley (1980)/USA	Waitresses wore flower in hair (versus not)	$1.49 per-person	$1.73 per-person	16%	
Jacob et al. (2012)/ France	Waitresses wore a decorative hair barrette (versus no barrette)	29.0% tipped 1.05 Euros	41.0% tipped 1.20 Euros	Tipping likelihood: 41% Size of tip: 14%	

(continued)

Table 8.1 (continued)

Author (year)/Country	Experimental treatment	Average tip in control condition	Average tip in treatment condition	Percentage increase in tip	Comments
#14 Wear red					
Gueguen and Jacob (2014)/France	Waitresses wore red t-shirt (versus other colored t-shirts)	37.2% tipped 1.02 Euros	58.0% tipped 1.30 Euros	Tipping likelihood: 56% Size of tip: 27%	Results are for male customers only; t-shirt color did not affect female customers' tipping; Lynn et al. (2016) failed to replicate this effect in a hypothetical scenario study conducted in the U.S
#15 Dress up					
Jacob and Gueguen (2014)/France	Pizza delivery driver wore suit (versus casual clothes)	3.23 Euros	6.01 Euros	86%	
Reciprocity inducing tactics					
#16 Give customers something					
Rodrigue (1999 S2)/USA	Restaurant servers gave customers candy (versus no candy)	14.1%	16.1%	14%	Effect was similar at lunch and dinner and for waiters and waitresses

Author (year)/Country	Experimental treatment	Average tip in control condition	Average tip in treatment condition	Percentage increase in tip	Comments
Strohmetz et al. (2002)/USA	Waiters gave customers candy (versus not)	15.1%	17.8%	18%	
Strohmetz et al. (2002)/USA	Waitress customers 1, 2 or 1 + 1 pieces of candy (versus no candy)	19.0%	21.4%	13%	Giving one piece of candy per-person and then adding another resulted in the best tips—23.0%
Frank (2020)/USA	Restaurant magician gave customers a card used in performance at their table (versus no gift)	27% tipped $6.89 when given	75% tipped $12.00 when given	Tipping likelihood: 178% Size of tip: 74%	These results are for tips to magician
Frank and Lynn (2020 S1)/USA	Restaurant magician gave customers a card used in performance at their table (versus no gift)	$2.71	$7.18	165%	These results are for tips to magician
Frank and Lynn (2020 S2)/USA	Restaurant magician gave customers a card used in performance at their table (versus no gift)	$2.20	$7.52	341%	These results are for tips to magician

(continued)

Table 8.1 (continued)

Author (year)/Country	Experimental treatment	Average tip in control condition	Average tip in treatment condition	Percentage increase in tip	Comments
#17 Inform customers					
Rind and Strohmetz (1999)/USA	Waitress wrote about an upcoming dinner special on check (versus not)	17.0%	19.9%	17%	
#18 Compliment customers					
Seiter and Dutson (2007)/USA	Hairstylist complimented customer (versus no compliment)	9.1%	12.7%	40%	
Seiter (2007)/USA	Waitresses complimented customers' food choices (versus not)	16.4%	18.9%	16%	
Seiter and Weger (2010)/USA	Restaurant servers complimented customers' food choices (versus not)	18.8%	20.3%	8%	Effect was smaller for large dining parties
Seiter and Weger (2023)/USA	Restaurant servers agreed with or complimented customers' choices (versus not)	20.1%	21.5%	7%	Effect was not significant

Author (year)/ Country	Experimental treatment	Average tip in control condition	Average tip in treatment condition	Percentage increase in tip	Comments
Mood enhancing tactics					
#19 Entertain customers					
Rind and Strohmetz (2001b)/USA	Waitress showed customers a card with an interesting puzzle (versus not shown the card)	18.5%	21.9%	18%	Letting customers keep the card did not increase tips further
Gueguen (2002)/ France	Nightclub servers gave customers a card with a joke printed on it (versus no card) when delivering the bill	24.6% tipped 16.4% of bill	41.7% tipped 23.1% of bill	Tipping likelihood: 100% Size of tip:41%	Giving a card advertising the nightclub did not increase tipping
Seiter and Weger (2023)/USA	Restaurant servers humorously asked "Mind if I take a seat?" (versus not) upon being told by a table that everything was fine or great	20.1%	24.6%	22%	
#20 Bring sunshine					

(continued)

Table 8.1 (continued)

Author (year)/ Country	Experimental treatment	Average tip in control condition	Average tip in treatment condition	Percentage increase in tip	Comments
Rind (1996)/USA	Casino hotel room server told customers weather was sunny (versus rainy)	18.6%	23.7%	27%	Telling customer weather was warm (versus cold) did not affect tipping
Rind and Strohmetz (2001a)/USA	Waitress wrote positive (and true) weather forecast with best wishes on check (versus no message)	18.7%	22.2%	24%	Writing a negative weather forecast with best wishes did not affect tipping
Gueguen and Legoherel (2000)/ France	Bar servers drew a sun on check (versus no drawing)	20.7% tipped 19.1% of bill	37.7% tipped 26.4% of bill	Tipping likelihood: 21% Size of tip: 38%	

customers, squatting down next to the table, introducing yourself by name, calling customers by their names, mimicking customers, thanking customers, highlighting identities shared with customers, and displaying charitableness. Each of these is discussed below.

Mega Tip #1: Smile. Smiling people are perceived as more attractive, sincere, sociable, and competent than unsmiling people, and smiling has been shown to increase service providers' rapport with their customers (Woo and Chan, 2020). Big, open-mouthed smiles have also been found to increase the tips given to a cocktail waitress (Tidd & Lockard, 1978), and drawing a smiley face on the check has been found to increase the tips of a restaurant waitress (Rind & Bordia, 1996). Comparable effects on tipping have not been demonstrated for male service workers, but the effects of smiling on interpersonal liking suggest that men as well as women will be rewarded with larger tips for smiling at their customers.[3]

Mega Tip #2: Touch Customers. Touching is a powerful non-verbal signal whose meaning depends on the manner and context in which it is done. As a part of positive social interactions, casual touches communicate appreciation, liking and/or social support, so casually touching customers should increase service workers' rapport with those customers and, with it, the tips those customers leave. Consistent with this expectation, several studies have found that touching customers does increase tips—typically by 25% or more (Cruscro and Wetzel, 1984; Stephen & Zweigenhaft, 1986; Gueguen and Jacob, 2005). This tip enhancing effect of touch has been found for waiters and waitresses and for male and female customers (Hornik, 1992). The effect is stronger for younger customers (Lynn et al., 1998) and when customers are touched by opposite sex servers (Hubbard et al., 2003), but it occurs for older customers and same-sex touching as well. The research testing these effects typically involved fleeting touches on the hand, arm, or shoulder, but one study found that even slightly prolonged touches (the waiter silently repeated "one Mississippi, two Mississippi, three Mississippi" before removing his hand from customers' shoulders) increased tips, so workers need not fear accidentally touching for too long (Lynn et al., 1998). Apparently, it is not just Midas whose touch turns things to gold.

Mega Tip #3: Stand Close to Customers. We generally stand or sit closer to acquaintances or friends than to strangers, so physical proximity signals interpersonal liking. Since liking is usually reciprocated, this suggests that

---

[3] However, drawing smiley faces on the check may be too "feminine" to work for waiters, because the study testing this technique found that it slightly decreased their tips.

servers may be able to increase their tips by standing physically closer to their customers (within limits of course). Consistent with this possibility, Jacob and Gueguen (2012) found that waitresses in France were more likely to get tips, and the tips they got were larger, when they stood approximately half a foot from the table than when they stood about one and half feet away.[4] Thus, service workers should keep their customers as well as their friends close.

Mega Tip #4: Squat Next to the Table. Servers usually stand throughout the service encounter, but they may want to rethink that practice. Squatting down next to the table or sitting down in an empty chair at the table does several things worth noting—it increases the similarity between the server's and customer's posture, facilitates eye contact by bringing the server's eye level down to that of the customer, and decreases subjective distance between the server and customer by bringing their faces closer together. Postural congruence, eye contact, and physical proximity are all associated with greater rapport and liking, so squatting down next to, or sitting down at, the table should increase tips. In fact, three studies tell us that squatting next to the table does increase tips to both waiters and waitresses (Davids et al., 1998; Lynn & Mynier, 1993). A fourth study found that sitting at the table also increased a waitress' tips, but only from her white customers (Leodoro & Lynn, 2007). Sitting at the table slightly decreased tips from the waitress' black customers, perhaps because of racial and ethnic differences in the sizes of personal space. Clearly some knowledge of cultural differences would be helpful when using this tactic, but research suggests that squatting next to the table is generally welcome in the U.S. and will increase tip income roughly 15–25%.

Mega Tip #5: Introduce Yourself by Name. Many waiters and waitresses introduce themselves by name to their customers, but only about half report doing so all the time and 17% report never doing so (Lynn & McCall, 2009). These missed opportunities are a mistake, because such introductions were shown to increase restaurant tips by over 50% in one study (Garrity & Degelman, 1990). A similar effect was also observed in tipping of hotel maids (Shih et al., 2019). In that study, maids received 50% more tips (though not larger tips) when a greeting card signed by and picturing a maid was left in the room than when the same card absent the signature and picture was left

---

[4] According to Jacob and Gueguen (2012) servers in France are trained to stand about one and half feet from the table, so that distance was normal and the half foot distance was much closer than usual.

in the room.[5] It is only two studies, but the lesson is clear—service workers should be more than a nameless face to their customers.

Mega Tip #6: Call Customers by Name. Our names are an important part of our identity and often one of the first things we tell people about ourselves. Consequently, remembering and using others' names makes them feel visible and appreciated by the name user (O'Brien et al., 2014). This probably explains why several studies have found that restaurant servers get larger tips when using customers' names than when not (Adams & Pettijohn, 2016; Rodrigue, 1999; Seiter et al., 2016; Seiter & Weger, 2013). Calling customers by their names increased tips by 10–36% in these studies with the largest effect coming from a study that had waitresses ask customers for their names and then use those names three times during the evening (Seiter et al., 2016).

Of course, calling customers by their first names could be perceived as presumptuous, especially when the names are obtained from reservations or credit cards rather than directly from the customer, so using titles and last names (e.g., Mr. Smith) is probably the safest bet in the latter conditions. This was certainly true for older customers in one study, which found that calling older customers by their titles and last names increased tips more than calling them by their first names (Seiter & Weger, 2013). On the other hand, younger customers in that study increased their tips more when called by their first names. These findings suggest that tipped workers should exercise judgment in deciding what name to use, but should call their customers by name whenever possible.

Mega Tip #7: Mimic Customers. Being copied or mimicked can be irritating when obvious and prolonged—that is why it is so popular among children as a means of tormenting their siblings. However, subtle copying of verbal and non-verbal behaviors has been shown to increase liking for the imitator (Kulesza et al., 2016). In retail settings, salesperson's verbal mimicry of customers results in higher sales rates and more positive evaluations of the salesperson and store (Jacob et al., 2011). Verbal mimicry in the form of repeating customers' orders back to them verbatim has also been shown to increase both tipping likelihood and the size of those tips left in Europe (van Baaren et al., 2003; Jacob & Gueguen, 2013). The effects on tipping of other forms of mimicry and of mimicry in non-restaurant contexts have not been tested, but mimicry's widely observed effects on liking and rapport

---

[5] The signature and picture were not those of the actual maid cleaning the room, but hotel guests did not know that. If they did, the effect would be even more remarkable as it would suggest that even proxied introductions increase personalization of the worker and tips to him or her.

suggest that the effect on tipping will generalize too. Thus, tipped workers in all service settings should try subtly mimicking their customers' verbal and/or non-verbal behaviors.

Mega Tip #8: Thank Customers. Expressions of gratitude increase perceptions of the expressers' interpersonal warmth (William & Bartlett, 2015). They also increase tips. Rind and Bordia (1995) found that a waitress in the U.S. increased her average tips from 16 to 18% of the bill simply by writing "Thank You" on her checks. This tactic did not work in another study conducted in Czechoslovakia (Alferovicova, 2016), but there is little downside to expressions of gratitude, so service workers should always thank customers for their patronage. In the U.S. at least, they will find that doing so gives them even more to be thankful for.

Mega Tip #9. Highlight Common Identities. Servers typically share one or more social identities with their customers. For example, they and their customers may be fans of a local sports team, members of a common religious faith, speakers of a foreign language, and/or lovers of their country. Highlighting these shared social identities can increase service workers' rapport with customers and one study suggests that it can also increase tips. Shortly after the terrorists attacks of 9/11, Seiter and Gass had waitresses write "United We Stand," "God Bless America," or "Have a Nice Day" on their checks and found that tips were significantly higher under the "United We Stand" than under the "Have a Nice Day" condition (20% versus 16%), with tips in the "God Bless America" condition (18%) being between those of the other two conditions (Seiter & Gass, 2005). Of course, these effects were almost certainly heightened by the wave of patriotic feelings following the 9/11 attacks. Nevertheless, they suggest that highlighting common identities with customers can increase service workers' tips from those customers.[6] Care should be taken not to alienate customers with different identities, but service workers should find ways to highlight shared identities with the majority of their customers—especially at times when those identities are particularly salient and valued.

Mega Tip #10: Display Charitableness. It seems obvious that we tend to like and help people who are generous and cooperative more than those who are selfish and non-cooperative. Research on indirect reciprocity (Albert et al., 2007) and competitive altruism (Hardy & Van Vugt, 2006) supports this idea and suggests that service workers will get more tips if they present themselves

---

[6] Also supporting this idea is a hypothetical scenario study finding that waitresses in Jordan got better tips when wearing a Hijab than when not wearing it (Shatnawi, 2019).

as compassionate and giving. Consistent with this expectation, one study found that a waitress in France got 21% more, and 133% larger, tips when she wrote "A good turn never goes amiss" on her checks than when she wrote nothing or a neutral message (Jacob et al., 2013).[7] Further supporting the expectation that displays of caring and giving increase tips, another study in Germany found that hairdressers got 28% more in tips on days when they told customers that they were collecting donations for a specific children's charity and invited the customers to make a donation than on days when they did not collect charitable donations (Khadjavi, 2017). Thus, logic and data both suggest that when it comes to tipping, workers' displays of charitableness pay.

Appearance Enhancing Tactics

The next set of tactics (or mega tips) to be discussed all revolve around servers enhancing their appearance. This is really a subset of rapport enhancing tactics because we tend to like and associate with physically attractive people more than unattractive ones, but the subset is large enough to deserve separate treatment. Our attraction to good looking people suggests that service workers' physical appearance is likely to affect consumers' altruistic and/or impression-management motivations for tipping them. Consistent with this possibility, several studies have found that naturally attractive restaurant servers get larger percentage tips, with the effect being stronger and more reliable for waitresses than for waiters (see Chap. 7). Building on this correlational research, field experiments have documented the effectiveness of several specific appearance-enhancing tactics for increasing tips. As discussed below, most of these particular mega tips are geared toward female service workers, but at least one is for male service workers.

Mega Tip #11: Go Blond (for Women). Research indicates that men tend to prefer light hair colors in the opposite sex, while women tend to prefer darker hair in the opposite sex (Feinman & Gill, 1978; Hinsz et al., 2013). This suggests that female service workers may increase their tips by changing their hair color to blond and at least two quasi-experiments support this possibility. One study had waitresses in France wear blond versus other colored wigs (Gueguen, 2012) while another study in the U.S. had waitresses dye their hair blond (versus not). Both studies found that blond waitresses got larger

---

[7] This manipulation actually backfired and reduced tips in a Czechoslovakian study (Alferovicova, 2016), but that study produced other unusual results that suggest Czechoslovakia is not like other countries when it comes to tipping.

tips. Unfortunately, similar quasi-experimental tests of hair color effects on the tips of male service workers are not available, but female service workers are likely to find that going blond increases their tips.

Mega Tip #12: Use Cosmetics (for Women). Make-up is designed to enhance physical attractiveness, so wearing it should increase tips (at least for women, who more traditionally wear cosmetics). Consistent with this expectation, researchers in France found that waitresses got more and larger tips on days that they had a cosmetician apply make-up to their faces than on days that they did not (Jacob et al. 2009; Gueguen & Jacob, 2011). In another study, these researchers found that waitresses got more and larger tips when wearing red lipstick (Gueguen & Jacob, 2012). All of these effects were limited to tips from male customers; wearing make-up did not increase tips from female customers. Nevertheless, female service workers should find that appropriate make-up improves not only their appearance but their tips.

Mega Tip #13: Ornament Your Hair (for Women). Hair ornaments are also designed to enhance physical appearance, so they too should increase tips for women. Consistent with this expectation, one quasi-experiment in the U.S. found that waitresses got larger tips when wearing a flower in their hair (Stillman & Hensley, 1980) and another in France found that waitresses got more and larger tips when wearing a decorative barrette in their hair (Jacob et al., 2012).

Mega Tip # 14: Wear Red (for Women). Research has found that exposure to the color red increases perceptions of the opposite sex's physical attractiveness in affiliative contexts (Lehmann et al., 2018). This suggests that service workers wearing red, should be perceived as more attractive by, and may receive more tips from, their opposite sex customers. Consistent with this expectation, one quasi-experiment in France found that waitresses got more and larger tips on days that they wore red t-shirts than on days when they wore different colored t-shirts (Gueguen & Jacob, 2014). Subsequent hypothetical scenario studies in the U.S. have failed to replicate this effect (Gourlay & Brewster, 2023; Lynn et al., 2016), so it is unclear how reliable and robust the effect is.[8] Nevertheless, female service workers may want to try this tactic out for themselves.

---

[8] The psychological effects of colors are context dependent. In contrast to its effects on perceived attraction in affiliative context, exposure to the color red has negative effects on perceived competence in achievement contexts (Elliot and Maier, 2012), so beware that this tactic could backfire and reduce tips!

Mega Tip #15: Dress Up. Researchers have found that wearing high status clothing and jewelry increases perceived physical attractiveness to the opposite sex as long as the wearer's physique is not highly salient (Hill et al., 1987). This suggests that service workers may get better tips if they wear more upscale clothing. Consistent with this possibility, Jacob and Gueguen (2014) found that a male pizza delivery driver got 86% more in tips when he wore a suit than when wearing more casual attire. Again, more research assessing the reliability and generalizability of this effect would be welcome, but dressing up as much as appropriate for the job is a tip enhancing tactic that service workers may want to try.

Reciprocity Inducing Tactics

A third set of mega tips rests upon the norm of reciprocity. People feel obliged to return favors even if they do not particularly like the person to whom they are indebted (Regan, 1971). This suggests that service workers can get larger tips by creating feelings of indebtedness in their customers. This is one of the key reasons that delivering better service increases tips. However, as we will see below, there are other (and arguably easier) ways of evoking the reciprocity norm and increasing tips.

Mega Tip #16: Give Customers Something. One obvious way to make people feel indebted to you is to give them something of tangible value. Such gifts are also an effective way to increase tips. Three field experiments by a high school student who worked as a restaurant magician found that he more than doubled his tips simply by giving the tables he performed at one of the cards he used in the performance (Frank, 2020; Frank & Lynn, 2020). Other field experiments have found that waiters and waitresses get larger tips if they give their customers after dinner candies (Rodrigue, 1999; Strohmetz et al., 2002). Particularly effective was giving each customer one piece of candy and then "spontaneously" increasing that to two pieces of candy each. That particular tactic increased average tips from 19% in the no candy condition to 23% (Strohmetz et al., 2002). These findings suggest that service workers can "sweeten the till" by giving their customers candies or other inexpensive gifts.

Mega Tip #17: Inform Customers. Not all favors or gifts to customers have to be tangible. Giving people useful information is enough to create an obligation to reciprocate and one study found that a waitress got larger tips simply by writing a message about an upcoming dinner special on the check (Rind & Strohmetz, 1999). This suggests that service workers should look for information that would interest and benefit their customers—such as food recommendations, upcoming community events, or curtain times for pre-theatre diners—and then share that information with them. Doing so should coax them into sharing more of their money in return.

Mega Tip #18: Compliment Customers. Another non-tangible gift that makes people feel good and, thus, creates a need to reciprocate is a compliment. Research has shown that complimenting people increases their compliance with a small request because it enhances the need to reciprocate—not because it increases moods or liking for the flatterer (though it does those things too) (Grant et al., 2022). A similar process probably also underlies the results of studies finding that complimenting customers' appearance increased tips to a hairstylist (Seiter & Dutson, 2007) and complimenting their food choices increased tips to waiters and waitresses (Seiter, 2007; Seiter & Weger, 2010). Regardless of the underlying processes, compliments are a means to larger tips, so service workers should not hesitate to flatter their customers shamelessly.

Mood Enhancing Tactics

The final set of server tactics proven to increase tips are likely to draw their effectiveness from elevating customers' moods. Social psychologists have found that positive moods predispose us to help others (Manucia et al., 1984), so elevating customers' moods should increase the tips they leave. Two mega tips based on this idea are described below.

Mega Tip #19: Entertain Customers. Entertained people tend to be happier than bored ones, so service workers should be able to increase their tips by entertaining their customers. That is not to say that they need to become professional entertainers—even modest efforts have been shown to increase tips. In one study, a waitress in the U.S. showed her customers a card reading *"Finished files are the result of years of scientific study combined with the experience of many years"* and challenged the customers to count the number of "F's" it contained. [Note: You might want to do that yourself before reading on.] Most of her customers were surprised to learn that the correct number was six. The customers (and perhaps you too) missed the F's at the end of the word "of" because it is pronounced with a V sound. They also gave her larger tips than did customers not shown the card—an average tip of 22% versus 19% (Rind & Strohmetz, 2001a, 2001b). In another study, nightclub servers in France got more and larger tips when the bill was randomly accompanied by a card with a lame joke printed on it than when it was not (Gueguen,

2002).⁹ A third study had restaurant servers in the U.S. randomly ask their customers "*Mind if I take a seat?*" (versus not) when being told everything was great at a table. That mildly humorous question increased tips by 22%! As these studies testify, workers don't have to be Robin Williams to entertain their way into bigger tips, so they should collect jokes or puzzles to share with their customers.

Mega Tip #20: Bring Sunshine. Sunny weather makes people happy and more inclined to help others (Cunningham, 1979). Even the idea of sunshine appears to have these effects. Different studies have examined the effects on tipping of (i) describing the current weather as sunny to indoor casino customers (Rind, 1996), (ii) sharing favorable weather forecasts with restaurant customers (Rind & Strohmetz, 2001a), and (iii) drawing a picture of the sun on checks given to bar patrons (Gueguen & Legoherel, 2000). All of these studies found that tips were larger in the "sunnier" conditions than in the control conditions. Thus, service workers should use these or other ways of bringing sunshine into the lives of their customers.

Concluding Remarks About Server Tactics

All of the techniques for increasing tips described above have been scientifically tested and found to be effective. However, it is unlikely that they will work in all circumstances. In fact, many of the techniques have been found to work better for some customers than others, as discussed above. In addition, many of the techniques were tested in casual-dining restaurants, and some of them, such as jokingly asking if you can join the table or actually sitting/squatting down at the table, would be inconsistent with and probably less effective for more formal, fine-dining service. This means that service workers will need to use judgment in deciding which techniques to use. Fortunately, there are many to choose from, so everyone should find something appropriate and effective for their circumstances.

---

[9] The joke was: "*An Eskimo had been waiting for his girlfriend in front of a movie theatre for a long time and it was getting colder and colder. After a while, shivering with cold and rather infuriated, he opened his coat and drew out a thermometer. He then said loudly, 'If she is not here at 15, I'm going!'*".

Managerial Tactics for Increasing Tips

In addition to testing the things service workers can do to increase their own tips, researchers have tested specific actions that managers can take to increase their employees' tips. First among these is encouraging workers to use the mega tips described above. Although people often tell me that these tactics are obvious, they are not employed as much as they should be. More than 40% of waiters and waitresses I surveyed said that they NEVER draw pictures on checks, touch customers, forecast good weather, wear flair, or squat next to the table. Even the more commonly tried tactics—like calling customers by name, writing "Thank You" on checks, telling jokes, complimenting customers' choices, and repeating customers' orders—are used only SOMETIMES (if ever) by one out of three servers (Lynn, 2009). Thus, increasing employees' use of these tactics is a clear way of helping them earn larger tips. Training is one way of accomplishing this, as demonstrated by a study conducted in Switzerland. In that study, a one and half hour training session focusing on many of the mega tips presented above increased waiters' and waitresses' use of the techniques and, through that, the tips they received (Fernandez et al., 2020).[10]

In addition to training workers to use the mega tips described above, executives and/or managers can increase their employees' tips by adopting some key policies and procedures related to tipping. Several specific policies and procedures that have been tested and shown to increase tips include reminding customers that tips are appreciated, displaying dueling tip jars, providing tip calculation assistance, adding emojis to printed or digital tip suggestions, using gold-colored, heart-shaped, or credit card logo embossed bill holders, and increasing the amounts of one-touch tipping options on digital screens. Each of these managerial tactics for increasing tips is discussed further below.

Inform/Remind Customers that Tips Are Appreciated

Consumers do not always know who they should tip and, even if they do know, often forget to leave a tip. For example, I once asked a sample of U.S. consumers why they (at least occasionally) failed to tip hotel maids and found that 28% said they did not know you were supposed to tip maids while 30%

---

[10] Sharing this book with tipped workers is another possible way to increase their use of the mega tips, so executives and managers in tipped industries might also consider gifting their employees with a copy of the book.

said they forgot to do so. This suggests that a simple way to increase tips in some less frequently tipped service settings is to inform/remind customers that tips are appreciated. A 2017 dissertation by I-hsuan Shih tested this tactic in an upscale Texas hotel and found that putting an envelope with a "Thank You" for choosing the hotel in rooms as an implicit reminder to tip increased tipping likelihood 33% (from 6 to 8% of stays) while putting a similar envelope that also explicitly stated "Gratuities Appreciated" in rooms increased tipping likelihood by 83% (from 6 to 11% of stays). Workers seeking tips in other service settings would likely benefit from similar reminders.

One particularly noteworthy reminder to tip that is becoming increasingly common takes the form of QR codes workers can leave for customers to scan with their smart phones and then leave a digital tip using Apple Pay or a credit card. This technology not only informs/reminds people that tips are welcome, but also facilitates tipping when consumers do not have cash at hand, so it may increase tips even more than do envelopes or other reminders. It is hard to get good evidence on this point because reliable tip records prior to the technology's adoption (for use as a comparison) are not readily available, but anecdotal testimony from hotels suggests that it does increase the frequency of guests' tipping.

Of course, some care needs to be taken about how to word messages informing/reminding customers that tips are appreciated in order to avoid pressuring them too much. Marriott provided a cautionary tale in this regard when its use of tip envelopes created a consumer backlash (Chappell, 2014).

> Marriott's envelopes read:
> THE ENVELOPE PLEASE
> *Thanks for staying at Marriott Hotels. Our caring room attendants enjoyed making your stay warm and comfortable. Please feel free to leave a gratuity to express your appreciation for their efforts.*
> ROOM ATTENDANT: _____.
>
>
> In comparison, Shih's (2017) explicit envelope read:
> GRATUITIES APPRECIATED
> *Dear Guest,*
> *Thank you for choosing (the study) Hotel. I hope you enjoyed your stay.*
> *Please let me know if you need anything, I will be more than happy to assist you.*
> *Warm Regards,*
> YOUR ROOM ATTENDANT: _____

American Hotel & Lodging Association Guest Gratuity Guide
www.ahia.com/uploadedfiles/_common.pdf/guestgratuityguide.pdf

I will leave it to readers to parse the differences between these two envelope messages for themselves, but Shih's (2017) work demonstrates that effective, low-pressure messages informing and reminding customers that tips are appreciated can be crafted and used without a consumer backlash.[11]

Display Dueling Tip Jars

In Chap. 2, we discussed five major motivations for tipping, but there is a way for clever managers to invoke a sixth (and much rarer) motive for tipping, namely self-expression. The way to do this is to display dueling tip jars that turn tips into votes of social preference. For example, label one tip jar "Cats" and another "Dogs" and put them side-by-side with a sign reading "Vote with your tips!." When researchers did this in one study and compared the resulting tips to those obtained when only a single, regular tip jar was used, they found that the proportion of customers leaving a tip was 88% higher in the dueling tip jar condition than in the control condition (0.77 versus 0.41 respectively). My guess is that the tip enhancing effects of any one duel will wane over time as consumers find themselves having already voted their preference on previous occasions. However, the social preferences listed on the tip jars can always be changed to refresh the duel. For example, instead of Cats versus Dogs, it could be Baseball versus Football, Mets versus Yankees, Vanilla versus Chocolate, Harvard versus MIT, Rock Music versus Country Music, etc. Given its effectiveness and low cost, I am surprised that this technique is not used more often. Managers of tipped counterworkers should give it a try.

Provide Tip Calculation Assistance

Many point-of-sale systems allow businesses to include tip calculation assistance on the bottom of checks. Specifically, dollar and cent amounts that constitute a 10, 15, and/or 20% of the check size can be printed on checks. Such calculation assistance implicitly communicates the tip percentages expected in a way that is hard for consumers to object to, and one field study found that including both 15 and 20% calculations on checks increased

---

[11] Shih (2017) did not explicitly measure or describe consumers' emotional reactions to the envelopes, but he ran several studies at the same hotel, which the hotel would almost certainly not have allowed if they had received any complaints from guests about the envelopes.

the tips restaurant customers left from 16.3% in the control condition to 18.7% in the experimental condition (Seiter et al., 2011). Another field study found that presenting similar information on a separate card—it identified 15, 20, and 25% tip amounts for various bill sizes—did not increase tips (Strohmetz & Rind, 2001). However, that card also explicitly labeled 15% tips as being for adequate service, 20% tips as being for better than average service, and 25% tips as being for outstanding service, and consumers may have perceived that as unwanted pressure. Thus, I recommend that managers print tip calculations (labeled as "calculation assistance") on checks but refrain from telling customers how much to tip for different levels of service.

Add Emojis to Tip Suggestions

Though I do not advise that businesses tell customers how much they should tip for different levels of service, I can recommend displaying increasingly positive emojis next to increasing tip suggestions at the bottom of checks or next to one-touch tip options on digital devices. One field study found that placing such stimuli at the bottom of restaurant checks increased tips by 11%—from 22.9% in the control condition to 25.4% in the experimental condition (Lefebvre et al., 2024). A follow-up study suggests that the emojis increase tip sizes by elevating customers' moods, so this managerial technique for increasing tips is akin to Mega Tips #19 and #20 for service workers.

Use Specific, Tested Bill-Folders or Tip-Trays

Among the decisions that managers are typically responsible for is what type of bill holders or tip trays to use. Surprisingly, even this seemingly innocuous decision can impact the tips customers leave. Two field experiments have shown that tips are over 20% higher when the bill is brought on a tray embossed with a credit card logo than when it is brought on a blank tray (McCall & Belmont, 1996). In one of the studies, restaurant tips increased from an average of 16% to 20% of the bill, and in the other study, café tips increased from an average of 18% to 22%. The authors speculate that this effect occurs because the repeated pairing of credit card logos with spending when we buy things on credit has conditioned us to spend more in the presence of those logos.

A third study found that bringing the bill in a gold-colored bill folder increased average restaurant tips by 14%—from 18.9% of the bill when a black folder was used to 21.5% when the gold folder was used (Lee et al.,

2018). Follow-up studies suggest that this effect occurs because the color gold increases consumers' perceptions of their own and the restaurant's status.

A fourth study conducted at a restaurant in France found that tip likelihood and the size of those tips left both increased when the bill was presented on a heart-shaped dish than when it was presented on round or square dishes (Gueguen, 2013). Specifically, the likelihood of tipping increased from 29% of customers in the round or square dish condition to 46% of customers in the heart-shaped dish condition, and the average size of those tips left went from 1.18 Euros to 1.38 Euros. The author attributed these effects to the heart-shaped dishes unconscious activation of the concept of love in consumers' minds. Given the demonstrated positive impact on tipping of using these particular types of bill holders, replacing existing trays or folders with one of them is clearly worth the cost and effort of doing so.

Display Larger Digital Tipping Options (Within Normative Expectations)

Another decision under businesses' control is the percentage or dollar amounts of the tone-touch tipping options used on digital screens that customers are increasingly facing when paying for services. Studies have examined the effects of increasing the average amounts of these tipping options in the context of taxicabs (Haggag & Paci, 2014), ride-share (Chandar et al., 2019), and pick-up/delivery services (Alexander et al., 2021). All three studies found that larger one-touch tipping options decreased the likelihood that customers would tip but increased tip sizes from those who did tip, with a net result of larger tip revenue. These findings provide a compelling rationale for using larger average tip options within the moderate ranges tested to date—i.e., $1–$10 or 5–30%. However, there must be a ceiling to how much you can effectively suggest tipping, and Alexander et al. (2021) found the negative effect of option-size on tipping likelihood was greater the larger those options were, so keeping the tip options within normative expectations seems advisable.[12]

---

[12] Of course, businesses care about tip-option-size effects on customer satisfaction as well as its effects on tip revenue. Hypothetical scenario studies suggest that larger tips options reduce customer satisfaction and Alexander et al. (2021) found some evidence for a similar effect in their field experiment, but the negative effects of tip-option-size on satisfaction in that experiment were small (less than 0.1 on a 5 point scale) and inconsistent across various conditions. Furthermore, that field experiment found no effect of tip-option-size on either consumer patronage frequency or spending. Thus, I do not believe that businesses need to fear a consumer backlash if they increase their tip options as long as the increases remain within normative expectations.

Concluding Remarks About Managerial Tactics

Like the Mega Tips for servers, all of the managerial tactics for increasing employees' tips presented in this chapter have been tested and supported by experiments or quasi-experiments in the field, but there is no guarantee that any given technique will work in all circumstances. Businesses may want to test these techniques on a small scale before deploying their use more widely. I would be happy to help any reader so inclined to design, execute, and analyze such tests in exchange for the anonymized data for use in academic research. If you are interested, you can reach me at WML3@Cornell.edu.

Concluding Note to Skeptics

Although the techniques presented here have been scientifically tested, and the evidence supporting their effectiveness is described along with the technique, some readers will have doubts. The simplicity of the techniques can be misleading. It just doesn't make sense to some people that simple little behaviors can have such a big effect on the amount of money that other people give away. For those readers unpersuaded by the scientific evidence, I provide the following testimonial sent to me by Joshua—a restaurant worker who found one of my earlier articles on ways to increase tips and shared that article with his co-workers.

> *Here's how it all happened: I was browsing around the Cornell website, Hotel School section, and came across your article. I read it, acknowledged it as a nice piece, and continued reading through the site. When I went to work (I work at a restaurant called Texas Roadhouse), I started to notice, after reading your paper, that people kept on and kept on complaining about not making lots of tips. I remembered some of the tips that you had in the paper, and I looked around to see if I saw people doing what you said worked: writing messages on the back of checks, using checkholders with credit card symbols on them, etc. I told a few people about the ideas, and two said that they would try some stuff out, because they were tired of making no tips. The other couple*

said that they were fine how they were and that the information in the article was "bull crap."

So, Bailey and John (their names, naturally) proceeded to follow your teachings, and at the end of the night, both came out between 8 and 10 percent higher in tips. I'd say that's very impressive, and they thought the same, but the others who did not believe me said it must just be a coincidence. Bailey and John, again the following night, brought in more tips than they had been before. Then the others started talking to each other, and giving hints to each other, and telling about how I'd told them about it, etc. So, I went to the site, printed it off, and hung it up on our nightly news board, for everyone to see. Of course, I gave complete credit to you (I printed it with full "Cornell" symbols at the top, as well as your name on it and whatnot), and people have thanked me about once a week since then, about three months ago. Overall, everyone was happy and definitely saw an increase, thanks to you."

Skepticism is good—it keeps you from falling prey to empty promises. However, too much skepticism can also make you miss out on worthwhile opportunities. That almost happened to some of Joshua's co-workers. Those who decided without evidence that my article was "bull crap" and refused to try the techniques would have continued making lousy tips if some of their less skeptical co-workers had not been willing to give the techniques a try and then shared their experiences. Don't let your skepticism get the better of you. Keep an open mind about these techniques, share them with tipped workers you know, and (if you are a tipped worker yourself) give them a try! If and when you do try these techniques, please send me an email at WML3@Cornell.edu to let me know how they worked out for you.

References

Adams, V. P., & Pettijohn, T. F., II. (2016). Using a customer's name to personalize checks and increase restaurant tipping behavior. *International Journal of Management Sciences, 6*(10), 491–497.

Albert, M., Güth, W., Kirchler, E., & Maciejovsky, B. (2007). Are we nice (r) to nice (r) people?—An experimental analysis. *Experimental Economics, 10*, 53–69.

Alexander, D., Boone, C. & Lynn, M. (2021). The effects of tip recommendations on customer tipping, satisfaction, repatronage, and spending. Management Science, 67 (1), 146–165.

Alferovicova, M (2016). Irrationality of consumer choice and the effect of nudging decision-making: A field experiment on tipping. Unpublished Masters Thesis, Charles University in Prague.

Bodvarsson, O. & Gibson, W. (1994). Gratuities and customer appraisal of service: Evidence from Minnesota restaurants. Journal of Socio-Economics, 23 (3), 287–302.

Butler, S. R., & Snizek, W. E. (1976). The waitress-diner relationship: A multimethod approach to the study of subordinate influence. *Sociology of Work and Occupations, 3*(2), 209–222.

Chandar, B., Gneezy, U., List, J.A. & Muir, I. (2019). The drivers of social preferences: Evidence from a nationwide tipping field experiment (No. w26380). National Bureau of Economic Research.

Chappell, B. (2014, Sept 16). *Marriott's new envelope for room tips stirs debate.* www.npr.org. Accessed 19 Sept 2024.

Conlin, M., Lynn, M. & O'Donahue, T. (2003). The norm of restaurant tipping. Journal of Economic behavior and Organization, 52, 297–321.

Crusco, A. H., & Wetzel, C. G. (1984). The Midas touch: The effects of interpersonal touch on restaurant tipping. *Personality and Social Psychology Bulletin, 10*(4), 512–517.

Cunningham, M. R. (1979). Weather, mood, and helping behavior: Quasi experiments with the sunshine samaritan. *Journal of Personality and Social Psychology, 37*(11), 1947.

Davis, S. F., Schrader, B., Richardson, T. R., Kring, J. P., & Kieffer, J. C. (1998). Restaurant servers influence tipping behavior. *Psychological Reports, 83*, 223–226.

Elliot, A. J., & Maier, M. A. (2012). Color-in-context theory. In *Advances in experimental social psychology* (Vol. 45, pp. 61–125). Academic Press.

Feinman, S., & Gill, G. W. (1978). Sex differences in physical attractiveness preferences. *The Journal of Social Psychology, 105*(1), 43–52.

Fernandez, S., Dufour, F., Costa, V., de Boer, C., Terrier, L., & Golay, P. (2020). Increasing Tips in Less Than Two Hours: Impact of a Training Intervention on the Amount of Tips Received by Restaurant Employees. Cornell Hospitality Quarterly, 61(1), 98–107.

Frank, D. G. (2020). To gift or not to gift: How providing a memento affects a restaurant magician's tips. *International Journal of Hospitality Management, 86*, 102368.

Frank, D. G., & Lynn, M. (2020). Shattering the illusion of the self-earned tip: The effect of a restaurant magician on co-workers' tips. *Journal of Behavioral and Experimental Economics, 87*, 101560.

Garrity, K., & Degelman, D. (1990). Effect of server introduction on restaurant tipping. *Journal of Applied Social Psychology, 20*(2), 168–172.

Gourlay, K., & Brewster, Z. W. (2023). Seeing red: color effects on restaurant tipping may not be as significant as thought. *Journal of Foodservice Business Research*, 1–18.

Grant, N. K., Krieger, L. R., Nemirov, H., Fabrigar, L. R., & Norris, M. E. (2022). I'll scratch your back if you give me a compliment: Exploring psychological mechanisms underlying compliments' effects on compliance. *British Journal of Social Psychology, 61*(1), 37–54.

Guéguen, N. (2002). The effects of a joke on tipping when it is delivered at the same time as the bill. *Journal of Applied Social Psychology, 32*(9), 1955–1963.

Guéguen, N. (2012). Hair color and wages: Waitresses with blond hair have more fun. *The Journal of Socio-Economics, 41*, 370–372.

Guéguen, N. (2013). Helping with all your heart: The effect of cardioid dishes on tipping behavior. *Journal of Applied Social Psychology, 43*, 1745–1749.

Guéguen, N., & Jacob, C. (2005). The effect of touch on tipping: An evaluation in a French bar. *Hospitality Management, 24*, 295–299.

Guéguen, N., & Jacob, C. (2011). Enhanced female attractiveness with use of cosmetics and male tipping behaviors in restaurants. *Journal of Cosmetic Science, 62*(3), 283–290.

Guéguen, N., & Jacob, C. (2012). Lipstick and tipping behavior: When red lipstick enhance waitresses tips. *International Journal of Hospitality Management, 31*, 1333–1335.

Guéguen, N., & Jacob, C. (2014). Clothing color and tipping: Gentleman patrons give more tips to waitresses with red clothes. *Journal of Hospitality & Tourism Research, 38*(2), 275–280.

Guéguen, N., & Legoherel, P. (2000). Effect on tipping of barman drawing a sun on the bottom of customers' checks. *Psychological Reports, 87*, 223–226.

Haggag, Kareem and Giovanni Paci (2014). Default tips. American Economic Journal: Applied Economics, 6 (3), 1–19.

Hardy, C. L., & Van Vugt, M. (2006). Nice guys finish first: The competitive altruism hypothesis. *Personality and Social Psychology Bulletin, 32*(10), 1402–1413.

Hill, E. M., Nocks, E. S., & Gardner, L. (1987). Physical attractiveness: Manipulation by physique and status displays. *Ethology and Sociobiology, 8*(2), 143–154.

Hinsz, V. B., Stoesser, C. J., & Matz, D. C. (2013). The intermingling of social and evolutionary psychology influences on hair color preferences. *Current Psychology, 32*, 136–149.

Hornik, J. (1992). Tactile stimulation and consumer response. *Journal of Consumer Research, Inc., 19*, 449–458.

Hubbard, A. S. E., Tsuji, A. A., Williams, C., & Seatriz, V., Jr. (2003). Effects of touch on gratuities received in same-gender and cross-gender dyads. *Journal of Applied Social Psychology, 33*(11), 2427–2438.

Jacob, C., & Guéguen, N. (2012). The effect of physical distance between patrons and servers on tipping. *Journal of Hospitality & Tourism Research, 36*(1), 25–31.

Jacob, C., & Guéguen, N. (2013). The effect of employees' verbal mimicry on tipping. *International Journal of Hospitality Management, 35*, 109–111.

Jacob, C., & Guéguen, N. (2014). The effect of employees' clothing appearance on tipping. *Journal of Foodservice Business Research, 17*, 483–486.

Jacob, C., Guéguen, N., Ardiccioni, R., & Sénémeaud, C. (2013). Exposure to altruism quotes and tipping behavior in a restaurant. *International Journal of Hospitality Management, 32*, 299–301.

Jacob, C., Guéguen, N., Boulbry, G., & Ardiccioni, R. (2009). Waitresses' facial cosmetics and tipping: A field experiment. *International Journal of Hospitality Management, 29*, 188–190.

Jacob, C., Guéguen, N., & Delfosse, C. (2012). She wore something in her hair: The effect of ornamentation on tipping. *Journal of Hospitality Marketing & Management, 21*, 414–420.

Jacob, C., Guéguen, N., Martin, A., & Boulbry, G. (2011). Retail salespeople's mimicry of customers: Effects on consumer behavior. *Journal of Retailing and Consumer Services, 18*(5), 381–388.

Jewell, C. N. (2008). Factors influencing tipping behavior in a restaurant. *Psi Chi Journal of Undergraduate Research, 13*(1), 38–48.

Jiang, C., & Galm, M. (2014). The economic benefit of being blonde: A study of waitress tip earnings based on their hair color in a prominent restaurant chain. *Journal of Behavioral Studies in Business, 7*, 1–6.

Kelley, K., & Byrne, D. (1976). Attraction and altruism: With a little help from my friends. *Journal of Research in Personality, 10*(1), 59–68.

Kerr, P.M. & Domazlicky, B.R. (2009). Tipping and service quality: Results from a large database. Applied Economic Letters, 16, 1505–1510.

Khadjavi, M. (2017). Indirect reciprocity and charitable giving—evidence from a field experiment. Management Science, 63(11), 3708–3717.

Kulesza, W., Dolinski, D., & Wicher, P. (2016). Knowing that you mimic me: The link between mimicry, awareness and liking. *Social Influence, 11*(1), 68–74.

Lee, N. Y., Noble, S. M., & Biswas, D. (2018). Hey big spender! A golden (color) atmospheric effect on tipping behavior. Journal of the Academy of Marketing Science, 46(2), 317–337.

Lefebvre, S., Boman, L., & Orlowski, M. (2024). Look on the bright side: Emojis impact tipping behaviour. International Journal of Hospitality Management, 117, 103653.

Lehmann, G. K., Elliot, A. J., & Calin-Jageman, R. J. (2018). Meta-analysis of the effect of red on perceived attractiveness. *Evolutionary Psychology, 16*(4), 1474704918802412.

Leodoro, G., & Lynn, M. (2007). The effect of server posture on the tips of whites and blacks. *Journal of Applied Social Psychology, 37*(2), 201–209.

Lynn, M. (2024). The Pro's and Con's of Working for Tips. *Cornell Hospitality Quarterly, 65*(2), 266–275.

Lynn, M. & McCall, M. (2009). Techniques for increasing tips: How generalizable are they? Cornell Hospitality Quarterly, 50, 198–208.

Lynn, M. (2011). MegaTips 2: twenty tested techniques to increase your tips. *CHR Tool, 2*(1).

Lynn, M. (2005). Increasing servers' tips: What managers can do and why they should do it. *Journal of Foodservice Business Research, 8*(4), 89–98.

Lynn, M., Giebelhausen, M., Garcia, S., Li, Y., & Patumanon, I. (2016). Clothing color and tipping: An attempted replication and extension. *Journal of Hospitality and Tourism Research, 40*(4), 516–524.

Lynn, M., & Gregor, R. (2001). Tipping and service: The case of hotel bellmen. *International Journal of Hospitality Management, 20*, 299–303.

Lynn, M., Le, J. M., & Sherwyn, D. S. (1998). Reach out and touch your customers. *Cornell Hotel and Restaurant Administration Quarterly, 39*(3), 60–65.

Lynn, M., & McCall, M. (2000). Gratitude and gratuity: A meta-analysis of research on the service-tipping relationship. *Journal of Socio-Economics, 29*, 203–214.

Lynn, M., & Mynier, K. (1993). Effect of server posture on restaurant tipping. *Journal of Applied Social Psychology, 23*(8), 678–685.

Lynn, M. (2009). Determinants and consequences of female attractiveness and sexiness: Realistic tests with restaurant waitresses. *Archives of Sexual Behavior, 38*(5), 737–745.

Manucia, G. K., Baumann, D. J., & Cialdini, R. B. (1984). Mood influences on helping: Direct effects or side effects?. Journal of Personality and Social Psychology, 46(2), 357.

McCall, M., & Belmont, H. J. (1996). Credit card insignia and restaurant tipping: Evidence for an associative link. *Journal of Applied Psychology, 81*(5), 609–613.

Millar, M.G. (2002). The effectiveness of the door-in-the-face compliance strategy on friends and strangers. The Journal of Social Psychology, 142 (3), 295-304.

O'Brien, M., Leiman, T., & Duffy, J. (2014). The power of naming: The multifaceted value of learning students' names. *QUT Law Review, 14*(1), 114–128.

Payscale (2015). *Restaurant report key stats*. http://www.payscale.com/data-packages/restaurant-report/full-data. Accessed 19 July 2017.

Regan, D. T. (1971). Effects of a favor and liking on compliance. *Journal of Experimental Social Psychology, 7*(6), 627–639.

Regner, T. (2014). Social preferences? Google Answers! Games and Economic Behavior, 85, 188–209.

Rind, B. (1996). Effect of beliefs about weather conditions on tipping. *Journal of Applied Social Psychology, 26*(2), 137–147.

Rind, B., & Bordia, P. (1995). Effect of server's "thank you" and personalization on restaurant tipping. *Journal of Applied Social Psychology, 25*(9), 745–751.

Rind, B., & Bordia, P. (1996). Effect on restaurant tipping of male and female servers drawing a happy, smiling face on the backs of customers' checks. *Journal of Applied Social Psychology, 26*(3), 218–225.

Rind, B., & Strohmetz, D. (1999). Effect on restaurant tipping of a helpful message written on the back of customers' checks. *Journal of Applied Social Psychology, 29*(1), 139–144.

Rind, B., & Strohmetz, D. (2001a). Effect of beliefs about weather conditions on restaurant tipping. *Journal of Applied Social Psychology, 31*(10), 2160–2164.

Rind, B., & Strohmetz, D. (2001b). Effect on restaurant tipping of presenting customers with an interesting task and of reciprocity. *Journal of Applied Social Psychology, 31*(7), 1379–1384.

Rodrigue, Karen M. (1999), "Tipping Tips: The Effects of Personalization on Restaurant Gratuity," Master's Thesis, Division of Psychology and Special Education, Emporia State University

Seiter, J. S. (2007). Ingratiation and gratuity: The effect of complimenting customers on tipping behavior in restaurants. *Journal of Applied Social Psychology, 37*(3), 478–485.

Seiter, J. S., Brownlee, G. M., & Sanders, M. (2011). Persuasion by way of example: Does including gratuity guidelines on customers' checks affect restaurant tipping behavior. *Journal of Applied Social Psychology, 41*(1), 150–159.

Seiter, J. S., & Dutson, E. (2007). The effect of compliments on tipping behavior in hairstyling salons. *Journal of Applied Social Psychology, 37*(9), 1999–2007.

Seiter, J. S., & Gass, R. H. (2005). The effect of patriotic messages on restaurant tipping. *Journal of Applied Social Psychology, 35*(6), 1197–1205.

Seiter, J. S., Givens, K. D., & Weger, H., Jr. (2016). The effect of mutual introductions and addressing customers by name on tipping behavior in restaurants. *Journal of Hospitality Marketing & Management, 25*, 640–651.

Seiter, J. S., & Weger, H., Jr. (2010). The effect of generalized compliments, sex of server, and size of dining party on tipping behavior in restaurants. *Journal of Applied Social Psychology, 40*(1), 1–12.

Seiter, J. S., & Weger, H., Jr. (2013). Does a customer by any other name tip the same? The effect of forms of address and customers' age on gratuities given to food servers in the United States. *Journal of Applied Social Psychology, 43*, 1592–1598.

Seiter, J. S., & Weger Jr, H. (2023). "Waiter, there'sa fly in my soup!": tipping behavior in restaurants as a function of food servers' humor, opinion conformity, and other-enhancement. Humor, 36(3), 355–373.

Shih, I.H. (2017). *Suggestion or coercion: gratuity envelopes and hotel guests' tipping behavior.* Dissertation, Texas Tech University.

Shih, I. H., Jai, T. M. C., Chen, H. S., & Blum, S. (2019). Greetings from Emily! The effects of personalized greeting cards on tipping of hotel room attendants.

International Journal of Contemporary Hospitality Management, 31(8), 3058–3076.

Shatnawi, H.S. (2019). Effects of a waitresses' headscarf (Hijab) on tipping behavior in restaurants. *African Journal of Hospitality, Tourism and Leisure,* 8 (4), 1–11.

Stephen, R., & Zweigenhaft, R. L. (1986). The effect on tipping of a waitress touching male and female customers. *The Journal of Social Psychology,* 126(1), 141–142.

Stillman, J. W., & Hensely, W. E. (1980). She wore a flower in her hair: The effect of ornamentation on nonverbal communication. *Journal of Applied Communications Research,* 8(1), 31–39.

Strohmetz, D. B., & Rind, B. (2001). The impact of tipping recommendations on tip levels. *Cornell Hotel and Restaurant Administration Quarterly,* 42(3), 71–73.

Strohmetz, D. B., Rind, B., Fisher, R., & Lynn, M. (2002). Sweetening the till: The use of candy to increase restaurant tipping. *Journal of Applied Social Psychology,* 32(2), 300–309.

Tedeschi, E. (2024, June 24). The "No Tax on Tips Act": Background on Tipped Wokers." https://budgetlab.yale.edu/news/240624/no-tax-tips-act-background-tipped-workers. Accessed 4 Sept 2024.

Tidd, K. L., & Lockard, J. S. (1978). Monetary significance of the affiliative smile: A case for reciprocal altruism. *Bulletin of the Psychonomic Society,* 11(6), 344–346.

van Baaren, R. B., Holland, R. W., Steenaert, B., & van Knippenberg, A. (2003). Mimicry for money: Behavioral consequences of imitation. *Journal of Experimental Social Psychology,* 39, 393–398.

Williams, L. A., & Bartlett, M. Y. (2015). Warm thanks: gratitude expression facilitates social affiliation in new relationships via perceived warmth. *Emotion,* 15(1), 1.

Woo, K. S., & Chan, B. (2020). "Service with a smile" and emotional contagion: A replication and extension study. *Annals of Tourism Research,* 80, 102850.

9

Winners a Losers (Who Does Tipping Benefit and How? Who Does It Harm and How?)

Tipping is often portrayed as pitting the interests of consumers, workers, and/ or businesses against one another. For example, readers may have heard or read that tipping empowers consumers, which benefits them by motivating workers to provide better service, but harms workers by compelling them to accept abuse from the customers they depend on for tips (ROC United, 2018; Skopic, 2024). Another common argument is that tipping enables businesses to pay lower wages, which benefits them but harms consumers by forcing them to fulfill the business's responsibility to pay its workers and harms workers by increasing their economic precarity (Hermann, 2024; Kelly, 2024; Mathwig, 2024; Schweitzer, 2021). While there is some truth to these and other claims about the benefits/beneficiaries and harms/victims of tipping, those claims are often presented in an overly simplistic and misleading way to support a particular policy being advocated. Rarely can interested parties find all the relevant issues brought together, looked at from multiple perspectives, and empirically assessed.

The current chapter fulfills the need for a more complete, complex, nuanced, and empirically based assessment of tipping's benefits and harms. Specifically, it discusses the pros and cons of tipping from a consumer, worker, and business perspective. In doing so, it will make clear to readers that tipping is a mixed blessing for each of these groups.[1] Moreover, the benefits and harms do not accrue equally to all members of these groups. Some informed

---

[1] Although a mixed blessing for consumers, workers, and businesses, tipping is an unambiguous negative for governments. Tipping lowers the price of services (as detailed later in the chapter), so it reduces state and local sales tax revenues. Furthermore, tip income is easy to hide, so tipping also lowers state and federal income tax revenues. In addition to lowering income tax revenue, evasion

members of each group will weigh the pros and cons to find tipping a net positive while others will find it a net negative. Read on to find out what those pros and cons are and to form your own educated assessment.

Pros and Cons of Tipping from a Consumer Perspective

My reading of the tipping literature indicates that the custom of tipping benefits consumers by: (i) improving service quality, (ii) reducing the perceived risks of services, (iii) reducing the costs of services, and (iv) allowing tippers to buy other psychological and social benefits. However, the custom harms consumers by: (v) forcing reluctant tippers to choose between a financial loss or losses of service, reputation, or pride, (vi) creating anxiety due to unclear tipping expectations, and (vii) motivating service discrimination against those expected to be poor tippers. Not all of these benefits and harms are equally strong or general, but there is evidence that each affects at least some consumers. That evidence and its implications are discussed below.[2]

Tipping Improves Service Quality

Tipping is supposed to be an incentive and reward for good service, but whether or not it actually improves service quality is an empirical question. Early research found that tip sizes were only weakly related to customers' ratings of service quality, leading me to doubt tipping's value as an incentive for better service (Lynn, 2011). However, more recent research has led me to modify that conclusion. Three surveys of restaurant waiters and waitresses indicate that many servers mistakenly believe the relationship between tips and service is strong (Kwortnik et al., 2009; Lynn, 2017a; Lynn et al., 2011). For example, the most recent of these surveys asked almost 700 restaurant servers from across the U.S. to rate how large an effect the quality of their service has on the size of tips they receive, using a seven-point scale. Seventy percent of the respondents rated the service-tipping relationship above the mid-point on this scale, indicating that they thought their service had moderately to large effects on their tips. Perhaps servers need to have

---

of taxes on tip income conditions those people to try to evade other taxes and it undermines the general public's perceptions about the fairness of the tax system.

[2] The writing in this section is drawn (with editing) from Lynn (2017b).

these inaccurate perceptions, because the perceptions contribute to servers' feelings of control and reduce servers' feelings that they depend on charity.

Regardless of how they are developed and maintained, servers' beliefs that tips are strongly related to service suggest that tipping does motivate servers to provide better service. Further supporting this conclusion are two other studies I conducted with Rob Kwortnik and Bill Ross (Kwortnik et al., 2009). In one study, 469 current or former servers read a scenario describing a restaurant and indicated (with 7-point scales) how often they would engage in various customer- and sales-oriented behaviors if they worked as a server in that restaurant. The customer-oriented behaviors included checking up on the table, complimenting customers' food choices, and thanking customers while the sales-oriented behaviors included recommending branded and high price selections and speeding up service to turn the table. The scenario was randomly varied to present respondents with one of three tipping policies: voluntary tipping, an automatic gratuity, or no tipping with high wages. The results are depicted in Fig. 9.1. Customer-oriented behavior was highest under a voluntary tipping policy (mean = 4.9), intermediate under an automatic gratuity policy (mean = 4.4), and lowest under a wages-only policy (mean = 3.9), with all of these differences being statistically reliable. Sales-oriented behavior was significantly higher under both voluntary tipping (mean = 4.8) and automatic gratuity policies (mean = 5.1), which did not reliably differ from one another, than under a wages-only policy (mean = 2.9). These findings suggest that replacing automatic service charges with tipping will increase customer-oriented, though not sales-oriented, behaviors and that replacing wages only with tipping will increase both customer- and sales-oriented behaviors.

In a second study, we asked over a thousand restaurant servers in the U.S. to indicate how often they engaged in nine positive service behaviors (such as introducing themselves by name, smiling at customers, and complimenting customers' food choices) and how large an effect they thought their service had on their tips. Consistent with a motivational effect of tipping, we found that the likelihood that servers would engage in seven of the nine service behaviors increased with their belief about how strongly service affects tip size. The observed correlations were not large ($0.06 \leq r's \leq 0.16$), but that may be because perceived service-tip contingency and service behaviors were measured at different levels of specificity—servers who thought service had little effect on tipping may nevertheless have thought the specific behaviors we measured do impact tips and servers who thought service did affect their tips may not have thought the specific behaviors we measured have such an effect.

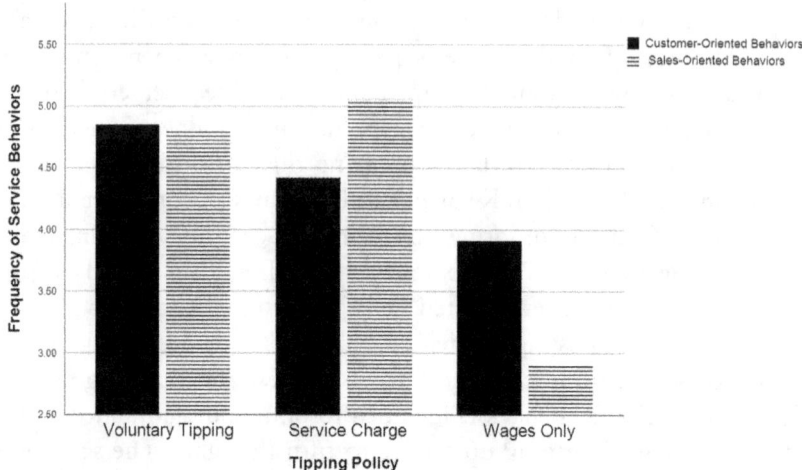

Fig. 9.1 Hypothetical sales- and customer-oriented behavior are lower under a wages-only policy than a voluntary tipping policy, and customer-oriented (but not sales-oriented) behavior is lower under a service charge policy than voluntary tipping policy. *Source* Lynn (2017b)

Although tipping motivates positive service behaviors, it is an extrinsic motivation. Psychological research has found that extrinsic rewards such as tips reduce intrinsic motivation (Deci et al., 1999). If the extrinsic motivation provided by tipping undermines intrinsic motivation, it could reduce service authenticity by motivating positive emotional displays that workers do not really feel. Other things being equal, such an effect would lower consumer perceptions of service quality, because researchers have found that consumers are able to distinguish authentic emotional labor from feigned emotional displays and prefer the former to the latter (Grandey et al., 2005; Houston et al., 2018; Hülsheger et al., 2015). Thus, it is possible that tipping reduces customer satisfaction with service even though it increases workers' service-oriented behaviors.

However, allaying such concerns are the previously discussed findings that servers believe they have control over their tip income (Kwortnik et al., 2009; Lynn, 2016; Lynn et al., 2011). Perceptions of empowerment and control have been shown to mitigate and even reverse the negative effects of extrinsic rewards on intrinsic motivation (Fang & Gerhart, 2012; Grandey et al., 2013). By enhancing servers' perceptions of control over their incomes, tipping is likely to increase not only positive service behaviors, but also servers' intrinsic motivation and the authenticity of their emotional displays.

Tipping Reduces Perceived Risks

Most tipped services are what is known as "experience goods"—goods that can be accurately evaluated only after being personally experienced. The intangible and customized nature of many services together with the inseparability of their production and consumption mean that consumers cannot be sure of what they will get when purchasing those services. Tipping can help consumers reduce the anxiety accompanying such risky purchases in two ways—by increasing consumer expectations of good service and by lowering the costs of bad service.

We have already seen that tipping does improve service, but that would not reduce consumers' perceptions of risk and accompanying anxiety if consumers did not believe that tipping improves service. Moreover, tipping can reduce consumers' perceptions of risk even if service levels are not really improved as long as consumers believe tipping improves service. So, what do consumers believe about tipping's effects on service? Research on this issue is surprisingly scant, but one survey found that 46% of US respondents believe that service is better under tipping than it would be under automatic service charges (Mills & Riehle, 1987). Another study I did with Shuo Wang provides additional, though qualified, evidence of such a belief. That study presented respondents with interior and exterior pictures of a restaurant as well as a restaurant menu describing the tipping policy as either (i) "Tipping 15% of the bill is customary," (ii) "A 15% gratuity (or service charge) will be added to the bill," or (iii) "No tipping—employees not allowed to accept tips," and then asked them to rate the expected service levels at that restaurant (Lynn & Wang, 2013). Study respondents rated the expected service quality higher (about half a point higher using a 7-point scale) when they believed the restaurant had a voluntary tipping policy than when they believed it had a no-tipping policy. The respondents' expectations of service quality were unaffected by whether they believed the restaurant had an automatic gratuity or a voluntary tipping policy, but perhaps they assumed (without being told) that the automatic gratuity could be dropped if service was unsatisfactory. More data on this issue is clearly needed, but it appears from the limited data we do have that many consumers do believe tipping improves service and this belief should reduce their perceptions of the riskiness of buying those tipped services.

Tipping also allows consumers to reduce the amount they tip if they are dissatisfied with the service, and consumers have long claimed that they do exercise that option. For example, 77% of respondents to a recent PEW Center survey reported that quality of service was a "major factor" in their decisions about whether or not to tip at all and about how much to tip (Desilver & Lippert, 2023). This ability to lower tips in response to bad service reduces the costs, and hence risks, of getting bad service. Perceived risk and the resulting anxiety are a function of both the amount potentially lost and the probability of that loss. As we have seen, tipping reduces both of these factors. Thus, it benefits consumers by bringing at least some peace of mind to transactions involving services that are experience goods.

Tipping Reduces the Prices/Costs of Services

Many people believe that tipping raises the costs of services by forcing customers to pay workers' wages in addition to the cost of the service. However, customers have to pay all of the costs of services (labor included) in one way or another if service providers are to stay in business. If service firms paid higher wages, then they would have to raise prices or add service charges to cover the costs. Conversely, economic theory tells us that competition ensures any labor-cost savings, such as those provided by tipping, tend to be passed on to consumers in the form of lower prices. You do not have to just take economic theory and my word on this. Figure 9.2 graphs the state level relationship between average restaurant prices in 2018 and the tipped minimum wage in that year.[3] As we can see, states with lower tipped minimum wages (or labor costs) also have lower average restaurant menu prices, and this relationship is moderately strong ($r = 0.57$, $n = 48$, $p < 0.001$). Moreover, this relationship is not just attributable to the effects of state differences in the costs of living on both restaurant prices and tipped minimum wages because it remains significant even after controlling for state differences in the costs of living (pr $= 0.36$, $p < 0.02$). Thus, both theory and data suggest that the labor savings that tipping provides businesses lowers the prices of services.

Of course, consumers pay for the lower prices that tipping brings via the tips they leave. However, the voluntary nature of tipping means that people can limit their payment for the service component of the service to an amount as low as they want. The hope (and reality) is that extremely low tips from price-sensitive customers will be (are) made up for with larger tips from price-insensitive customers. In essence, tipping enables wealthy and price-insensitive customers to subsidize the service experiences of poor and price-sensitive customers.

---

[3] Menu prices by state are from Business Insider. (August 12, 2019). Average menu price in the United States as of 2018, by state [Graph]. In *Statista*. Retrieved March 10, 2023, from https://www.statista.com/statistics/1079053/us-menu-price/

9 Winners a Losers (Who Does Tipping Benefit ... 163

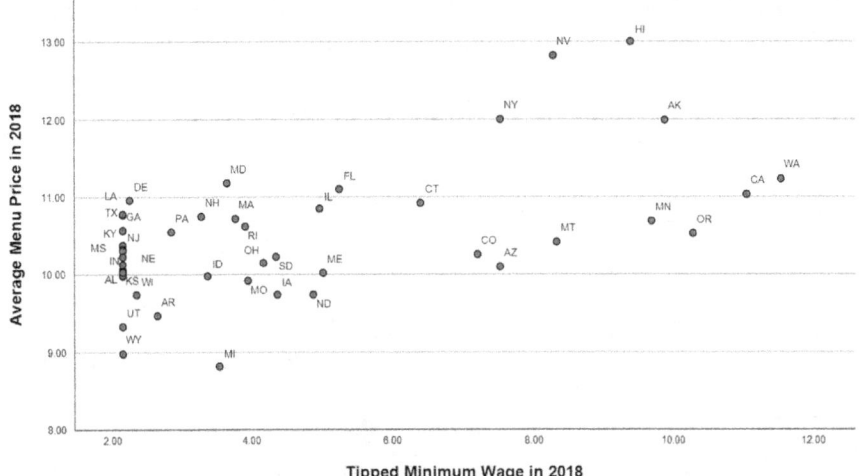

Fig. 9.2 States with higher tipped minimum wages (or labor costs) also have higher average restaurant menu prices ($r = 0.57$, $n = 48$, $p < 0.001$)

To get some sense of how many consumers benefit from this subsidy, I used April 2013 charge sales and tip data from seven restaurant chains (provided by NCR) and calculated the proportion of customers who tipped less than 15, 18, and 20% of their bills. Collectively, the restaurant chains operated in 48 states (and the District of Columbia) and spanned a wide range of price-tiers, with median check sizes ranging from $13 to $135. Overall, 24% of the restaurants' patrons tipped less than 15% of the bill, 46% of them tipped less than 18% of the bill, and 66% of them tipped less than 20% of the bill.[4] These percentages varied only a little with restaurant price-tier (see Fig. 9.3) and they suggest that almost all restaurants replacing tipping with revenue neutral service charge or service-inclusive menu pricing systems would raise prices on a substantial proportion of their customers. Many big tippers would pay less under no-tipping systems, but their voluntary generosity suggests that they would benefit less than poor tippers would be harmed by the elimination of tipping.[5]

---

[4] Time has not changed the numbers at the lower end of tipping much. A 2022 survey by YouGov found that 22, 40, and 44% of respondents reported that they usually tip less than 15, 18, and 20% of their bills respectively.

[5] Consistent with this idea, a survey I did a few years back found that consumers' sensitivity to restaurant prices was negatively related to the amounts they tipped ($r_{\text{with cash tip}} = -0.21$, $n = 160$, $p < 0.008$; $r_{\text{with percent tip}} = -0.14$, $n = 493$, $p < 0.003$). This is an unpublished finding from a survey used and described in Lynn (2009).

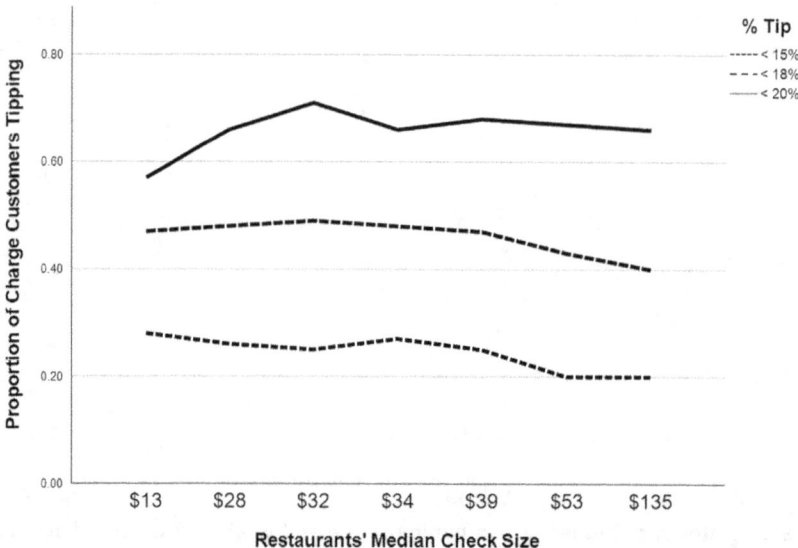

Fig. 9.3 Across a wide range of restaurant price-tiers, roughly 25, 45, and 65% of restaurant customers tip less than 15%, 18%, and 20% of the bill respectively and would face higher prices under corresponding service charges or higher service-inclusive prices. *Source* Lynn (2017b)

Tipping Provides Opportunity to Buy Psychological and Social Benefits

The altruistic, reciprocity, and social-esteem motives for tipping discussed in Chap. 2 identify additional psychological or social benefits that at least some consumers derive from tipping—i.e., warm-glow, enhanced gratitude, equitable relationships, and social-approval/esteem. Research in social psychology and other disciplines tells us that (i) helping others provides positive "warm glow" feelings in the helper (Crumpler & Grossman, 2008), (ii) expressing gratitude enhances feelings of well-being (Sheldon & Yu, 2020), (iii) maintaining equitable relationships (where the ratio of what we give and receive is equal to the ratio of what the other person gives and receives) is more psychologically comfortable than being in inequitable relationships (Adams & Freedman, 1976), and (iv) that the approval and esteem of others is rewarding (Fershtman & Weiss, 2012; Leary & Kowalski, 1990). Tipping provides all of these psychological and social benefits by allowing the tipper to help the tip recipient, express gratitude to the tip recipient, maintain equity in the relationship with the tip recipient, and buy the approval/esteem of the tip recipient and other observers. Supporting the idea that tipping delivers these benefits to at least some consumers are the results of a 2023 OnePoll survey conducted for Forbes Advisor asking 2000 Americans how they felt about tipping over the last year. It found that 36% of respondents reported feeling happy, 33% reported feeling grateful, 22% reported feeling content, and 18% reported feeling proud (Miranda, 2023). Additional support comes from several other studies finding that people with stronger altruistic, gratitude/reciprocity, and social-esteem motivations for tipping report greater liking for the custom than do people in whom these motives are weaker (Lynn, 2015, 2018, 2021; Lynn & Brewster, 2020). This is correlational data and correlations do not prove causality, but it makes sense that people with these motivations like tipping more than others because they get more of the aforementioned psychological and social benefits from it.

Tipping Pressures Consumers

While generous tips bring the tipper positive benefits such as better future service, greater social-esteem, and pride, less generous tips can lead to negative outcomes such as poor future service, loss of social-status, and guilt. As a consequence, tipping forces many consumers to choose between either a financial loss or losses of service, reputation, and/or pride. Basically, reluctant tippers are pressured to tip more than they would like in order to avoid those negative outcomes. Putting consumers in such a loss-loss situation is a clear harm. The previously mentioned OnePoll survey conducted for Forbes provides some evidence about how widespread that harm was in 2023. When asking 2000 Americans how they felt about tipping over the last year, it found that 31% of respondents reported feeling pressured, 23% reported feeling embarrassed, and 23% reported feeling guilty (Miranda, 2023). Additional support comes from other studies finding that people with stronger loss-avoidant and/or duty motivations for tipping report lower liking for the custom than do people in whom these motives are weaker (Lynn, 2015, 2021; Lynn & Brewster, 2020). Again, this is only correlational data, but it makes sense that people with these motivations like tipping less than do others because they feel more pressure to part with money they would rather keep.

Tipping Creates Unclear Social Expectations

The pressures to tip described above come from social expectations and the negative consequences of failing to live up to those expectations. Unfortunately, such unwanted pressure is not the only harm tipping expectations inflict on consumers. Another harm is the anxiety that comes from not knowing what those tipping expectations are in a given situation. Although advice about tipping expectations is publicly available in the form of online and press articles, etiquette books, and tipping guides, those sources of information are not always immediately available in tipping situations, so they require some foresight to be of use. Furthermore, as discussed in Chap. 5, these sources are of questionable reliability because they provide conflicting advice. Add to that the fact that tipping expectations of service providers can and do change over time—as evidenced by post-Covid-19 expansions in the numbers and types of services asking U.S. consumers for tips (tip-creep) and increases in the amounts they are asked to tip for traditionally tipped services (tip-flation)—and it is easy to understand why 11–20% of respondents to recent polls in the U.S. reported being confused about who and how much to tip (Gillespe, 2023; Kelton, 2024; Miranda, 2023). Few people find such uncertainty pleasant, so it must be added to the ways that tipping harms consumers.

Tipping Motivates Service Discrimination

Although tipping generally enhances servers' motivation to deliver good service, many people argue that it has the opposite effect on servers' motivation to serve groups that are perceived to be poor tippers. Indeed, there is a growing body of both qualitative and quantitative research documenting the effects of servers' expecting low tips on their service discrimination against foreigners, ethnic minorities, and other customers (Barkan & Israeli, 2004; Brewster, 2013; Kim, 2012; Shrestha, 2010). Some indication about the pervasiveness of such tipping-based service discrimination can be found in the responses to two questions from a survey of 700 servers previously mentioned.

One question asked the servers to rate a number of different consumer groups on a scale of "very bad" to "very good" tippers. Foreigners, teenagers, coupon users, Blacks, Hispanics, Christians, and the elderly are all widely perceived to be below-average tippers. The sample was not representative, but regression analyzes indicated that servers' perceptions of various groups' tipping behavior did not vary much across servers' geo-demographic and workplace characteristics (Lynn, 2017b). Thus, these perceptions are held by a wide range of restaurant servers.

The second question asked servers how often they had given substandard service to customers expected to be poor tippers. Thirty-eight percent of the servers acknowledged at least sometimes doing so. This tendency to give substandard service to customers perceived to be poor tippers did not vary much across servers' geo-demographic and workplace characteristics, but was greater for servers who were younger, lived in the northeast (especially compared to the south), and had lots of ethnic minority customers (Lynn, 2017b). Overall, if servers' self-reports are to be believed, tipping-motivated service discrimination is not common, but is not rare either. Since this service discrimination is most likely to be directed at foreigners, teenagers, coupon users, Blacks, Hispanics, Christians, and the elderly, members of these groups may find that tipping lowers rather than raises the quality of service they receive.

Net Effects on Consumers

The different benefits and harms described above each affect different consumers to different degrees, so their combined impact will also differ across consumers. There is no net benefit or harm of tipping common to every consumer, but what about consumers as a whole? Does tipping increase or decrease overall consumer satisfaction and happiness? Are most consumers helped or hurt by tipping? Are the net benefits that accrue to some consumers greater or lesser than the net harms that accrue to others?

I used to believe that the benefits of tipping to consumers were better established, stronger, and more generalizable than the harms to consumers. Thus, I believed that tipping has a net positive effect on satisfaction and happiness for consumers as a whole (Lynn, 2017a, 2017b, 2018a, 2018b, 2018c). Four studies of tipping-policy effects on customer satisfaction in the real world (as opposed to hypothetical scenarios) that I did with various co-authors supported this conclusion (see Lynn & Kwortnik, 2015; Kwortnik et al., 2009; Lynn, 2018; Lynn & Brewster, 2017). Those studies found that:

- Carnival cruises' online reviews were higher before the cruise line replaced voluntary tipping with automatic service charges than afterward (average ratings = 4.0 vs. 3.7),
- Miami Beach restaurants with voluntary tipping had higher Zagat service ratings than did those with service charges after controlling for food, décor, and cost ratings (average ratings = 19.5 vs. 18.5),
- Joe's Crab Shack restaurants that replaced tipping with service-inclusive pricing in 2015 saw their collective online ratings go down relative to those of control restaurants (by 0.30 out of 5 points) only to see those ratings go up again (by 0.25 out of 5 points) after returning to voluntary tipping,

- 41 independent restaurants in the U.S. that operated under tipping and no-tipping policies at different times from 2014 to 2016 had collectively higher online ratings under tipping than under service charges or service-inclusive pricing. Low, medium, and high priced restaurants that replaced tipping with automatic service charges saw their online ratings go down by 0.30, 0.21 and 0.16 out of 5 points respectively. Low and medium priced restaurants that replaced tipping with service inclusive pricing saw their online ratings go down by 0.10 and 0.18 out of 5 points respectively. High priced restaurants that replaced tipping with service inclusive pricing did not see their online ratings go down.

Also supporting a positive net effect of tipping on consumer satisfaction and happiness is the fact that most consumers in the U.S. report liking tipping more than its alternatives. For example, one survey I did asking U.S. consumers how much they liked or disliked a variety of different tipping policies in full-service restaurants found that voluntary tipping was clearly the most liked policy—with a net favorability (% liking minus % disliking) of + 39% as compared to + 17% for service-inclusive menu pricing, and − 12% for automatic service charges (Lynn, 2017a, 2017b).

Taken together, the evidence that tipping has a net benefit to consumers as a whole was pretty compelling. However, a subsequent study indicates that conclusion must be significantly qualified. In that study, Rob Kwortnik and I compared the online ratings of Royal Caribbean Cruises before and after its abandonment of voluntary tipping on March 1, 2013 (Lynn & Kwortnik, 2020). At first glance, this might seem like just an uninteresting repetition of the study examining the effects of tipping policies on Carnival's ratings described above. However, there is an important difference between this study and that other one. The Carnival study examined tipping-policy effects at a time when voluntary tipping on cruises was common—during the early 2000s when the cruise industry had just started to shift from voluntary tipping to end-of-cruise service charges. The other studies described above also occurred in a context where tipping is ubiquitous—U.S. restaurants. It is possible that the net effects of tipping on consumers found in these studies depend on how common and familiar the practice is.

Royal Caribbean's abandonment of voluntary tipping in 2013 allowed us to test this possibility because by that time tipping had become rare in the cruise industry. We found that Royal Caribbean's online ratings were not affected by its change in tipping policy. This failure to replicate the earlier research suggests that the previously observed effects probably had more to do with adopting counter-normative policies than with abandoning tipping per se. More research is needed to be sure, but it appears that tipping enhances overall customer satisfaction and happiness in contexts where it is common but not in contexts where it is rare. This qualification suggests that expansions of tipping into new service contexts will not necessarily enhance overall consumer satisfaction and well-being. It may also help explain why tipping has remained rare in many countries around the world—because tipping in non-tipping countries does not improve overall consumer satisfaction.

Pros and Cons of Tipping from a Worker Perspective

A critical reading of the evidence suggests that compensation via tips and tipping benefits workers by: (i) paying more per hour than most other jobs requiring comparable qualifications, (ii) allowing workers to hide much of that income from tax authorities, (iii) giving workers unusual control over their own incomes, and (iv) providing immediate feedback about job performance that can help workers get better and that is satisfying when they do well. On the downside, however, there is also evidence that tip income: (v) brings social pressure from co-workers to under-report that income, (vi) is less stable and certain than wages, (vii) allows businesses to pay less than regular minimum wages, (viii) empowers consumers to be abusive, and (ix) gives managers control over workers' incomes that is greater and easier to abuse than their control over wages. Again, not all of these benefits and harms are equally strong or general, but there is evidence that each affects at least some tipped workers. That evidence and its implications are discussed below.[6]

High Income Levels

Many people believe that working for tips contributes to low worker incomes. Supporting this belief, Allegretto and Cooper (2014) analyzed data from the U.S. government's Current Population Survey and found that the median hourly wage for tipped workers is only about 60% of that for all workers ($10.22 vs. $16.48) and that the percentage of tipped workers whose family incomes fall below the poverty level is twice that of other workers (12.8% vs. 6.5%). However, these statistics are misleading, because tipped workers are more likely than others to be members of demographic groups that typically earn less per hour even for non-tipped work—i.e., to be young, female,

---

[6] The writing in this section is drawn heavily (with editing) from Lynn (2024).

non-white, non-college graduates, and part-time employees (Allegretto & Cooper, 2014). In addition, tipped work requires less training and skill than does much non-tipped work and low training/skill jobs typically pay less than higher training/skill jobs even if both are non-tipped (Neumark & Yen, 2021). Moreover, even if appropriate comparison groups of tipped and non-tipped workers were obtained, these data rely on self-reports to the government of workers' wages and incomes. As will be discussed more below, tipped income is easy to hide and an estimated half of it is never reported to the IRS (Department of Treasury, 2018). It seems unlikely that tipped workers would be substantially more forthcoming in reports of their incomes to other government offices, so it is almost certain that this data significantly understates the incomes of tipped workers compared to those of similar non-tipped workers.

My own experiences as a tipped worker while in college and graduate school were that I earned more in tip income than I could possibly have made in wages for any other job I was qualified to do. Furthermore, several studies suggest that my experiences were not unusual—tipped workers often make more than similarly situated non-tipped workers. First, a 2015 compensation and benefits survey of NYC restaurant companies conducted by a local industry association found that the median hourly income (including tips) of bartenders and waiters/waitresses exceeded that of all other non-tipped hourly employees of those companies (NYC Hospitality Alliance, 2015). For example, waiters/waitresses' median hourly income exceeded that of porters by 175%, of cashiers by 129%, of line cooks by 112%, of hosts/hostesses by 99%, of reservationists by 83%, of office managers by 62%, and of accounting clerks by 10%. These hourly income differences were not limited to fine-dining restaurants but were also observed at casual-dining restaurants.

Second, a survey of over 1000 restaurant managers from large metro areas across the U.S. conducted by Cornell and the Ohio State University researchers found that median weekly wages (including tips) of front-of-house employees (who typically receive tips) exceeded that of back-of-house employees (who typically do not receive tips) (Batt et al., 2014). This income difference was greater at upscale fine-dining restaurants where F-O-H workers earned a median of $792 per week and B-O-H workers earned a median of $441 per week, but it was also observed at moderately priced restaurants where F-O-H workers earned a median of $464 per week and B-O-H workers earned a median of $360 per week.

Finally, a 2013–2014 survey of 15,000 restaurant workers across the U.S., conducted by the compensation company Payscale (2014), found that restaurant jobs getting higher percentages of their pay from tips paid more per hour

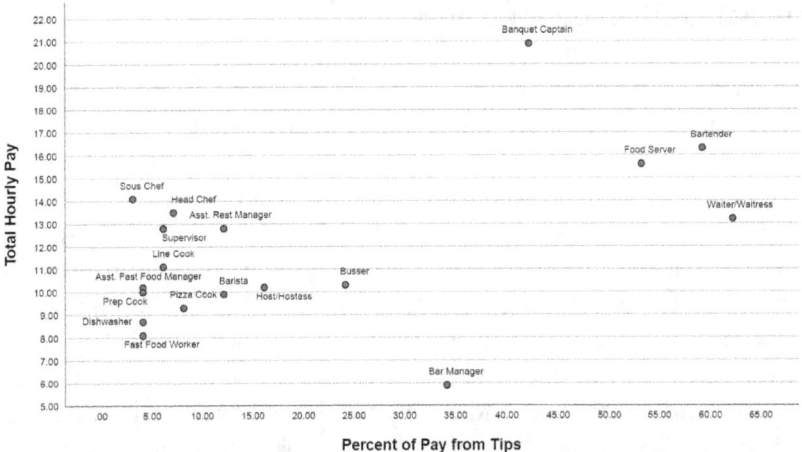

Fig. 9.4 Across the U.S., restaurant workers with a high percentage of their pay coming from tips make more than those with a low percentage of their pay coming from tips. *Source* Lynn (2024)

(including tips) than did jobs getting lower percentages of their pay from tips (see Fig. 9.4).

The data from all three of the surveys described above involved unverified income information, but the respondents had less motivation to lie to the surveyors than they would to lie to the government, so these data are more trustworthy than government data on tip incomes. This more trustworthy data consistently supports my own experiences and indicates that most tipped restaurant workers earn substantially more, not less, than non-tipped workers with comparable training and skills.

Tax Evasion

All tip income is taxable (IRS, 2021). Evading payment of those taxes is unlawful, and I do NOT recommend that anyone attempt or encourage it. Nevertheless, cash tips are easy to hide from the government, and many servers view this opportunity to unlawfully evade taxes as a perk of tipped work. In fact, the IRS estimates that less than half of all tip income is reported (Department of Treasury, 2018), so many servers do take advantage of that perk.

Personal Control over Income

Many workers have little control over the incomes their jobs provide. If workers want to make more money, they must typically work more hours (which is not always possible) or find other, better-paying jobs. However, the compensation for some jobs is structured so that workers who produce or sell more get paid more. Tipping is one of those compensation systems; it allows workers to make more money not only by working more hours, but also by working smarter and getting customers to leave larger tips. Although how much a consumer tips is largely determined by his or her own characteristics, service workers can still influence those decisions. What is more, that ability to influence tips extends beyond simply providing better service, though that does help too. Researchers have identified dozens of specific, easy-to-perform behaviors that service workers can use to increase their tips—often by 20% or more (see Chap. 8). The point here is that tipping gives workers many more opportunities to increase their incomes than do other compensation methods. Furthermore, servers do not have to wait until their next paychecks to see the increased compensation—they take it home with them after each work shift! Thus, people who value the opportunity to personally control their earnings (and are willing to engage in the behaviors that increase tips), should find working for tips more appealing than others.

Performance Feedback

While the primary motive for working is to make money, that is not the only motive. Most people take pride in their work and want to do as good a job as possible. In order to become the best they can be and to maximize their intrinsic job satisfaction, workers need meaningful feedback on their job performance. As Peter Drucker is often mistakenly quoted as saying, "You can't manage what you can't measure." (Zak, 2013). The job of service workers is to satisfy customers while also conforming to organizational policies and expectations. The latter goal is usually pretty straightforward and often explicitly spelled out in training documents. For example, it is clear that good servers or bartenders should usually refrain from giving customers free drinks even though it would please those customers. However, the former goal is more abstract and vague. What does it take to satisfy customers? How do servers know if they are satisfying their customers? How do they know if their performance is getting better or worse over time and how their performance compares to that of co-workers?

Customers' verbal and non-verbal behaviors are certainly a clue about servers' performances. For example, rarely do dissatisfied customers smile at or verbally thank workers for poor service. On the other hand, words are cheap, and sometimes customers say everything is okay when it isn't. Furthermore, not all customers are verbally or non-verbally expressive, so reading their statements and expressions is difficult and error prone. Most importantly, it is virtually impossible to quantify the sentiments expressed in customers' naturally occurring verbal statements and non-verbal expressions, so they cannot be meaningfully compared across time and people.

Servers could look to their managers for feedback about their performance. After all, monitoring and motivating worker performance is part of a manager's job. However, not all managers are observant, insightful, objective, and articulate enough to provide good feedback. Furthermore, even the best managers have a hard time telling if service workers have done a good job, because services are fleeting, intangible, and customized. Monitoring the many short, inter-personal interactions involved in providing most services would require too many watchers. Moreover, differences in customers' desires mean that those watchers would have a difficult time telling if a particular service behavior was wanted by the customer or not. For example, is a waiter who rarely visits a table ignoring the table or giving them the space and privacy they want? These issues make managers a relatively poor source of feedback to servers about their performance (Azar, 2004).

Where other sources fall short, tips can help fill servers' needs for meaningful feedback on their performances, because tips come from the customers that servers are supposed to satisfy and are supposed to reflect those customers' satisfaction with the service. In fact, many economists believe that this is why tipping exists in the first place—because it is easier and more efficient for customers than for managers to monitor and reward service worker performance (Azar, 2004; Jacob & Page, 1980). While there is reason to question how good tips are at measuring performance on some aspects of service, research has made it clear that they do reflect service workers' social connection with customers as well as customers' overall affective reactions to service encounters. Furthermore, tips are easily quantified and compared across time and workers. This means that servers can compare their tips with those of co-workers to see how much room for improvement in their performance there is and to get ideas about how to improve by trying to identify behaviors that differentiate those who get good and bad tips. They can also compare their tips across customers and time periods to discover what behaviors seem to make their customers' happiest. Thus, tips are a valuable source of feedback to servers about their own performance and about ways to get better at their jobs. For those workers who take pride in their work and want to maximize their performance for intrinsic reasons, the feedback provided by tipping should add to the attractiveness of working for tips above and beyond that attributable to its financial benefits.

Pressure to Break the Law

We have already noted that cash tips are easy to hide from the government and that many find this opportunity to unlawfully evade taxes to be a perk of tipped work. However, it can also put social pressure to break the law on workers who do not want to (Kipp et al., 2023). Servers and their employers financially benefit from under-reporting tip income, so many do under-report it. Remember, the IRS estimates that less than half of all tip income is reported (Department of Treasury, 2018). Unfortunately, that under-reporting becomes more obvious if other servers at the establishment fully report their tips, so there is likely to be pressure from co-workers, and sometimes even employers, to get on board and under-report tip income like everyone else. For those with less flexible morals, this social pressure to break the law is a reason to avoid tipped employment.

Income Instability and Uncertainty

Although tip income often exceeds what workers can make in non-tipped jobs, that income depends on how many customers a server has and how much those customers decide to tip, both of which can vary from day to day even when work hours are stable. These unique sources of variability in tip income mean that tipped workers face much more income instability and uncertainty than do other workers. The greater instability of tipped income makes it harder for tipped workers to plan and secure loans for major purchases such as cars and houses, but those difficulties can be overcome with proper records. More problematic for some people is the psychological toll of income uncertainty and/or the emotional ups and downs accompanying frequent rises and falls in tip income.

To help get an idea of just how big those rises and falls in tip income typically are, I turn to data provided to me by Upserve (a point-of-sale or payment systems company) on the total daily charge tip amounts for each of 164 servers from seven, casual-dining, California restaurants who worked and received charge tips on at least 21 days over the course of the year in 2017. Figure 9.5 plots those servers by the top and bottom quartile of their daily

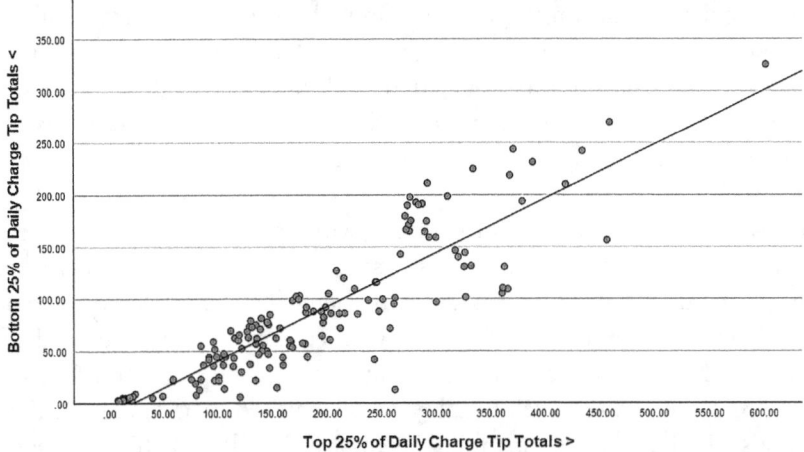

Fig. 9.5 The bottom quarter of servers' daily tip totals were typically half or less of the amounts they got on the top quarter of days. Each dot represents a server whose 25th and 75th percentile of daily charge tip totals are shown on the corresponding axes. *Source* Lynn (2024)

charge tip totals. Although this data does not include cash tips and, therefore, understates the servers' tip incomes, it does illustrate how much tips can vary across work shifts.

Typically, the bottom quarter of these servers' daily tip totals were half or less of the amounts they got on the top fourth of days. Some servers saw less variability in their daily tip totals (those above the line in Fig. 9.5), but others saw more (those below the line), and none had the income stability provided by traditional wages or salaries. Though not representative of all servers, these data illustrate the kind and extent of income variability that working for tips can entail.

Sub-minimum Wages

In addition to income uncertainty, tipped workers must also cope with substandard hourly wages. In the United States, federal law stipulates the minimum wage an employer can pay workers. However, within their own jurisdictions, states and cities can mandate higher minimum wages than are required by federal law, and many (though not all) do so. Thus, the minimum legal wage varies across cities and states within the U.S. Most of these minimum wage laws allow employers to pay tipped workers less than non-tipped workers as long as the employees' tip earnings amount to at least $30 a month and bring the total compensation of tips plus wages to the regular minimum wage level. Only the states of Alaska, California, Minnesota, Montana, Nevada, Oregon, and Washington require employers to pay the same minimum wage to tipped and untipped employees. The difference between the regular and tipped minimum wages allowed by federal and most state laws is known as the tip credit, and it varies across states (see Fig. 9.6).

These sub-minimum wages for tipped workers are usually not a problem for the employees. As previously discussed, most tipped workers earn more than the regular minimum wage when their tips are taken into account. Nevertheless, tip amounts, which vary across employers, workers, and shifts, sometimes fail to cover the tip credit and bring total compensation to the regular minimum wage level. Employers are required by federal law to make-up any such shortfalls in tips for a given work-week with higher wages for that week, but this requirement is difficult to enforce—as acknowledged in a White House (2014) report on the minimum wage. As a result, some tipped employees find themselves working for less than the regular minimum wage on a given week, even though this is unlawful.

No one knows for sure how often these violations of tipped minimum wage laws occur, but the available evidence suggests that they are not rare. The U.S. Department of Labor's Current Population Surveys have found that over 10% of workers in predominately tipped occupations reported total compensation (tips plus wages) that fells below the federal minimum wage when that compensation was converted to hourly wages by dividing by the respondent's reported number of hours usually worked. Problems with self-reports of income and work hours mean that this 10% number cannot be taken at face value. However, it is more than twice the percentage of all surveyed workers whose similarly calculated total compensation fells below the federal minimum wage, so it is clear that tipped workers are much more likely than others to be paid unlawfully low wages (Allegretto & Cooper, 2014).

Furthermore, tip totals vary more from shift to shift than from week to week, because there are fewer tips in a shift than in a week and chance affects small samples more than large ones. This means that tipped workers are more likely to find themselves working for less than the regular minimum wage on a given work-shift than on a given work-week. Such shortfalls on shifts are legally acceptable and do not have to be made up by the employer as long as surplus tips on other shifts mean that the tip credit is covered for the week. Thus, even tipped workers with law-abiding employers may find themselves occasionally working shifts for compensation that it is below the federal minimum wage. To be sure, those bad days are made up by good days, but some people have a hard time looking at the big picture and resent having

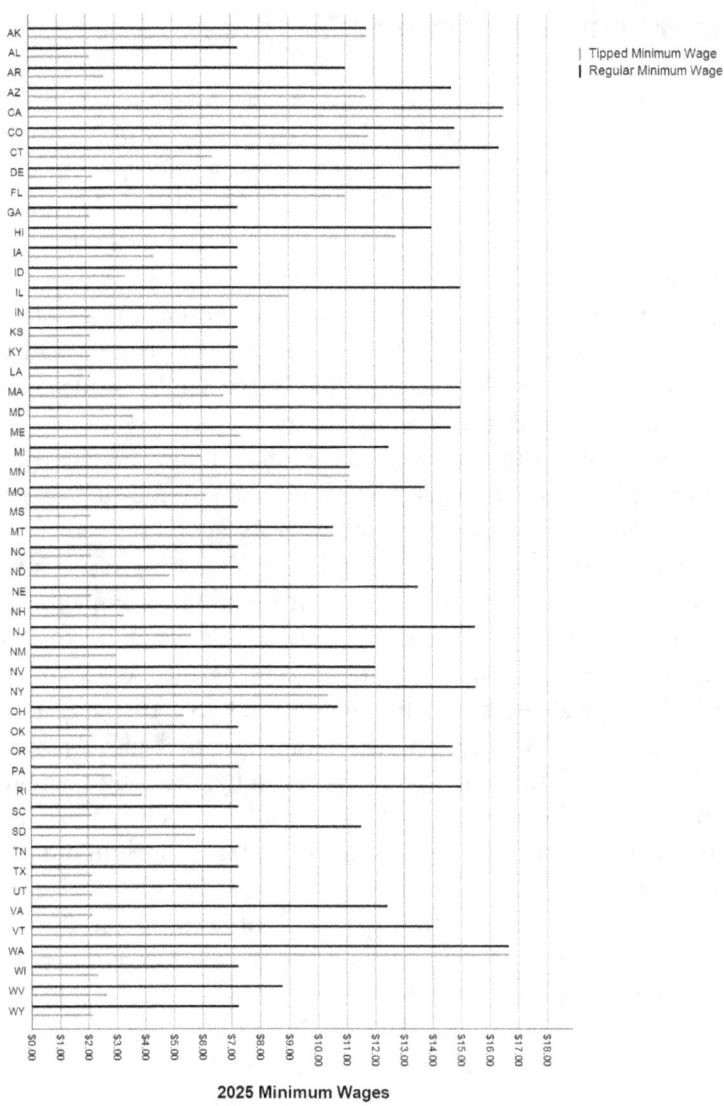

Fig. 9.6 Effective minimum wages for tipped and non-tipped workers, and the differences between those minimum wages, vary across states in the United States. *Source* https://www.paycor.com/resource-center/articles/minimum-wage-tipped-employees-by-state/

to work shifts for which they are poorly paid. To be happy working for tips, workers need to be able to keep the big picture in mind and not be bothered by occasional work shifts that are under-compensated.

Consumer Control over Income

Tips are voluntary—meaning that consumers can tip large or small amounts or even nothing at all as they see fit. This discretionary nature of tipping gives customers power over workers who depend on those tips for a portion of their incomes, and some customers abuse that power. This abuse takes many forms.

Often customers are merely inconsiderate. For example, they may wait until the last minute to ask for things they should have foreseen but now urgently need—necessitating the temporary abandonment of other tables as servers run back into the kitchen to fulfill their request. Other times customers are excessively picky, demanding, messy, and/or rude, and servers quietly put up with all of it for the sake of their tips.

Not infrequently, customer rudeness can reach levels that are truly offensive. For example, I still feel angry when I think about one customer I waited on during a New Year's Eve party many years ago. This customer put a generous stack of $5 bills on the table and told me that stack was my tip, but that he would remove a bill anytime his or his dining companions' glasses became empty during the evening. He then left the stack on the table and ostentatiously removed a bill on each of the few instances that I did not refill someone's glass quickly enough. Although I ended up getting a good tip from this customer, I hated waiting on him because he rubbed his power in my face and because he insulted my professionalism by assuming I would not do a good job without the incentive of losing tips. [Note: There was a scene like this on the television comedy show Third Rock from the Sun, but it actually happened to me.]

As distasteful as I found the experience of waiting on the customer described above, I am a white male and had it easy compared to the treatment that many female servers and servers of color must endure. For example, female servers routinely put up with sexual innuendo, requests for dates (or their phone numbers), and inappropriate touching from the people they need to tip them. One survey of restaurant workers in 2014 found that about 80% of women experienced some form of sexual harassment from customers, with 33% experiencing such sexual harassment on a weekly basis (ROC United, 2014). Men were sexually harassed by customers too, but at a lower rate than were women. Most importantly for the current discussion, rates of sexual harassment were higher for tipped than for non-tipped restaurant workers (ROC United, 2014).

Except in the most egregious cases, management is unlikely to risk the ire of customers by calling the customer out and stopping their inappropriate behavior, so workers must usually deal with that unwanted behavior on their own. In the case of tipped workers, fear of getting a smaller tip adds to the fears all employees have that customers who are called out on their inappropriate behavior will try to humiliate the worker or will complain to management about the worker. As a result, most servers simply ignore and endure the customer misbehavior (ROC United, 2014). Thus, working for tips requires a relatively thick skin and a greater tolerance for mistreatment by customers than does other work.

Managerial Control over Income

Managers determine their employees' work shifts and hours as well as their wages or salaries, and this gives them a fair amount of power over those workers. Managers can abuse this power—for example, by favoring employees who resemble them in terms of sex and race or who come across as more "friendly and compliant" to their wishes. Fortunately, employment laws prohibiting sexual harassment and discrimination provide some protection against such abuse, but enforcement of these laws is difficult, costly, and uncertain, and this is particularly true for tipped jobs. Tipped work tends to be part-time, which gives managers more latitude in the assignment of hours and shifts. In addition, shift assignments matter more for tipped work because tips (unlike wages) vary considerably with how busy the establishment is. This means that managers can affect tipped employees' pay in a way that is harder to complain about and get redress for than is simple wage or salary discrimination.

Further heightening managers' extraordinary control over tipped workers' incomes is their ability to determine how many and which customers a worker serves in any given shift. In restaurants, for example, servers are assigned to sections comprised of different numbers and configurations of tables (e.g., tables for 2 vs. 4 vs. 6) and this assignment decision alone can affect a server's tip-take for a shift. Add to that the impact of having groups of diners known to be good (or bad) tippers assigned to their sections or not and managerial control over the incomes of waiters and waitresses is considerably greater and easier to hide than their control over the incomes of non-tipped employees. If power corrupts, then the extraordinary managerial control over tipped workers' incomes is more likely to encourage than discourage its abuse, so tipped workers must be prepared to put up with that abuse or to quit in the hopes of finding a better job elsewhere.

Net Effect on Workers

Different workers will evaluate the mixed bag of benefits and harms from working for tips and reach different conclusions about its net benefits or harms to them personally. In fact, a survey asking members of the general U.S. population if they would like or dislike working under tips with sub-minimum wages found opinions evenly split—— 45% said they would like it but 44% said they would dislike it (Lynn, 2017b). Fortunately, working for tips is voluntary, so those who find working for tips more harmful than beneficial do not have to do it. Those with no better options may feel compelled to work for tips, but if tipped work is their best option, then tipping does provide them with a net benefit. Thus, although tipping may be a net harm to some workers in the general population, it is almost by definition a net benefit to those working in tipped jobs.

Pros and Cons of Tipping from a Business Perspective

Of course, tipping's effects on the satisfaction and happiness of consumers and workers impact businesses, because they need both customers and workers to survive. In particular, the previously discussed effects of tipping on service quality, service discrimination, the prices/costs of services to consumers, and customer satisfaction are important benefits and costs to businesses too. Since these have already been discussed, we will focus on tipping's other benefits and costs to businesses in this section. The additional benefits to businesses of tipping are that it (i) helps them attract and retain better workers, (ii) decreases their sales-contingent costs, and (iii) increases consumers' perceptions of their price competitiveness. The additional costs to businesses of tipping are that it (iv) reduces teamwork and increases conflict among workers, (v) increases their employees' theft from the business, (vi) subjects them to additional, costly regulation, and (vii) increases their risk of being sued for unlawful employment discrimination. Not all of these benefits and costs are equally strong or general, but there is evidence that each impacts at least some businesses that allow consumer tipping of their employees. That evidence and its implications are discussed below.[7]

---

[7] The writing in this section is drawn (with editing) from Lynn (2017b).

Tipping Attracts and Retains Better Workers

Some people argue that tipping reduces the quality of workers attracted to, and staying in, the tipped jobs. As we saw above, tip income is inherently variable, which may be unappealing to workers seeking to support themselves and a family (Parise, 1987). Thus, tipping may attract single workers with a part-time or temporary mentality, thereby undermining efforts to build a professional wait-staff. However, other people argue that tipping helps attract and retain better workers. One rationale for this belief is that the pay premium discussed in a previous section of this chapter may attract higher quality workers into the profession (Eater Staff, 2015; NBC News, 2013). A second rationale is that the performance-contingent nature of tip income should appeal to and reward competent workers more than less competent ones (Lynn et al., 2011). What does the evidence say about these competing beliefs? Continue reading to find out.

Pay premium and performance-contingent pay effects on employee recruitment and retention are consistent with theory and data in economics and human resources management, but it is not clear that these general effects apply to tipping because (as we saw above) it has other costs to workers not typically associated with other forms of compensation. If tipping does help to attract and retain better workers, then we should find that better workers are more willing to work for tips and get larger tips than less capable workers and that the latter factors increase job satisfaction and retention as depicted in Fig. 9.7. Evidence about one or more of these assumed relationships is available from several studies described below.

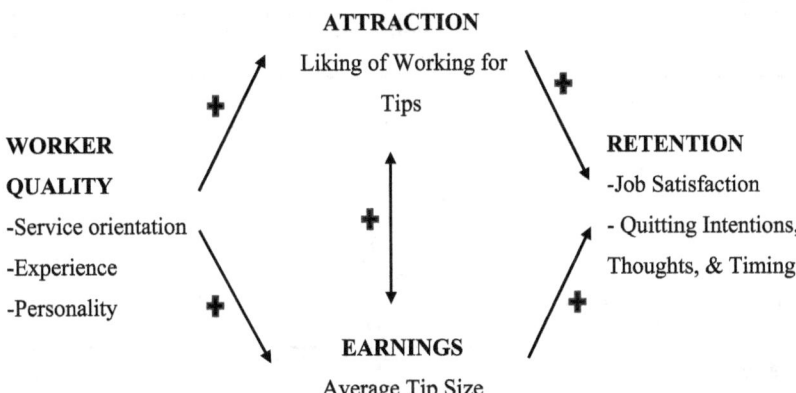

Fig. 9.7 Model showing how tipping may help to selectively attract and retain better workers

Specifically, three studies have surveyed restaurant servers to examine the relationships of their average tip sizes or their attitudes toward working for tips with their service or guest orientation, years of waiting experience, job satisfaction, and intentions or thoughts about quitting (Lynn et al., 2011; Lynn, 2003, 2017a, 2017b). The results of these studies are summarized in Table 9.1. Overall, more experienced and service-oriented waiters and waitresses earn larger average tips and like working for tips more than do less experienced and service-oriented waiters and waitresses. Furthermore, servers who earn larger tips and prefer working for tips like their jobs more, think less about quitting, and intend to stay in the job longer. These findings are all consistent with the idea that tipping helps to attract and retain more experienced and service-oriented workers. The observed correlations are weak and the selective attraction and retention effects of tipping depend on sequentially linking these weak relationships together (see Fig. 9.7), which suggests that the selective attraction and retention effects of tipping are likely to be small. However, restaurants that have abandoned tipping report loss of their better service workers to other restaurants with tipping (Bowen, 2020; Dai, 2018), so these studies may underestimate the impact of tipping on employee retention.

While tipping may be more important to employee retention than the studies reviewed above suggest, there is additional evidence that it may not be as important for attracting competent staff. Using job performance as an indicator of worker quality, I tested the effects of the pay premiums

Table 9.1 Tip averages and attitude toward working for tips are only weakly correlated with desirable server characteristics

	Average tip size	Prefer working for tips over service charges
Service/guest orientation	$r = 0.14$[a] $r = 0.18^{**}$[b] $r = 0.06$[c]	$r = 0.14^{**}$[b] $r = 0.17^{**}$[c]
Years experience as a server	$r = 0.26^{**}$[b] $r = 0.17^{**}$[c]	$r = 0.19^{**}$[b] $r = 0.18^{**}$[c]
Job satisfaction	$r = 0.26^{**}$[a] $r = 0.24^{**}$[c]	$r = 0.32^{**}$[c]
Intentions/thoughts/timing of quitting	$r = -0.29^{**}$[a] $r = -.03$[c]	$r = 0.03$[c]

Source Lynn (2017b)
** $p < 0.01$
[a] From unpublished data collected by Alex Susskind ($n = 130$) and reported in Lynn (2003)
[b] From Lynn et al. (2011) ($330 \leq n's \leq 336$)
[c] From Lynn (2016) ($685 \leq n's \leq 694$)

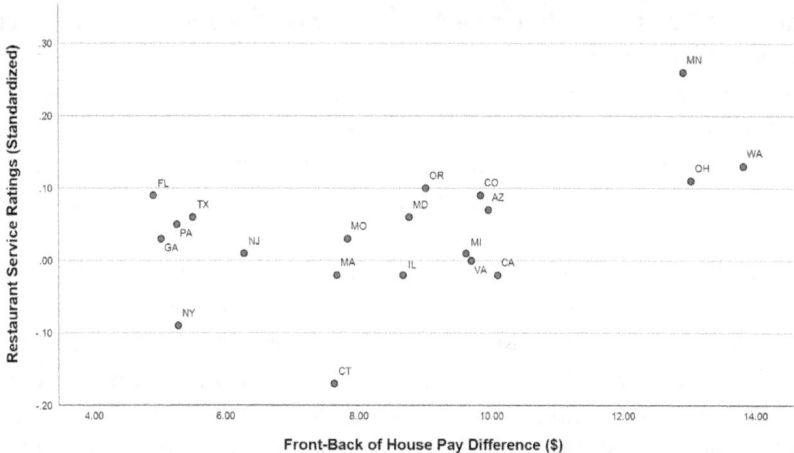

Fig. 9.8 States with larger differences in pay (tips plus wages) between front- and back-of-house restaurant staff have slightly better restaurant service ($r = 0.49$, $n = 20$, $p < 0.03$). *Source* Lynn (2017b)

tipping provides on worker quality by seeing if customer-rated service is higher in states with higher server pay (tips plus wages) relative to that of back-of-house workers (Lynn, 2017b). Using such data, I found that average customer service ratings for family-dining and full-service restaurants in 32 states did increase with the gap between front- and back-of-house restaurant employees' average pay (see Fig. 9.8). The bigger the pay premium servers got the better the service. However, the increment in average service rating was less than 0.02 out of 5 points for every dollar that front-of-house employees' hourly pay exceeded that of back-of-house employees (Lynn, 2017b). In other words, cutting the excess pay going to servers by $10 per hour would reduce average service ratings by only one-fifth of one point on a five-point scale. These analyses suggest that the pay premiums associated with tipping do attract somewhat better service workers as reflected in customer ratings of the service levels those workers provide, but probably not enough to justify those premiums.

Tipping Lowers Some Sales-Contingent Costs of Business

The taxes, rent, and marketing costs that a business must pay are often tied to sales figures. Tipping's previously discussed reduction of prices (thus, sales totals) reduces these sales-contingent costs (or commissions). The benefit of those commission reductions is hidden by the reduced sales, but they are real. Basically, tipping allows businesses to avoid paying commissions on a portion of their labor costs, which increases their profits. The following hypothetical example explains why.

Say that a restaurant with service-inclusive menu pricing generates $10,000/month in sales from which it pays $3500/month in labor costs, $3500/month in food costs, and $2500/month in rent. Further, say that 20% of its sales come from Grub Hub, which charges a 13.5% commission. This restaurant would make a profit of $230/month [$10,000 sales − $3500 labor − $3500 food − $2500 rent − ($2000 × 0.135 = $270) commission = $230 profit]. Next assume that tipping is introduced at the restaurant allowing labor costs to be reduced by 15% of the old sales and all of the savings would go to reduced menu prices, with no other changes. Now the restaurant would make a profit of $270.50/month [$8500 sales − $2000 labor − $3,500 food − $2500 rent − ($1700 × 0.135 = $229.50) commission = $270.50 profit].

As this example illustrates, tipping does allow real savings on fixed commissions, and that is a benefit (at least in the short term). However, in the long term, commissions are often negotiated rather than fixed, and no-tipping businesses may be able to negotiate lower commissions than those paid by businesses with tipping. In that case, the savings on fixed commissions do not provide a long-term reason for businesses to allow or encourage tipping of their employees.

Tipping Increases the Perceived Competitiveness of Pricing

We have already seen that tipping reduces the prices of services, which reduces their total costs to poor tippers. However, tipping also reduces the perceived expensiveness of services even to generous tippers whose total costs are not reduced. The reasons for this effect vary depending on whether we are comparing tipping with service-inclusive pricing or with service charges.

Service-inclusive menu prices present customers with one consolidated price, while voluntary tipping and service charges present them with separate prices for the food and service components of the dining experience. Marketing researchers have found that presenting separate prices for each component in a bundle of components (as opposed to presenting one total price) often reduces perceptions of expensiveness. This occurs because consumers tend to focus on the more salient or expensive component's price and fail to fully process or integrate the other components' prices (Greenleaf et al., 2016). In the context of restaurants, these effects mean that consumers tend to focus on menu prices and perceive restaurants with no-tipping and higher, service-inclusive menu prices as more expensive than restaurants with voluntary tips or service charges that are offset with lower prices.

As just mentioned, automatically adding service charges presents customers with separate prices for the food and service components of the dining experience, so it should decrease perceptions of restaurant expensiveness in the same way that tipping does. However, the mandatory nature of service charges may draw more attention to them than is drawn to voluntary tips, so consumers may incorporate service charges into their perceptions of restaurant expensiveness more than they incorporate voluntary tips. If so, then restaurants with automatic service charges should be perceived as more expensive than comparably priced restaurants with voluntary tipping.

Shuo Wang and I tested these expected effects in a series of experiments presenting subjects with information about hypothetical restaurants—including information about their tipping policies, which were randomly varied across subjects—and asking them to rate the expensiveness of the restaurants (Lynn & Wang, 2012, 2013). The results of those studies are summarized in Table 9.2. We found that restaurants with voluntary tipping were perceived as significantly less expensive than restaurants with service charges or higher service-inclusive menu prices even when the total costs of each were comparable. Importantly, these effects held for big and small tippers alike, which means that even customers whose total costs (including tips) were higher under the tipping system nevertheless thought the restaurant with voluntary tipping was less expensive. Furthermore, the reductions in perceived expensiveness were obtained even when customers were aware of the total combined costs of eating at the restaurant. Such reductions of perceived expensiveness are a benefit to individual businesses because they confer an advantage over competitors that do not permit tipping. However, this advantage is diminished as more competitors adopt tipping and it can even be perceived as a disadvantage to those businesses that would otherwise prefer to be no-tipping establishments. This is because those businesses are compelled to adopt tipping in order to keep their perceived expensiveness comparable to that of competitors that do permit tipping.

Tipping Adversely Impacts Relationships Among Workers

Press reports and qualitative studies by academics suggest that tipping adversely impacts the relationships among business' workers in two ways. First, the previously discussed pay premiums it gives tipped workers compared to non-tipped workers create jealousy and a sense of being unfairly

Table 9.2 Consumers perceive restaurants with voluntary tipping as less expensive than restaurants with automatic service charges or higher service-inclusive pricing even when the total costs of each are comparable

Source/type of service/restaurant information provided	Voluntary tipping	No tipping (15% higher menu prices)	15% Service charge	18% Service charge	22% Service charge
Lynn and Wang (2012:S1)/menu service/pictures & menu	3.9	4.7*	4.3*	4.4*	4.7*
Lynn and Wang (2012: S2)/menu service/pictures & menu	4.6	4.9*	4.7*	4.9*	
Lynn and Wang (2013)/menu service/pictures & menu	3.5	4.1*	3.6		
Wang (2013: S1)/brunch service/flyer only	3.3	4.2*	3.6*		
Wang (2013:S2)/brunch service/flyer only	3.4		3.7*		
Wang (2013:S3)/brunch service/flyer only	2.7	3.0*			

Source Lynn (2017b)
* Means (from a 7-point scale) in each row with an asterisk are significantly greater than the voluntary tipping mean at a one-tailed $p < 0.05$ level

compensated by those not receiving tips (Wilson, 2019; Wilson & Setter, 2020). Such feelings can be expected to negatively impact the attitudes, performance, and retention of the non-tipped staff and lead to conflict between tipped and non-tipped staff. Second, tipping reduces teamwork among tipped workers by focusing their attention on satisfying their own customers and increases competition among tipped workers for the best shifts, stations, customers, and other resources (Frumkin, 1988; Mount, 2018; Paules, 1991). Unfortunately, I could find no quantitative empirical tests of these effects, so it is unclear how large and widespread they are. This is yet another issue deserving of future research.

Tipping Increases Employee Theft

Tipping is an unusual form of employee compensation in that it comes from someone other than the employer.[8] Pay is the principal source of control employers have over their employees' behavior, so giving a substantial portion of this control over to others is risky. By giving customers direct control over employee income, tipping makes employees agents of the customer as well as the firm (Kwortnik et al., 2009), which can create role conflict as employees face competing demands of customers and managers (Shamir, 1980) and can encourage employees to collude with consumers against the interests of the firm (Eddleston et al., 2002).

One form that such collusion can take is employee failure to fully charge customers for goods and services ordered (Brady et al., 2012). Such gifting of complementary items, known as "service sweet hearting" or "comping," should be discouraged by the fact that consumers often tip a percentage of their bills. Failing to charge for items that customers order reduces bill size, which might be expected to reduce the monetary amount tipped. However, a hypothetical scenario study I did to examine this issue found that comping desserts increased tips more than enough to make up for the comp's reduction in bill size—tips on the $46 bill with comped desserts averaged $11.39 while those on the $56 bill with no comps averaged only $10.39 (Lynn, 2023). Thus, tipping does give employees an incentive to steal from their employers and approximately 30% of restaurant servers admit that they "fail to ring up food items" (Hawkins, 1984) or have at least occasionally "given customers free food and/or drinks in order to increase the tips they leave" (Lynn, 2017a, 2017b).

---

[8] The writing in this subsection on employee theft is drawn (with editing) from Lynn (2023).

Tipping Brings Costly Regulation

The rules and regulations surrounding tipping are numerous and complex. Employers are required by law to report all their employees' incomes (including tips), withhold employee taxes on that income, and pay the employer share of FICA taxes on that income, even though the employer cannot be certain how much an employee makes in cash tips (Anonymous, 2013). Furthermore, various employment laws and regulations either now require, or have in the past required, employers of tipped workers to (1) notify affected employees of their intention to claim a tip credit and of any tip pooling or sharing arrangements, (2) apply the tip credit allowance only for employees earning sufficient tips and only for hours worked in which 80% or more of employees' time was spent on tip earning duties, and (3) ensure that only tip-eligible employees participate in tip pooling or sharing arrangements (Ruzal, 2014).

Documenting compliance with these requirements is costly and failure to comply or to document that compliance can be even more costly. Data on the total tipping-related tax penalties, lawsuit settlement amounts, court-ordered judgments, and legal fees incurred by restaurants each year are unavailable, but it is clear that the costs are often substantial for those restaurants involved. For example, Lehigh Valley Restaurant Group (a Red Robin franchisee) settled a tipping-related lawsuit for $1.3 million, Sushi Yasuda settled for $2.4 million, and Mario Batali for $5.25 million (Follow, 2014; Harris, 2015; Weiser, 2012).

Tipping Increases the Risk of Employee Discrimination Lawsuits

Another potential legal risk of tipping deserves discussion. As discussed in Chap. 7, there is some evidence that consumers' tip ethnic minority servers less than they do white servers, and this may represent an adverse impact that would make the use of tipping to compensate employees an unlawful business practice under Title VII of the Civil Rights Act of 1964. The legal issues involved are complex and beyond the scope of this book, but both legal scholars and practicing lawyers have acknowledged that this theory of the law is plausible and that a class-action lawsuit alleging adverse impact from tipping could prevail (see Kline, 2016; Pandya, 2015). Thus, I believe that such a lawsuit is a real risk that businesses should be aware of and might want to get ahead of by (i) seeing if their data indicates an adverse impact and (ii) dealing with the problem if it does. I would, of course, be happy to help any interested businesses with the necessary data analyzes in exchange for permission to use the anonymized data in my academic research.

Net Effect on Businesses

The size and strength of the benefits and costs to businesses of tipping will vary across service industries and across businesses within industries. Therefore, no valid conclusions about their net effect for all businesses are possible. To make tip policy decisions that maximize their interest, businesses need to assess and weigh the impact of each of these benefits and costs for their particular industry and circumstances.

Conclusions

When doing television, radio, blog, and press interviews for stories on tipping, I am often asked for my personal attitude toward the practice. Since I study the issue, people seem to want to know whether I think it is good or bad—for consumers, workers, businesses, or society as a whole. I recall giving different answers to those questions at different times, because my opinions depended on the particular issues that my research focused my attention on at the time as well as on the state of my ever-growing knowledge about tipping. Today, I would say that tipping is a mixed bag of benefits and harms for all parties involved and that no generalizable claims about its goodness or badness for any of the parties mentioned above are possible. After reading this chapter, you know why I say this. You also have the knowledge to form your own educated opinion.

References

Adams, J. S., & Freedman, S. (1976). Equity theory revisited: Comments and annotated bibliography. *Advances in Experimental Social Psychology, 9*, 43–90.

Allegretto, S., & Cooper, D. (2014). *Twenty-three years and still waiting for change*. Economic Policy Institute Report. https://www.epi.org/publication/waiting-for-change-tipped-minimum-wage/. Accessed November 30, 2021.

Anonymous. (2013). Three challenges tipped employees present to employers. http://www.paychex.com/articles/payroll-taxes/three-challenges-tipped-employees-present. Accessed October 15, 2024.

Azar, O. H. (2004). Optimal monitoring with external incentives: The case of tipping. *Southern Economic Journal, 71*(1), 170–181.

Barkan, R., & Israeli, A. (2004). Testing servers' roles as experts and managers of tipping behavior. *Service Industries Journal, 24*, 1–18.

Batt, R., Lee, J. E., & Lakhani, T. (2014), *A National Study of Human Resource Practices, Turnover, and Customer Service in the Restaurant Industry*. Unpublished manuscript, Cornell University. https://archive.ilr.cornell.edu/sites/default/files/National-Study-of-Human-Resource-Practices-High-Turnover-and-Customer-Service-in-the-Restaurant-Industry.pdf. Accessed November 30, 2021.

Bowen, K. C. (2020, September 1). Gratuity (still) not included. https://www.eater.com/21398973/restaurant-no-tipping-movement-living-wage-future. Accessed October 27, 2024.

Brady, M. K., Voorhees, C. M., & Brusco, M. J. (2012). Service sweethearting: Its antecedents and customer consequences. *Journal of Marketing, 76*(2), 81–98.

Brewster, Z. (2013). The effects of restaurant servers' perception of customers' tipping behaviors on service discrimination. *International Journal of Hospitality Management, 32*, 228–236.

Crumpler, H., & Grossman, P. J. (2008). An experimental test of warm glow giving. *Journal of Public Economics, 92*(5–6), 1011–1021.

Dai, S. (2018, February 6). Danny Meyer admits large portion of staff left over no-tipping changes. https://ny.eater.com. Accessed October 27, 2024.

Deci, E., Koestner, R., & Ryan, R. (1999). A meta-analytic review of experiments examining the effects of extrinsic rewards on intrinsic motivation. *Psychological Bulletin, 125*, 627–668.

Department of Treasury. (2018). *Billions in tip-related tax noncompliance are not fully addressed and tip agreements are generally not enforced*. Report of the U.S. Department of Treasury, Reference Number 2018-30-081. https://www.treasury.gov/tigta/auditreports/2018reports/201830081fr.pdf. Accessed November 30, 2021.

Desilver, D., & Lippert, J. (2023, November 9). *Tipping culture in America: Public sees a changed landscape*. Pew Research Center. Available at: https://www.pewresearch.org/wp-content/uploads/2023/11/SR_23.11.09_tipping-culture_report.pdf. Accessed October 10, 2024.

Eater Staff. (2015). A restaurant server explains why we shouldn't abolish tipping. http://www.eater.com/2015/3/13/8187659/restaurant-server-explains-why-we-should-not-abolish-tipping. Accessed October 14, 2024.

Eddleston, K. A., Kidder, D. L., & Litzky, B. E. (2002). Who's the boss? Contending with competing expectations from customers and management. *Academy of Management Perspectives, 16*(4), 85–95.

Fang, M., & Gerhart, B. (2012). Does pay for performance diminish intrinsic interest? *International Journal of Human Resource Management, 23*, 1176–1196.

Follow, C. R. (2014). Sushi Yasuda agrees to pay $2 million to settle tipping lawsuit. http://www.grubstreet.com/2014/05/yasuda-lawsuit.html. Accessed October 15, 2024.

Frumkin, P. (1988, July). The great tipping debate. *Restaurant Business* (pp. 113–120).

Gillespe, L. (2023, June 8). Survey: 66% of Americans have a negative view of tipping. https://www.bankrate.com/personal-finance/tipping-survey/. Accessed October 13, 2024.

Grandey, A., Chi, N., & Diamond, J. (2013). Show me the money! Do financial rewards for performance enhance or undermine the satisfaction from emotional labor? *Personnel Psychology, 66*, 569–612.

Grandey, A. A., Fisk, G. M., Mattila, A. S., Jansen, K. J., & Sideman, L. A. (2005). Is "service with a smile" enough? Authenticity of positive displays during service encounters. *Organizational Behavior and Human Decision Processes, 96*(1), 38–55.

Greenleaf, E. A., Johnson, E. J., Morwitz, V. G., & Shalev, E. (2016). The price does not include additional taxes, fees, and surcharges: A review of research on partitioned pricing. *Journal of Consumer Psychology, 26*(1), 105–124.

Harris, J. (2015). Red Robin franchisee settles tip-sharing lawsuit for $1.3 million. http://www.mcall.com/business/mc-red-robin-settles-wage-lawsuit-20151203-story.html. Accessed October 15, 2024.

Hermann, A. (2024, February 7). Tipping culture perpetuates harm for workers, consumers. https://standard.asl.org/29401/opinions/tipping-culture-perpetuates-harm-for-workers-consumers/. Accessed October 28, 2024.

Houston, L., III., Grandey, A. A., & Sawyer, K. (2018). Who cares if "service with a smile" is authentic? An expectancy-based model of customer race and differential service reactions. *Organizational Behavior and Human Decision Processes, 144*, 85–96.

Hülsheger, U. R., Lang, J. W., Schewe, A. F., & Zijlstra, F. R. (2015). When regulating emotions at work pays off: A diary and an intervention study on emotion regulation and customer tips in service jobs. *Journal of Applied Psychology, 100*(2), 263.

IRS. (2021). Tip Record Keeping & Reporting. https://www.irs.gov/businesses/small-businesses-self-employed/tip-recordkeeping-and-reporting#:~:text=All%20cash%20and%20non%2Dcash,be%20reported%20to%20the%20employer. Accessed November 30, 2021.

Jacob, N., & Page, A. (1980). Production, information costs, and economic organization: The buyer monitoring case. *American Economic Review, 70*, 476–478.

Kelly, K. (2024, April 3). Tipping is out of control. It's also a serious labor issue. https://time.com/6962665/tipping-labor-issue-kim-kelly/. Accessed October 28, 2024.

Kelton, K. (2024, June 5). Survey: More than 1 in 3 Americans think tipping culture has gotten out of control. https://www.bankrate.com/credit-cards/news/tipping-culture-survey/. Accessed October 13, 2024.

Kim, K. (2012). *The effects of perceived visible characteristics of customers on servers' tipping expectations.* Unpublished Masters thesis, University of Missouri.

Kipp, P., Mathew, J., Sapkota, K., & Sapkota, P. (2023). Self-reporting cash tip income for income tax purposes. *Journal of Forensic and Investigative Accounting, 15*(2).

Kline, J. (2016). Fifteen percent or less: A Title VII analysis of racial discrimination in restaurant tipping. *Iowa Law Review, 101*, 1651.

Kwortnik, R., Lynn, M., & Ross, B. (2009). Buyer monitoring: A means to insure personalized service. *Journal of Marketing Research, XLVI*, 573–583.

Leary, M. R., & Kowalski, R. M. (1990). Impression management: A literature review and two-component model. *Psychological Bulletin, 107*(1), 34.

Lynn, M. (2003). Tip levels and service: An update, extension and reconciliation. *Cornell Hotel and Restaurant Administration Quarterly, 42*, 139–148.

Lynn, M. (2009). Individual differences in self-attributed motives for tipping: Antecedents, consequences, and implications. *International Journal of Hospitality Management, 28*, 432–438.

Lynn, M. (2011). Mega Tips 2: Twenty tested techniques to increase your tips. *Cornell Hospitality Tools, 2*(1), 4–22. https://ecommons.cornell.edu/handle/1813/71274. Accessed November 30, 2021.

Lynn, M. (2015). Explanations of service gratuities and tipping: Evidence from individual differences in tipping motivations and tendencies. *Journal of Behavioral and Experimental Economics, 55*, 65–71.

Lynn, M. (2016). Why are we more likely to tip some service occupations than others? Theory, evidence, and implications. *Journal of Economic Psychology, 54*, 134–150.

Lynn, M. (2017a). Does tipping help to attract and retain better service workers? *Journal of Foodservice Business Research, 20*(1), 82–89.

Lynn, M. (2017b). Should US restaurants abandon tipping? A review of the issues and evidence. *Psychosociological Issues in Human Resource Management, 5*(1), 120–159.

Lynn, M. (2018). The effects of tipping on consumers' satisfaction with restaurants. *Journal of Consumer Affairs, 52*(3), 746–755.

Lynn, M. (2021). Effects of the Big Five personality traits on tipping attitudes, motives, and behaviors. *International Journal of Hospitality Management, 92*, Article 102722.

Lynn, M. (2023). Service sweethearting: An effective way to increase tips? *International Journal of Hospitality Management, 114*, Article 103551.
Lynn, M. (2024). The pro's and con's of working for tips. *Cornell Hospitality Quarterly, 65*(2), 266–275.
Lynn, M., & Brewster, Z. W. (2020). The Tipping behavior and motives of US travelers abroad: Affected by host nations' tipping norms? *Journal of Travel Research, 59*(6), 993–1007.
Lynn, M., & Kwortnik, R. J. (2015). The effects of tipping policies on customer satisfaction: A test from the cruise industry. *International Journal of Hospitality Management, 51*, 15–18.
Lynn, M., & Kwortnik, R. J. (2020). Tipping policy effects on customer satisfaction: An informative failure to replicate. *International Journal of Hospitality Management, 86*, Article 102448.
Lynn, M., Kwortnik, R. J., Jr., & Sturman, M. C. (2011). Voluntary tipping and the selective attraction and retention of service workers in the USA: An application of the ASA model. *The International Journal of Human Resource Management, 22*(9), 1887–1901.
Lynn, M., & Wang, S. (2012). *The effects of tipping on perceived restaurant expensiveness: Implications for price partitioning and employee compensation*. Unpublished manuscript, Cornell University.
Lynn, M., & Wang, S. (2013). The indirect effects of tipping policies on patronage intentions through perceived expensiveness, fairness, and quality. *Journal of Economic Psychology, 39*, 62–71.
Mathwig, J (2024, May 1). Contrary to popular belief, tipping culture hurts workers. https://www.thetriangle.org/opinion/contrary-to-popular-belief-tipping-culture-hurts-workers/. Accessed October 28, 2024.
Mills, S., & Riehle, H. (1987). What customers think about tips vs. service charges. *Restaurants USA*, 20–21.
Miranda, D. (2023, September 19). 2023 U.S. Digital Tipping Survey: 1 in 3 people feel pressured to tip. https://www.forbes.com/advisor/business/digital-tipping-culture/. Accessed October 12, 2024.
Mount, L. (2018). "Behind the Curtain": strip clubs and the management of competition for tips. *Journal of Contemporary Ethnography, 47*(1), 60–87.
NBC News. (2013). Should American restaurants abolish tipping? http://www.nbcnews.com/business/should-american-restaurants-abolish-tipping-6C10285252. Accessed October 14, 2024.
Neumark, D., & Yen, M. (2021). *Tipped workers, minimum wage workers, and poverty*. Employment Policies Institute, white paper. https://epionline.org/studies/tipped-workers-minimum-wage-workers-and-poverty/. Accessed November 30, 2021.
NYC Hospitality Alliance. (2015). *2015 NYC Restaurant Industry Compensation and Benefits Report*.

Pandya, S. (2015). Tipping as employment discrimination? http://lawprofessors.typepad.com/laborprof_blog/2015/11/tipping-as-employment-discrimination.html. Accessed October 15, 2024.

Parise, M. (1987). Optional tipping has seen its day. *Nation's Restaurant News*, March 9, F50.

Paules, G. F. (1991). *Dishing it out: Power and resistance among waitresses in a New Jersey restaurant* (Vol. 105). Temple University Press.

Payscale. (2014). *PayScale's restaurant report: The agony and ecstasy of food service workers*. https://www.payscale.com/data-packages/restaurant-report/full-data, accesses November 30, 2021.

ROC United. (2014). *The glass floor: Sexual harassment in the restaurant industry*. https://chapters.rocunited.org/publications/the-glass-floor-sexual-harassment-in-the-restaurant-industry/. Accessed November 30, 2021.

ROC United. (2018, May). *Take us off the menu*. https://rocunited.org/wp-content/uploads/sites/7/2020/02/TakeUsOffTheMenuReport.pdf. Accessed October 28, 2024.

Ruzal, J. (2014). Tip-related claims will continue to be served up as the lawsuit du jour against the hospitality industry in 2015. http://www.ebglaw.com/news/tip-related-claims-will-continue-to-be-served-up-as-the-lawsuit-du-jour-against-the-hospitality-industry-in-2015/. Accessed October 15, 2024.

Schweitzer, J. (2021, March 30). Ending the tipped minimum wage will reduce poverty and inequality. https://www.americanprogress.org/article/ending-tipped-minimum-wage-will-reduce-poverty-inequality/. Accessed October 28, 2024.

Shamir, B. (1980). Between service and servility: Role conflict in subordinate service roles. *Human Relations, 33*(10), 741–756.

Shrestha, J. (2010). *Tipping differences of domestic and foreign customers in casual dining restaurants: An investigation of customers' and servers' perception*. Unpublished Masters thesis, Oklahoma State University.

Skopic, A. (2024, February 23). Abolish the tipped minimum wage. https://www.currentaffairs.org/news/2024/02/abolish-the-tipped-minimum-wage. Accessed October 28, 2024.

Wang, S. (2013). *The effects of price partitioning and its implications for menu pricing*. Unpublished doctoral dissertation, Cornell University.

Weiser, B. (2012, March 7). Mario Batali agrees to $5.25 million settlement over employee tips. https://archive.nytimes.com/dinersjournal.blogs.nytimes.com/2012/03/07/mario-batali-agrees-to-5-25-million-settlement-over-employee-tips/. Accessed October 15, 2024.

White House. (2014). *The impact of raising the minimum wage on women and the importance of ensuring a robust tipped minimum wage*. https://obamawhitehouse.archives.gov/the-press-office/2014/03/26/new-white-house-report-impact-raising-minimum-wage-women-and-importance-. Accessed November 30, 2021.

Wilson, E. R. (2019). Tip work: Examining the relational dynamics of tipping beyond the service counter. *Symbolic Interaction, 42*(4), 669–690.

Wilson, E. R., & Setter, D. (2020). Working through tips: Examining labor dynamics in tipped workplaces. *Population change and public policy* (pp. 259–275).

Zak, P. (2013). Measurement myopia. https://www.drucker.institute/thedx/measurement-myopia/. Accessed November 30, 2021.

10

Cornucopia of Controversies (What Controversies Arise from Tipping? What Should People Know About Them?)

Debates about the benefits/beneficiaries and harms/victims of tipping are not the only controversies raised by this behavior. Other controversies (some long-standing and some nascent) generated by tipping include disagreements about:

- the moral status of tipping,
- the existence and boundaries of a social obligation to tip,
- the desirability of a subminimum wage for tipped workers,
- the fairness of mandatory tip sharing,
- the desirability of exempting tip income from taxation, and
- the impact and desirability of digital tipping screens.

While I have personal opinions about these issues, which I will share, my principal goal in this chapter is to identify the key considerations and ideas underlying each controversy along with relevant facts so that you can form your own educated opinions and can see where more research is needed. Let's get started.

Disagreement About the Ethics of Tipping

One of the most longstanding debates about tipping concerns its ethical or moral status. This debate occurs at two levels—(i) How ethical is the *system* of tipping? and (ii) How ethical is the *behavior* of tipping given current tipping systems? However, the first of these questions has considerable overlap with previous chapters' discussions about inequities in tip income (Chap. 7) and the pros and cons of tipping from different perspectives (Chap. 9). Furthermore, you have more control over your own tipping behaviors than you do over the system of tipping. Therefore, I will focus on the second question here and only briefly address the first as it bears on the focal question.

Tipping is a Moral Duty

Many people believe that we have a moral duty to tip in contexts where it is socially expected and the service is adequate. Advocates of this position can be found among average consumers (Quora, 2024), theologians (Grisez, 1997), and philosophy scholars (Kershnar, 2014). There are two basic arguments supporting this position—a humanitarian argument and a promissory argument.

The Humanitarian Argument. The humanitarian argument is that (i) failing to tip materially harms service workers for whom tips are a large part of their pay and (ii) harming people is morally wrong, so (iii) failing to tip is morally wrong. An alternative framing of the same argument is that tipping materially helps service workers for whom tips are a large part of their pay and helping people is morally good, so tipping is morally good.

The main counters to this argument challenge the first premise. One specific counterargument is that an individual's tipping decisions do not substantially help or harm tipped workers more than any other worker because the former's low wages are already supplemented by tips from other customers. Another counterargument is that giving tips hurts workers more than not tipping them does because tipping helps perpetuate an abusive compensation practice. See Ikema (2016) for a more elaborate version of this counterargument. Also, recall that empirical evidence relevant to both these counterarguments is presented in Chap. 9. Finally, see Mailer (1993) for still more counterarguments to humanitarian or sympathetic claims that tipping is a moral duty.

The Promissory Argument. The promissory argument for a moral duty to tip is that (i) accepting services from a traditionally tipped worker is an implicit promise to tip that worker (unless you explicitly tell the service provider otherwise ahead of time) and (ii) breaking promises that are beneficial or desirable to the recipient is morally wrong, so (iii) failure to tip in this circumstance is morally wrong. See Kershnar (2014) for a more detailed philosophical exposition and defense of this second argument.

The main counters to this argument challenge one of its two premises. One counterargument is that accepting services from traditionally tipped workers is not an implicit promise to tip because tipping is explicitly voluntary and post-service. Servers know that customers do not have to tip and do not have to disclose their tipping intentions pre-service, so receiving services is not a promise to tip. A second counterargument is that breaking promises is morally acceptable if keeping those promises would do more harm than good, and keeping implicit promises to tip does more harm than does breaking the promise because giving tips helps perpetuate a system that abuses workers and puts unwelcome social pressures on consumers. Again, see Ikema (2016) for a more elaborate version of this counterargument and Chap. 9 for evidence relevant to its empirical claims.

Data on the Prevalence and Predictors of the Belief That Tipping Is a Moral Duty. Although it does not bear on the validity of the preceding arguments about a moral duty to tip, I have surveyed people from across the U.S. about these matters and want to take this opportunity to share for the first time what I found. Specifically, one study asked 100 people whether or not they "feel morally obligated to tip" each of 108 different service occupations. The percentage of survey respondents who felt morally obliged to tip ranged from 1% (for veterinarians) to 92% (for waiters/waitresses), with over 70% of respondents feeling a moral obligation to tip bartenders, barbers, bellhops, hairdressers, pizza delivery drivers, taxi drivers, and waiters/waitresses. Average feelings of moral obligation to tip an occupation were almost perfectly predicted by the average likelihood that other people reported tipping that occupation ($r = 0.96$, $n = 108$, $p < 0.001$), so it is only commonly tipped occupations that most people feel morally obliged to tip.

In a second study, I asked 400 people about their belief that tipping was a moral obligation as well as about their motivations for tipping and their beliefs about various aspects of service work and workers. Analyses of the data indicated that the strongest predictors of individuals' beliefs that they were morally obligated to tip were their (i) perceptions that service workers are under-paid, (ii) motivations to make up for low server wages with their tips, and (iii) motivations to fulfill a social duty to tip.[1] These results underscore

---

[1] The correlations of perceived moral obligation to tip with these other measures were 0.40, 0.53, and 0.54, respectively (all n's = 400, all p's < 0.001). The perception that bad tippers were viewed negatively also strongly predicted individuals' perceptions that tipping was a moral obligation ($r = 0.41$, $n = 400$, $p < 0.001$), perhaps because people believe that moral/immoral behaviors as more subject to public scrutiny and judgement than are amoral behaviors.

the importance of server harm (low pay) and social norms to people's perceptions of a moral obligation to tip, which essentially mirrors the role of these factors in the philosophical arguments supporting such a moral obligation.

Tipping is Immoral

While many people think tipping is a moral duty, others consider it a moral abomination. As with the former position, advocates of the latter position can be found among average consumers (Quora, 2024) and philosophy scholars (Ikema, 2016). The argument is that (i) the system of tipping harms workers and/or consumers, (ii) giving tips supports and enables the system of tipping, and (iii) supporting or enabling harmful institutions is morally wrong, so (iv) giving tips is morally wrong.

All three premises of this argument can be challenged. First, opponents can argue that tipping is a mixed bag of benefits and harms to all involved and there is no compelling evidence that the harms outweigh the benefits (see Chap. 9). Second, opponents can argue that individual tipping does not materially support the custom of tipping because the impact of one person's (or even several people's) tipping behavior on the majority of other people's tipping (and, hence, the institution of tipping) is negligible. Nor does individual tipping symbolically support the custom of tipping because people can and do think the system is morally bad, but that its existence nevertheless makes individual tipping a social or a moral duty. See Grisez (1997) for an example of such a person. Finally, opponents can argue that supporting a harmful institution is morally acceptable if failure to do so results in even more harm and refusing to tip hurts the would-be-tipped worker more than it benefits the anti-tipping cause.

Tipping is Amoral

A final group of people (myself-included) think tipping is amoral—neither moral nor immoral. Those holding this position believe that there may be a social obligation to tip, but not a moral one (see Mailer, 1993). The basic argument for this position is that (i) the burden of proof lies on those making affirmative claims that tipping is moral or that it is immoral and (ii) none of the arguments for these positions meets that burden, so (iii) tipping is amoral. Whether or not you agree with me and accept this argument depends on your own evaluation of the arguments for tipping's morality or immorality. Hopefully, this section leaves you better equipped to make that evaluation.

Disagreement About Social Obligation to Tip

Tipping is a social norm in the U.S. as well as in many other countries, so many people feel a social (if not a moral) obligation to tip. However, uncertainty about what the tipping norms are and about the basis for determining them leads to differing opinions about who should be tipped and how much. These differences of opinion have undoubtedly sparked many private debates like the one featured in the film Reservoir Dogs, where a group of mobsters sitting around a restaurant table discuss the tip they are about to leave their waitress. They have also spilled over into larger societal debates (as detailed in Seagrave, 1998). Furthermore, recent expansions in the types of workers asking for tips via the digital screens used in point-of-sale payment systems (aka, tip-creep) and in the amounts of the suggested tips on those screens (aka, tip-flation) has begun to bring these public debates back into the fore (c.f., Ermey, 2023; Jonjopop, 2022).

In interviews with the public media, I have been asked numerous times to weigh in on the current debate about who we should tip and how much. I usually decline that invitation on the grounds that I have no authority or desire to tell people how they should (or should not) tip. Furthermore, I point out that no one else has that authority either—not Emily Post, or Miss Manners, or anyone! As pointed out in Chap. 5, there is no God of tipping. Rather, tipping norms emerge from the behaviors of individuals—with those behaviors that are widely adopted or copied eventually becoming seen as normative and socially required. This means that there is no hard-and-fast demarcation of tipping norms. Ultimately, it is up to you to decide for yourself how common tipping for a given service must be for you to accept some social obligation to tip the providers of that service. Similarly, you must decide for yourself how common a particular tip size is (or range of tip sizes is) for you to accept some social obligation to tip that amount. For me personally, roughly 2 out of 3 consumers must tip a service provider before I feel socially obliged to do so as well, but that reflects my own tolerance of stiffed workers' disapproval and my own tendency to react negatively to social pressure.[2] Different people can and should have different demarcation lines.

How does one set a personal demarcation line for the acceptance of a social obligation to tip? That too is a personal matter. Most people probably just go with their affective reactions or gut feelings. Feelings are neither right nor wrong, but they can be affected by correct and incorrect beliefs.

---

[2] Note that I am talking here only about my feelings of social obligation to tip. I do often tip workers for reasons other than social obligation—see Chap. 2.

For example, 68% of respondents to a recent survey reported feeling pressured to tip for restaurant carryout if the point-of-sale system prompts them to (Treanor, 2023). In all likelihood, those people feel social pressure to tip because they assume that most other people in that situation do tip. However, another survey tells us that only 22% of U.S. consumers usually or always tip for restaurant carryout (Gillespie, 2023). My guess is that most of the respondents to the first survey would feel less social pressure and less of a social obligation to tip for restaurant carryout if they knew how rare such tipping really is. Therefore, I recommend that you look at data on actual, or at least reported, tipping likelihood for various services before trusting your gut feelings of social obligation to tip the providers of those services. To make doing that a little easier for you, I have summarized relevant data from two surveys conducted in 2023 by YouGov and the Pew Research Center respectively in Table 10.1.

Table 10.1 The percentage of people who tip varies widely across service settings/providers

Service setting or provider	YouGov survey[a] % who tip most of the time or always	Pew research center survey[b] % who tip often or always
Restaurant waiters	83	92
Food delivery drivers	75	76
Hair stylists and barbers	72	78
Bartenders or cocktail waitresses		70
Taxi or ride-share drivers	63	61
Hotel maids	47	
Coffee shop baristas/workers	48	25
Furniture or appliance delivery workers	35	
Home services/repair workers (e.g., plumbers, electricians, cable installers, etc.)	26	
Restaurant carryout workers	22	
Fast casual restaurant workers		12

[a]Source Gillespi (2023)
[b]Source DeSilver and Lippert (2023)

Disagreement About the Tipped Minimum Wage

In 2014, Sylvia Allegretto and David Cooper wrote a report for the Economic Policy Institute, titled "Twenty-Three Years and Still Waiting for Change." In that report, they pointed out that the federal minimum wage for tipped workers had been stuck at $2.13 per hour since 1991 and they advocated for elimination of the tip credit that allows employers to pay tipped workers less than the regular minimum wage.[3] Ten years later, the federal tipped minimum wage still sits at its 1991 levels. State minimum wages can be, and in many cases are, more generous than the federal minimum wages, but tipped workers in 42 states are still paid less than the regular minimum wage with tipped workers in 15 of those states guaranteed only the federal minimum of $2.13 per hour.

This lack of any federal action, and only limited state action, on tipped minimum wages for 33 years now has helped fuel a controversy over the desirability of having a lower minimum wage for tipped workers than for non-tipped ones. Liberals and labor advocates generally call for elimination of the tipped sub-minimum wage on the grounds that it lowers incomes, increases poverty (especially among ethnic minorities and women), and increases sexual harassment of women (c.f., Jayaraman, 2021; ROC United, 2018). Conservatives and restaurant industry groups generally advocate for its retention on the grounds that it increases employment (especially among young and unskilled workers) and lowers prices (c.f., Kiley, 2024; NRA, 2024). Evidence about these claims, as well as about other relevant effects of the tipped sub-minimum wage, is examined below. [Note: The terms "tipped minimum wage," "tipped sub-minimum wage," and "tip credit" all refer to essentially the same thing, but you should remember that larger tip credits mean smaller tipped minimum wages.]

Effects on Income and Poverty

Eliminating the tip credit will obviously increase the hourly wages of tipped workers earning the tipped sub-minimum wage, but its impact on tipped workers' incomes is less clear because it might also induce employers to reduce work hours for those workers and/or consumers to tip those workers less. The

---

[3] Remember from Chap. 9 that federal and most state minimum wage laws allow employers to pay tipped workers less than non-tipped workers as long as the employees' tip earnings amount to at least $30 a month and bring the total compensation of tips plus wages to the regular minimum wage level. The difference between the regular and tipped minimum wages allowed by these laws is known as the tip credit and its size varies across states.

only study I know of to examine tip minimum wage effects on hours worked found that larger tipped minimum wages were associated with fewer work hours (Jones, 2016) and, as mentioned in earlier chapters, several studies have found that larger tip credits are associated with smaller tips in U.S. restaurants (Lynn, 2020, 2022; Tang et al., 2022). Thus, the possibility that positive tip credit effects on hourly wages are offset by negative impacts on work hours and/or tips cannot be dismissed out of hand.

That said, the academic studies of tipped sub-minimum wage effects on total income (wages + tips) have found that weekly earnings of tipped workers do tend to be higher the larger the tipped minimum wage (Allegretto & Nadler, 2015; Even & Macpherson, 2014; Neumark & Yen, 2023).[4] This effect together with the fact that over 10% of tipped workers in the U.S. have incomes below the poverty line (Schweitzer, 2021) suggests that higher tipped minimum wages will also decrease the percentage of tipped workers in poverty. A few academic studies indicate that it does—with caveats. Sabia et al. (2018) found that increases in the tipped minimum wage decrease the risk of tipped restaurant workers living in **families** (people related by blood, marriage or adoption) whose income is below the federal poverty levels. However, many tipped workers whose family income falls below the poverty line live in households with non-relatives whose incomes they benefit from and the risk of tipped workers living in **households** whose income is below the federal poverty levels was not reliably affected by tipped minimum wages (Sabia et al., 2018). Other researchers have found that increases in tipped minimum wages are associated with reductions in poverty-related stress among women, but only for those without college degrees who were also unmarried and/or women of color (Andrea et al., 2020b). In another study, the same research team found that increases in tipped minimum wages are also associated with reductions in an informative poverty-related health risk among women—namely giving birth to under-weight or over-weight infants (Andrea et al., 2020a). More data is always welcome, but what we

---

[4] Jones (2016) obtained separate measures of wages and tips from workers' w-2 tax forms and found that increasing the tipped minimum wage decreased tip income by the same amount that it increased wage income, so that there was no net income effect. However, the validity of her tip data is suspect because tipped workers often hide their tip income from tax authorities. The reductions in tips she found could reflect differences in tip reporting rather than differences in tip income. This is plausible in my experience because servers often report only enough cash tips to make their total hourly income (wages + charge tips + cash tips) equal the regular minimum wage, which their employers require of them in order to qualify for the tip credit. In that case, every dollar per hour increase in the tipped minimum wage (reduction in the tip credit) reduces the tips per hour that employers require servers to report by one dollar.

have makes a reasonably compelling case that elimination of the tipped sub-minimum wage would increase tipped workers' incomes and would reduce the poverty that some of them live under.

Effects on Sexual Harassment

Advocates of eliminating the tipped minimum wage argue that it would reduce tipped workers' dependence on tips, which in turn would reduce consumers' power to sexually harass and abuse them. To support this argument, the Restaurant Opportunities Centers (ROC) United (2014) present data and analyses indicating that tipped workers, and all workers in states with tip credits, report higher rates of being sexually harassed than do non-tipped workers and workers in states without tip credits. This leaves the impression that tipping increases consumer power, which many consumers use to sexually harass tipped workers, and that this effect is greater in states with tipped sub-minimum wages. However, that impression is misleading.

There is little doubt that tipping empowers consumer sexual harassment of tipped workers, but the effects of the tipped sub-minimum wage are more questionable. States with tipped sub-minimum wages differ from those without them in many other ways that could be responsible for the difference in their overall levels of sexual harassment. If tipped sub-minimum wages increase sexual harassment in the way claimed or implied, then the difference in sexual harassment experienced by tipped vs non-tipped workers (not their combined level of sexual harassment) should be greater in states with tipped sub-minimum wages. In other words, tipped sub-minimum wages should be associated with greater sexual harassment of tipped, but not of non-tipped, workers. I can find no evidence of such an interaction effect. Even the data reported by ROC United shows that the greater harassment experienced by workers in states with tipped sub-minimum wages is roughly the same across tipped and non-tipped workers!

The absence of evidence that eliminating the tipped sub-minimum wage would reduce sexual harassment is not evidence that it would not do so. However, common sense also suggests that such an effect is unlikely. Even tipped workers earning the regular minimum wage depend on tips for a substantial portion of their incomes, so consumers are still likely to feel empowered to sexually harass those workers. Thus, without evidence to the contrary, it is reasonable to reject claims that eliminating the tipped sub-minimum wage would reduce sexual harassment.

Effects on Employment

Economic theory suggests that increasing prices reduces demand, so it is reasonable to expect that eliminating the tipped sub-minimum wage (increasing the price of tipped workers' labor) would reduce the number of tipped jobs available. However, businesses could cover the increased labor costs with higher consumer prices instead of reductions in employment. Thus, the effect of eliminating the tipped sub-minimum wage on employment is an issue that must be determined empirically rather than by relying on theory alone.

Several studies have examined this issue, but with very different results. Some studies have found that employment declines with increases in the tipped minimum wage as expected (Evan & Macpherson, 2014; Neumark & Yen, 2023), but others have found no effects of tipped minimum wages on employment (Allegretto & Nadler, 2015; Lynn & Boone, 2015), and still others have found that employment first increases with movement in the tipped minimum wage from low to moderate levels but then decreases with movement in the tipped minimum wage from moderate to high levels (Jones, 2016; Wessels, 1997). Much of the differences in these outcomes is due to differences in the ways the researchers tried to separate the effects of tipped minimum wages from the effects of the many other ways that those states differed from one another, and there is no clear consensus about which of those statistical controls is best. Thus, the effect of eliminating the tipped minimum wage on the overall employment of tipped workers remains open to dispute. That said, some scholars have argued that "the basic economic question is the same" as the effect of raising the regular minimum wage on employment (Wicks-Lim & Kerrissey, 2024), and a much larger body of research on the latter question suggests that this effect in the United States is negligible (Belman & Wolfson, 2014). Personally, I remain agnostic on this issue, but I am not terribly concerned about harmful effects on overall employment of eliminating the tipped sub-minimum wage because those effects must be small or we would have more definitive evidence of them.

Effects on Prices

Businesses can meet the costs of rising wages by increasing consumer prices as well as by reducing the number of workers they employ. Thus, advocates of keeping the tipped sub-minimum wage often argue that eliminating it would lead to higher prices instead of, or in addition to, higher unemployment.

I could find no published studies examining this claim, but my analysis of unpublished data in Chap. 9 shows that restaurant prices do tend to be higher in states with larger tipped minimum wages (see Fig. 9.2) and this remains true even after controlling for state differences in the costs of living. Furthermore, a study of regular minimum wage effects on restaurant pricing found that increasing the minimum wage "unambiguously" increases both quick-service and full-service restaurant prices (Aaronson et al., 2008). Together, these results incline me to believe the argument that eliminating the tipped sub-minimum wage would increase the prices of tipped services.

Other Miscellaneous Effects

Although less commonly heard in political debates about the issue, and also less studied, there are a number of other potential consequences of eliminating the tipped sub-minimum wage that should be mentioned (even if only to encourage more research testing them). First, Azar (2012) argued that lower minimum wages for tipped workers make tipping more attractive to businesses, so that eliminating the tip credit would make tipping a less commonly used form of worker compensation. Whether this effect is good, bad, or neutral depends on one's view of tipping, but there are no academic studies testing it, so either way, more research on the issue would be welcome.

Second, McKenzie (2019) argued that raising tipped minimum wages would motivate businesses to find cheaper alternatives to labor intensive service, so would lead to more service automation and fewer table-service restaurants relative to counter-service ones. This claim is reasonable, but I could find no directs tests of it, so this too would be a good subject for future research.

Third, a study by Compton and Compton (2024) suggests that elimination of the tipped sub-minimum wage would increase the quality of applicants seeking tipped work. Specifically, they found that larger gaps between the regular and tipped minimum wages were negatively associated with the likelihood that tipped waiters, waitresses, and bartenders were heads of a household, college educated, older, and non-immigrants. In comparison, the regular vs tipped minimum wage gap was less negatively related to the likelihood that non-tipped cashiers or retail salespersons were from these groups. This suggests that the tipped sub-minimum wage makes tipped jobs less attractive to high-quality workers with other prospects, so those tipped jobs are more likely to go to marginal workers with more restricted job options (such as younger, less educated, and immigrant workers). Arguably, this makes the subminimum wage a good thing—it not only benefits marginal workers with fewer other job opportunities but also increases economic efficiency by directing higher quality workers to jobs where their skills are more needed. Personally, I find these effects credible, but would welcome more research testing them.

Fourth, a master's thesis by Sienkiewicz (2016) found that larger gaps between the tipped and regular minimum wages were associated with shorter job tenures among restaurant servers. Again, more research on this effect would be welcome, but it suggests that eliminating the tipped sub-minimum wage would reduce turnover in tipped jobs. Since turnover is a major cost to restaurants and other service businesses, they may want to reconsider their opposition to that change in minimum wage laws.

Finally, recent changes in federal U.S. labor law have expanded the types of hourly workers that businesses can require their tipped workers to share tips with as long as those businesses do not take the tip credit and pay their tipped workers at least the regular minimum wage (Yang, 2020). This provides advocates of tip pooling a reason to support elimination of the tipped sub-minimum wage. However, as discussed below tip sharing/pooling has its own benefits and costs that deserve more research attention.

Summary about Tipped Minimum Wages

Overall, I come away from the academic literature believing that the clearest and best reason to support elimination of the tipped sub-minimum wage is to increase tipped workers' incomes while the clearest and best reason to oppose its elimination is that doing so would increase prices. In essence, eliminating the tipped sub-minimum wage would redistribute wealth from consumers to tipped workers. Whether that is a good or a bad thing is something I leave for you to decide for yourself.

Disagreement About Mandatory Tip Sharing

Another contentious topic is whether or not tipped workers should be required to share their tips with non-tipped co-workers. Some see tip sharing as a way to reduce problems stemming from tipping-related pay-disparities (Estreicher & Nash, 2018). Recall from Chap. 9 that restaurant servers often make substantially more than other equally or more qualified co-workers who do not receive tips and that (allegedly) this pay-disparity negatively impacts the attitudes, performance, and retention of the non-tipped staff and increases their conflict with tipped co-workers. The effectiveness of tip sharing as a remedy to these problems is supported by a study finding that back-of-house restaurant workers' perceptions that they were compensated fairly was greater when they shared in tip pools (Watt, 2017).[5] Its fairness is also supported by a study I conducted with a high school student. The student was a restaurant magician and we found that waiters and waitresses got larger tips from the tables he performed magic at than from tables he did not (Frank & Lynn, 2020). This finding demonstrates that tips are not solely determined by the efforts of the tipped worker but also by the efforts of other workers, who arguably deserve a share of the largesse they help create.

However, mandatory tip pools tend to be opposed by consumers (DeSilver & Lippert, 2023; Lynn & Ni, 2022) as well as by tipped workers (Lin & Namasivayam, 2011). In addition, at least one study suggests that tip pooling decreases individual motivation to deliver good service when those service efforts are difficult for co-workers or managers to monitor (Barkan et al., 2004). More research on this topic is needed, but until more promising findings emerge, tip pooling appears to be a risky way for restaurateurs to mitigate the negative effects of tipping on staff relations.

Disagreement About Taxing Tips

The 2024 Presidential Election saw both of the major parties' candidates campaign on exempting tips from income taxes, and several bills were introduced in Congress that year to implement such a policy (McDermott, 2024; The Budget Lab at Yale, 2024). The idea is popular among the general public and was supported by over 70% of Democrats, Republicans, and Independents alike in one election year poll (Jackson & Mendez, 2024). Presumably, this support stems from a desire to help low-income workers. However, economists and tax experts are less enthusiastic about the idea (Duke, 2024; The Budget Lab at Yale, 2024; Thorndike, 2024). They argue that tax proposals should be evaluated in terms of how well they promote equity, efficiency, and revenue and that the exemption of tips from taxation fails on all three criteria (Thorndike, 2024). First, exempting tips from income taxation fails a horizontal equity or fairness criterion because it favors those who earn tips over equally low-paid workers who do not.

Second, exempting tips from taxation fails several different definitions of efficiency. Most importantly, this policy is not an efficient way to achieve its

---

[5] Watt's (2017) study found non-significant effects of back-of-house participation in tip pools on other measures of work morale, but the sample was small and these could be Type 2 errors.

goal of helping the poor because it would benefit only about 3% of families, and those benefits would be disproportionately enjoyed by relatively well-off tipped workers. According to The Budget Lab at Yale University, the average family seeing some benefit from the policy would gain about $1700 a year, but those with incomes in the bottom fifth of tipped workers would see a gain of only $200 (The Budget Lab at Yale, 2024). Depending on how it is implemented, exemption of tips from taxes might also cause some poorer tipped workers to lose other federal benefits—thus counteracting any potential income gains (McDermont, 2024). There are simply better and more cost-effective ways to help the lowest income workers. In addition, exempting tips from income taxation would encourage more people to seek and claim income in the form of tips, which would distort the labor market (reducing economic efficiency) and would make taxes harder to collect (reducing administrative efficiency).

Finally, exempting tips from income taxation would reduce government revenues. The exact amount of the revenue loss depends on many factors and cannot be known for sure. However, if compensation, tax avoidance, and tipping behavior are unaffected, then exemption of tips from income taxes alone would cost an estimated $107 billion over the next 10 years and exempting tips from income and payroll taxes would cost an estimated $195 billion over the same time period. The former number could be reduced to about $65 billion if only workers in specific leisure and hospitality industries were eligible, but (again) that assumes behavior remains unchanged and that assumption need not hold. Exempting tips from income tax could alter compensation, tax avoidance, and/or tipping behavior in ways that bring the costs up even higher than the preceding "static" estimates suggest (The Budget Lab at Yale, 2024).

Neither I nor anyone else can confidently predict the precise behavioral effects of exempting tips from income taxation. However, there are two reasons to believe that those effects may be modest. First, the effects on workers seeking tip compensation and on consumers' tip sizes are likely to have opposite effects on the revenue costs of the policy. We know that people seek to minimize their income taxes, so more businesses and workers will try to use tipping as part of their compensation model, which would increase the revenue loss from the tax policy. However, we also know that consumers leave smaller tip percentages when service workers make more in wages (see Chap. 5), so effectively increasing workers' wages by reducing their taxes is likely to reduce the tip percentages consumers give, which would reduce the revenue loss from the tax policy. It is not clear how big either of these effects will be, but their opposite direction means that they will at least partially offset and moderate one another.

Second, efforts to take advantage of the tax policy by expanding tipping to new occupations are likely to meet with limited success if the characteristics of those occupations do not support consumers' motivations for tipping. We have seen that tipping is more common for occupations with low worker status and income, happier customers than workers, less customer-worker contact time, and more customized services—presumably because these occupational characteristics enhance consumers altruistic, reciprocity and duty motives for tipping (see Chap. 6). Occupations with these characteristics are likely to already be tipped and occupations without them are unlikely to ever be frequently tipped. This means that even though exempting tips from taxes is likely to increase the occupations seeking tip compensation, it is likely to alter consumers' willingness to tip only a few of those new occupations and to increase their tip income only a little. These two considerations lead me to believe the revenue costs of exempting tips from income taxation will not be substantially ballooned by behavioral changes and will be close to the static estimates above.

Although I do not fear the extremely large revenue losses that some do, I nevertheless come away from my reading about this issue seeing little reason to support the exemption of tips from income taxation and good reasons to oppose it. I know from the survey data reported above that I am in the minority on this, but I hope this is one of those campaign promises that politicians do not keep.

Disagreement About Digital Tipping

Recent years have seen a growth in the frequency of digital screens asking consumers for tips. Such digital tip requests appear in point-of-sale systems when customers pay with credit, in the interfaces of many online and app-based services, and in screens that consumers can voluntarily bring up on their phones by scanning QR codes provided for that purpose. The requests typically take the form of presenting consumers with several one-touch tipping options, a custom tip option, and a no tip option and their impact and desirability have become topics of debate (Escobar, 2024). Proponents of the digital tipping screens argue that they benefit businesses and their employees by increasing tips. They also argue that digital tipping screens benefit consumers by (i) enabling cashless tipping in contexts such as hotel room cleaning service where consumers want to tip but do not have cash at hand and (ii) making the process of tipping easier by providing one-touch options and by removing consumers' need to do complicated math to translate percentage tips into dollar amounts. Opponents of the digital tipping screens argue that they put unwanted social pressures to tip on consumers and have contributed to the recent expansions in the types of services asking for tips (called "tip-creep") and in the sizes of tips expected (called "tip-flation"), which have led to increasing consumer dissatisfaction with the whole custom of tipping (called "tip-fatigue"). Let's examine these arguments in more detail.

Increases Tips

The producers of POS systems and digital tipping solutions report that their clients see an increase in tips after adopting their technologies, and some client reviews of those companies that I have read online support that claim. Unfortunately, independent verifications of these claims are not available. Real-world tests of the effects of digital tip requests (versus analog or no tip requests) are difficult to do because tipping data in the pre-adoption (non-digital) conditions is unreliable and hard to get. Hypothetical scenario and survey data are easier to get but less trustworthy. One hypothetical scenario study found that people said they would tip a barista the same amounts regardless of whether the tip was collected via a digital tipping options screen, a credit card slip, or a tip jar (Goh et al., 2021). However, this study showed each subject all the scenario conditions and asked how much they would tip in each. This approach creates massive demand effects and makes the results uninformative.

A 2023 survey conducted by YouGov for Bankrate found that 9% of respondents in the US said they tip more and 18% said they tip less or not at all when "presented with a pre-entered tip screen (e.g., at coffee shops, food trucks, in mobile apps, etc....)" (Gillespie, 2023). This finding too suggests that digital tip requests do not increase tipping, but another 2023 survey found different results. In the latter survey, the median tip respondents said they would leave was 15% if facing a digital tipping screen but was only 10% if facing a tip jar (PYMNTS, 2023). These conflicting findings underscore the main problems with such surveys—people may not know how these screens affect their behavior and cannot be relied upon to give an honest answer if they do know. For now, the best evidence we have is the anecdotal testimony of businesses using the systems together with the growing numbers of such businesses, which suggest that digital tipping screens probably do increase tips.

Enables Cashless Tipping

Less open to dispute is the idea that QR-code and other digital tipping systems enable customers to give digital tips to workers that had previously received only cash tips. This is a real benefit to at least some consumers who want to tip but do not have cash at hand. It is also a benefit to those workers, such as parking valets and hotel maids, who do not process bill payment and, therefore, have traditionally missed out on the opportunity to get such non-cash tips. However, I am aware of no evidence quantifying those benefits. More research is needed to identify how often consumers want to tip but do not have cash at hand to do so. More research is also needed to find out how much the opportunity to get non-cash tips increases the tip incomes of workers who were traditionally tipped in cash only.

Saves Consumers' Effort

Digital tipping clearly saves consumers' effort in two ways. First, the ability to give digital tips in situations where it was not previously possible saves committed tippers the effort of making sure they have enough cash on hand to tip parking valets, hotel maids, and other workers who traditionally received only cash tips. Second, the provision of several specific one-touch tip options saves consumers the mental effort of having to generate their own tip amounts. This later benefit may seem small but should not be underestimated. Using sophisticated analyses of NYC taxicab data to estimate how different a default tip option had to be compared to a tippers' preferred amount before the tipper elected to use the custom tip option, Donkor (2021) estimated that the average value that riders placed on the ease of using the default options was between 63 and 90 cents per ride. If that result even roughly generalizes to other digital tipping transactions, then the combined economic value of the saved mental effort that one-touch digital tipping options provide is enormous.

Pressures Consumers

Requests for tips are not new; they have existed in the forms of tip jars, tip trays, and/or tipping lines on credit card slips for many years. However, digital tipping requests typically differ from these more traditional tip requests in four ways that are likely to increase felt social pressures to tip. First, tip jars, tip trays, and tipping lines on credit card slips usually provide no hint about the expected tip amount while digital tipping requests typically present several one-touch tipping options that are seen as defining social expectations. This communication of tip expectations is likely to be seen as social pressure by consumers wanting to tip less than the expected amounts (Fan et al., 2024; Warren et al., 2021a). That is probably why 40% of Americans surveyed in 2023 opposed, while only 24% favored, businesses suggesting tip amounts to their customers (DeSilver & Lippert, 2023).

Second, tip trays and tipping lines on credit card slips (though not tip jars) allow the consumer to leave tips outside the immediate scrutiny of the service provider while digital tip requests often require the customer to tip in front of the service worker providing them access to the digital screen. This lack of privacy has been shown to increase felt social pressures to tip and to decrease intended re-patronage while increasing tip amounts (Warren & Hanson, 2025).

Third, consumers not wanting to tip can simply not add anything to tip jars, tip trays, and tipping lines on credit card slips, but must actively select a "no tip" option or enter a custom tip of "0" on digital tipping screens. In other words, digital tipping requests turn what had previously been an act of omission (failure to tip) into an act of commission. Since we tend to judge acts of commission more harshly than acts of omission (Ramalingam et al., 2019), this probably increases felt social pressures to tip.

Finally, cash tips in tip jars and tip trays (though not credit card tips) publicly display the tipping behavior of others while digital tipping requests typically do not. The former's transparent display of actual tipping likelihood reduces social pressures to tip in contexts where tipping is rare (such as retail counters, coffee shops, and restaurant carryout). In contrast, digital tipping's hiding of this information leaves people to assume that requested tips are commonly given, which should increase social pressures to tip in such contexts. These increased social pressures accompanying digital tip requests have been shown to negatively impact consumers' emotional states and possibly their future patronage (Fan et al., 2024; Warren et al., 2021a), so businesses may want to redesign their digital tip requests in ways that reduce those felt social pressures as discussed in Chap. 2.

Disrupts Tipping Customs

Digital tip requests have begun (i) appearing even in contexts where tipping is not traditional and (ii) providing tip options that are larger than traditionally expected. Objective documentation of these phenomena (called "tip-creep" and "tip-flation" respectively) is not available, but recent surveys of the US population found that 72% said tipping was expected in more places today than was the case five years ago (DeSilver & Lippert, 2023) and 48% said they were being asked to tip larger amounts than they were 6 months ago (Zuluaga, 2024). These apparent expansions of tipping norms have fueled a growing dissatisfaction with digital tipping and with the custom of tipping itself (the latter phenomenon is called "tip-fatigue"). Surveys indicate that 34% of U.S. consumers are "annoyed about pre-entered tip screens" (Kelton, 2024) and 40% oppose "businesses giving their customers suggestions about how much to tip" (DeSilver & Lippert, 2023). Furthermore, surveys of consumers from across the U.S. that I conducted in 2016, 2018, and 2022 found that 32, 41, and 52% of respondents (respectively) agreed or strongly agreed to the statement "I would like to see tipping abolished." These considerations have led at least some to argue that digital tipping is a major disruptor of tipping customs (Warren & Hansen, 2023).

There is little doubt that the growth in digital tipping has enabled, and thus contributed to, the tip-creep, tip-flation and tip-fatigue described above. However, there are good reasons to question the extent of this digital revolution's impact on tipping. First, the Covid-19 pandemic and the post-pandemic economic-conditions are also likely drivers of the trends in tip-creep, tip-flation and tip-fatigue, and it is unclear whether or not digital tipping's impact can sustain these trends in the absence of their other, more transitory causes.[6,7] Second, growing tip-fatigue and businesses' increasing

---

[6] The Covid-19 pandemic is likely to have contributed to tip-flation and tip-creep by increasing altruistic desires to (i) help service workers whose incomes were harmed by the pandemic, (ii) equitably reward service workers for the health risks they faced during the pandemic, and/or (iii) appear compassionate and equitable to others during this time of need. Indeed, several studies have found that consumers tipped more to both traditionally-tipped and non-tipped workers during the Covid-19 pandemic than they had previously (Conlisk, 2022; Lynn, 2021a, 2023b). This consumer display of willingness to tip more than typical no doubt contributed to businesses' willingness to request larger tips and tips for previously non-tipped workers. However, it seems more likely that the return to non-pandemic conditions and the growing tip-fatigue will prompt consumers to return to their pre-pandemic tipping habits. Press reports of TOAST's 2024 point-of-purchase data and YouGov/Bankrate's 2024 survey data provide some support for this expectation because that data shows restaurant tip amounts and the likelihood of tipping for various other services have declined from pandemic highs (Blake, 2024; Taylor, 2024). The reported changes in restaurant tip sizes are very small (about 1/10th of 1%) and could be due to chance, but the changes in tipping likelihood are less trivial. As consumers tipping habits return to pre-pandemic levels, so too should businesses' willingness to request larger tips and tips for previously non-tipped workers.

[7] The aftermath of the pandemic brought high levels of inflation together with a tight labor market. These economic conditions put businesses in a bind—they needed to attract scarce workers by paying them more, but they also needed to attract price sensitive customers by keeping prices (and, therefore, labor costs) low. Businesses could address both these needs by asking their customers to tip larger amounts and a wider range of workers. Asking for tips should increase income to employees without requiring the business to increase costs and prices. Since they are voluntary, tips are disproportionately paid by price insensitive customers and should have less impact on demand than would higher wages paid for with price increases (Lynn, 2017b). While the reductions in labor costs and prices allowed

awareness of it will likely exert a counter-force that slows and perhaps even stops current tip-creep and tip-flation.

Finally, tip-creep and tip-flation refer to expansions in tip requests and do not necessarily imply expansions in tipping behavior. Although one survey found that half of U.S. consumers have felt manipulated by checkout tablets to tip more generously than they had intended (Burke, 2023), those people may successfully resist such manipulation on most occasions. We have already seen that less than half of consumers report usually or often tipping at coffeeshops and only 22% of consumers report usually or often tipping for restaurant carryout (see Table 10.1) even though requests for tips in these contexts are becoming ubiquitous. These findings suggest that requests for tips are not enough by themselves to appreciably alter tipping behavior and norms. Furthermore, it makes sense that digital technologies have had only modest effects on actual tipping behavior and norms because tipping is affected by a multitude of motivations (see Chap. 2) and factors (see Chap. 3–8), which can override and mute the digital technology effects. For all these reasons, I personally believe that the behavioral and cultural impact of digital tipping is over-blown, but I have been wrong before and time will tell.

Summary about Digital Tipping

In summary, digital technology has given businesses new opportunities to explicitly ask for tips, and the ways they make those digital tip requests undoubtedly impact consumer tipping behavior and sentiment. However, the extent and desirability of those impacts is debatable. Some people see digital tipping as putting unwanted social pressures to tip on consumers and as causing tip-creep, tip-flation, and tip-fatigue, which threaten to fundamentally change the custom. Others, like myself, question the larger cultural effects attributed to digital tipping and see it as enabling and effort saving for consumers as well as beneficial to workers and their employers. Hopefully, you now see the issues in this debate with greater clarity and are better equipped to form your own judgements on those issues and the overall debate. Even more hopefully, we can and will do more research on the issues and use that information to design and use digital tipping screens that maximize their benefits while minimizing their costs.

---

by tipping are always a benefit to businesses, they were particularly valuable during the high inflation and tight labor market following the pandemic and the pressure on businesses to request larger tips and tips for previously non-tipped workers is likely to weaken as the labor market loosens.

References

Aaronson, D., French, E., & MacDonald, J. (2008). The minimum wage, restaurant prices, and labor market structure. *Journal of Human Resources, 43*(3), 688–720.

Andrea, S. B., Messer, L. C., Marino, M., & Boone-Heinonen, J. (2018). Associations of tipped and untipped service work with poor mental health in a nationally representative cohort of adolescents followed into adulthood. *American Journal of Epidemiology, 187*(10), 2177–2185.

Andrea, S. B., Messer, L. C., Marino, M., Goodman, J. M., & Boone-Heinonen, J. (2020). The tipping point: could increasing the subminimum wage reduce poverty-related antenatal stressors in US women?. *Annals of Epidemiology, 45*, 47–53.

Allegretto, S., & Cooper, D. (2014). Twenty-three years and still waiting for change. In *Economic policy institute and center for wage and employment dynamics briefing paper*. Economic Policy Institute.

Allegretto, S. & Nadler, C. (2015). Tipped wage effects on earnings and employment in full-service restaurants. *Industrial Relations, 54* (4), 622–647.

Azar, O. H. (2012). The effect of the minimum wage for tipped workers on firm strategy, employees and social welfare. *Labour Economics, 19*(5), 748–755.

Barkan, R., Erev, I., Zinger, E., & Tzach, M. (2004). Tip policy, visibility and quality of service in cafes. *Tourism Economics, 10*(4), 449–464.

Belman, D., & Wolfson, P. J. (2014). *What does the minimum wage do?*. WE Upjohn Institute.

Blake, S. (2024, Sept 10). *Why Americans are tipping less and less*. www.newsweek.com. Accessed 19 Nov 2024.

Burke, M. (2023, July 6). 70% of Consumers are tired of tipping and it's pushing your most valuable customer away: here's how to respond. https://www.capterra.com/resources/tip-fatigue/. Accessed 6 Dec 2024.

Compton, J., & Compton, R. A. (2024). Disentangling customer and employer discrimination using state variation in the tipped minimum wage. *Journal of Economics, Race, and Policy, 7*(2), 65–81.

Conlisk, S. (2022). Tipping in crises: Evidence from Chicago taxi passengers during COVID-19. *Journal of Economic Psychology*, 102475.

Desilver, D., & Lippert, J. (2023, Nov 9). *Tipping culture in America: Public sees a changed landscape*. Pew research center. Available at https://www.pewresearch.org/wp-content/uploads/2023/11/SR_23.11.09_tipping-culture_report.pdf. Accessed 10 Oct 2024.

Donkor, K. B. (2021). *The economic value of norm-adherence and menu opt-out costs: Evidence from tipping*. https://ideas.repec.org/p/ecl/stabus/3960. Accessed 12 June 2024.

Duke, B. (2024, June 17). Sen. Ted Cruz's no tax on tips act does little for low- and moderate-wage workers but opens door to tax abuse by wealthy. https://www.americanprogress.org/article/sen-ted-cruzs-no-tax-on-tips-act-does-little-for-low-and-moderate-wage-workers-but-opens-door-to-tax-abuse-by-wealthy/. Accessed 6 Dec 2024.

Ermey, R. (2023, Aug 24). *You don't need to tip when you buy coffee at a counter, etiquette experts say—Why workers disagree.* https://www.cnbc.com/2023/08/24/workers-customers-and-etiquette-experts-debate-tipping-at-the-counter.html. Accessed 12 Nov 2024.

Escobar, C. (2024, Apr 30). *Tipping turmoil: The debate over digital tipping.* https://hospitalitytech.com/tipping-turmoil-debate-over-digital-tipping. Accessed 6 Dec 2024.

Estreicher, S., & Nash, J. R. (2018). The case for tipping and unrestricted tip-pooling: Promoting intrafirm cooperation. *BCL Review, 59*, 1.

Even, W.E. & Macpherson, D.A. (2014). The effect of the tipped minimum wage on employees in the U.S. restaurant industry. *Southern Economic Journal, 80* (3), 633–655.

Fan, A., Wu, L., & Liu, Y. (2024). To display tip suggestion or not? Examining tip suggestion's impact in technology-facilitated preservice tipping encounters. *Journal of Hospitality & Tourism Research, 48*(1), 32–57.

Frank, D. G., & Lynn, M. (2020). Shattering the illusion of the self-earned tip: The effect of a restaurant magician on co-workers' tips. *Journal of Behavioral and Experimental Economics, 87*, 101560.

Gillespe, L. (2023, June 8). Survey: 66% of Ameicans have a negative view of tipping. https://www.bankrate.com/personal-finance/tipping-survey/. Accessed 13 Oct 2024.

Goh, F. W., Jungck, A. C., & Stevens, J. R. (2021). Pro tip: Screen-based payment methods increase negative feelings in consumers but do not increase tip sizes. *European Journal of Behavioral Sciences, 4*(4), 1–21. https://doi.org/10.33422/ejbs.v4i4.678

Grisez, G. (1997). Question #99: What morals norms should one follow in tipping? *The Way of the Lord Jesus, Volume 3: Difficult Moral Questions.* Franciscan Press, Quincy University, Quincy IL. Available online at http://www.twotlj.org/G-3-99.html

Ikema, M. (2016). To tip or not to tip? that's a philosophical question! (Doctoral dissertation, San Francisco State University).

Jackson, C., & Mendez, B. (2024). *Proposed policy to end federal income tax on tips has bipartisan support.* https://www.ipsos.com/en-us/proposed-policy-end-federal-income-tax-tips-has-bipartisan-support. Accessed 6 Dec 2024

Jayaraman, S. (2021). *One fair wage.* The New Press.

Jonjopop (2022). Alright let's talk about the tipping debate …. https://www.reddit.com/r/KitchenConfidential/comments/111ia5a/alright_lets_talk_about_the_tipping_debate/?rdt=42050. Accessed 24 Nov 2024.

Jones, M. R. (2016). Measuring the effects of the tipped minimum wage using W-2 data. *US Census Bureau, May, 26*.

Kelton, K. (2024, June 5). *Survey: More than 1 in 3 Americans think tipping culture has gotten out of control*. www.bankrate.com. Accessed 22 Aug 24.

Kershnar, S. (2014). A promissory theory of the duty to tip. *Business and Society Review, 119*(2), 247–276.

Kiley, K. (2024). Chair kiley highlights how the tip credit protects millions of livelihoods. Press Release of the Committee on Education and the Workforce. U.S. House of representatives. Available at https://edworkforce.house.gov/news/documentsingle.aspx?DocumentID=411930. Accessed 26 Nov 2024.

Lin, I. Y., & Namasivayam, K. (2011). Understanding restaurant tipping systems: A human resources perspective. *International Journal of Contemporary Hospitality Management, 23*(7), 923–940.

Lynn, M. and Boone, C. (2015). Have minimum wages hurt the restaurant industry? The evidence says no! Cornell Hospitality Report, 15(22).

Lynn, M. (2017b). Should US restaurants abandon tipping? A review of the issues and evidence. *Psychosociological Issues in Human Resource Management, 5*(1), 120–159.

Lynn, M. (2020). The Effects of Minimum Wages on Tipping: A State-Level Analysis. *Compensation & Benefits Review, 52*(3), 98–108. https://doi.org/10.1177/0886368720908959.

Lynn, M. (2021a). Did the COVID-19 pandemic dampen Americans' tipping for food services? Insights from two studies. *Compensation & Benefits Review, 53*(3), 130–143.

Lynn, M. (2022). How tip credits affect consumer tipping behavior. *International Journal of Hospitality Management, 103*, 103214.

Lynn, M. (2023b). How did the Covid-19 pandemic affect restaurant tipping? *Journal of Foodservice Business Research*, 1–20.

Lynn, M., & Ni, X. (2022). The effects of tip distribution policies: Servers' keeping vs sharing/pooling tips affects tippers' sentiments but not tip-giving. *International Journal of Hospitality Management, 100*, 103087.

Mailer, M. P. (1993). The morality of tipping. *Public Affairs Quarterly, 7*(3), 231–239.

McDermott, B. (2024, Oct 28). *Taxation of tip income*. https://crsreports.congress.gov/product/pdf/IF/IF12728. Accessed 6 Dec 2024.

McKenzie, R. B. (2019). *Tipped workers and the minimum wage. Regulation*. https://www.cato.org/regulation/spring-2019/tipped-workers-minimum-wage. Accessed 26 Nov 2024.

Neumark, D., & Yen, M. (2023). The employment and redistributive effects of reducing or eliminating minimum wage tip credits. *Journal of Policy Analysis and Management, 42*(4), 1092–1116.

NRA (2024). How tip credit helps restaurant employees, operators, and customers. National Restaurant Association Public Affairs Policy Brief. Available at https://restaurant.org/getmedia/38f3e0dc-3f22-4a0f-a825-d2454768e7bc/tip-credit.pdf. Accessed 26 Nov 2024.

PYMNTS (2023, Nov). *Consumer inflation sentiment report*. https://www.pymnts.com/study_posts/27percent-of-consumers-at-self-checkout-say-theyve-been-asked-to-tip/. Accessed 6 Dec 2024.

Quora (2024). *Should tipping be considered unethical or wrong?* https://www.quora.com/Should-tipping-be-considered-unethical-or-wrong. Accessed 23 Nov 2024.

Ramalingam, A., Morales, A. J., & Walker, J. M. (2019). Peer punishment of acts of omission versus acts of commission in give and take social dilemmas. *Journal of Economic Behavior & Organization, 164*, 133–147.

ROC United (2018). Restaurants flourish with one fair wage. *Report of Restaurant Opportunities Centers United*. Available at https://workercenterlibrary.org/resources/better-wages-better-tips-restaurants-flourish-with-one-fair-wage/. Accessed 26 Nov 2024.

Sabia, J. J., Burkhauser, R. V., & Mackay, T. (2018). Minimum cash wages, tipped restaurant workers, and poverty. *Industrial Relations: A Journal of Economy and Society, 57*(4), 637–670.

Schweitzer, J. (2021). Ending the tipped minimum wage will reduce poverty and inequality. *Center for American Progress Report*, https://www.americanprogress.org/article/ending-tipped-minimum-wage-will-reduce-poverty-inequality/. Accessed 27 Nov 2024.

Seagrave, Kerry (1998), Tipping: An American History of Gratuities, Jefferson, NC: McFarland & Company.

Sienkiewicz, J. H. (2016). *Waiting on you: A study of tipped minimum wages' effects on job tenure among white restaurant servers* (Master's thesis, Loyola University Chicago).

Tang, J., Raab, C., Zemke, D. M. V., & Choi, C. (2022). The effect of the minimum server wage on restaurant guest tipping behavior. *Journal of Foodservice Business Research, 25*(1), 1–32.

Taylor, C. (2024, July 2). *Tipped off: American consumers grapple with tip creep*. https://www.usnews.com/news/top-news/articles/2024-07-02/tipped-off-american-consumers-grapple-with-tip-creepwww.reuters.com. Accessed 19 Nov 2024.

The Budget Lab at Yale. (2024, Sept 16). *"No tax on tips": Budgetary, distributional, and tax avoidance considerations*. https://budgetlab.yale.edu/research/no-tax-tips-budgetary-distributional-and-tax-avoidance-considerations. Accessed 6 Dec 2024.

Thorndike, J. (2024, Sept 30). *Tax history: no tax on tips: A bad idea with a long history*. https://www.forbes.com/sites/taxnotes/2024/09/30/tax-history-no-tax-on-tips-a-bad-idea-with-a-long-history/. Accessed 6 Dec 2024.

Treanor, B. (2023, Apr 28). *Guilt tips: Are we being pressured to tip more?* https://time2play.com/blog/guilt-tips/. Accessed 24 Nov 2024.

Warren, N. B., & Hanson, S. (2025). Tipping privacy: The detrimental impact of observation on non-tip responses. *Journal of Business Research, 186*, 115008.

Warren, N. B., & Hanson, S. (2023). Tipping, disrupted: The multi-stakeholder digital tipped service journey. *Journal of Service Research, 26*(3), 389–404.

Warren, N. B., Hanson, S., & Yuan, H. (2021a). Who's in control? How default tip levels influence customer response. *Marketing Science Institute Working Paper Series, 21*(126).

Watt, C. (2017). *Tip pooling practices and quality of life for back of the house restaurant employees.* https://digital.lib.washington.edu/server/api/core/bitstreams/492ca6c0-64dd-42a2-8e3d-9840e4492229/content. Accessed 30 Nov 2024.

Wessels, W.J. (1997), "Minimum Wages and Tipped Servers," *Economic Inquiry, 35*, 334–349.

Wicks-Lim, J. & Kerrissey, J. (2024). Potential impacts of a full minimum wage for tipped workers in Massachusetts. Policy Brief, Political Economy Research Institute, University of Massachusetts Amherst.

Yang, Y. D. (2020). *Share the tip jar: Department of Labor finalizes rule opening tip-pooling to back-of-the-house workers.* https://www.laboremploymentlawblog.com/2020/12/articles/tip-pooling/dol-tip-credit/. Accessed 28 May 2021.

Zuluaga, T. (2024). *How restaurant guests really feel about tipping in America.* https://pos.toasttab.com/blog/on-the-line/tipping-in-america?srsltid=AfmBOootAhI57Ie8X8LluIdUSKCF2fSwheZ6nEGFGTwAYpdIwEWgGHoY. Accessed 6 Dec 2024.

11

Past as Prologue (When and Where Did Tipping Arise? How Might It Change Going Forward?)

George Santanya (1905) famously said that "Those who cannot remember the past are condemned to repeat it." That is not to say that knowledge of history necessarily frees us from the forces that have driven our collective journey to date, but an awareness of the past does alert us to those forces and informs our efforts to shape them going forward. As William Shakespear's character Antonio says in The Tempest, "What's past is prologue" and knowledge of history helps us both to understand the present and to predict and shape the future. Thus, all those involved in tipping today stand to benefit from some understanding of its history. I am neither a historian nor a futurist, but I have picked up bits and pieces of information about the history of tipping in my studies and I am better able than most others to make educated guesses about the likely future of this custom. Therefore, with lots of caveats and disclaimers, I share what I know and think about these issues in this final chapter of the book.

Origins of the Word "Tip"

The word "tip" is often described as being an acronym for the words "To Insure Promptitude," which were supposed to have been written on notes wrapped around coins given to servers (or printed on bowls or boxes into which coins for servers were dropped). However, this idea is almost certainly incorrect, because the use of acronyms did not become common until the twentieth century and use of the terms "tip" and "tipping" substantially predates that time. For example, Jonathan Swift mentions "tipping" an inn keeper in his 1733 poem, "The Legion Club" (Seagrave, 1998).

Other ideas are that the term may come from (i) "stips" the Latin word for "gift," (ii) "tippen" a Dutch word meaning "to tap" as in tapping a coin on a glass to get the waiters' attention, (iii) "tip" a word from seventeenth-century thieves cant meaning "give me," or (iv) "tipple" an English word meaning "to drink" so that tips represent money intended to allow service workers to buy drinks for themselves (Azar, 2004). Although I do not have a position about its correctness, I do want to note that the last idea is consistent with the observation that the word for tip in many different countries (e.g., Austria, Belgium, Bosnia, Croatia, Czech Republic, Estonia, Finland, France, Germany, Iceland, Israel, Kazakhstan, Latvia, Norway, Slovakia, Spain, Sweden, and Vietnam) translates to "drink money" or its equivalent (Foster, 1972).

Origins of Tipping

Ideas about the origins of tipping as a practice (not a just word) are also numerous, but difficult to verify or falsify. Some say it originated in feudal times when traveling lords threw coins to crowds on the roads to insure safe passage (Schein et al., 1984). Others say that tipping grew out of the English custom of vails, which started when lords would occasionally give coins to serfs, and eventually evolved into a social expectation that visitors to private British homes would give gifts of money (called, vails) to the host's servants on account of the extra work their visit imposed on those servants (Seagrave, 1998). However, even if they are correct, these ideas describe phenomena very different from modern-day tipping and do not really explain when, how, or why they evolved into the practice we know today.

A more proximate account of the origins of tipping might be inferred from the previously noted fact that the word for tipping in different languages so often translates to "drink money" or its equivalent and from George Foster's previously noted theory that restaurant and bar tips are an attempt to buy off the envy of waiters and bartenders. Specifically, these points suggest that tipping may have begun in hospitality establishments as a way to appease workers who might otherwise envy customers enjoying themselves eating, drinking, and socializing while the workers toiled to serve them. Essentially tippers were saying, "Don't envy me for enjoying myself while you work—here is some money for you to have a drink on me later." However, there are records of "bibalia" or "drinksilver" (money for drinks) given to construction workers in the fourteenth and fifteenth centuries (Wikipedia,), so the terminology of tipping need not indicate an origin in taverns and inns or a grounding in fear of envy. Ultimately, the origins of tipping remain obscure and this would seem to be a rich topic of future research for historians.

History of Tipping in the U.S.

Although we know little about the global history of tipping, more is known about the history of tipping in the United States. That history literally fills a book (Seagrave, 1998) and cannot be recounted in full here.[1] Instead, I will highlight what I consider to be particularly interesting facts and takeaways from that history. Those highlights include the following.

Origins and Spread of Tipping in the U.S.

Thomas Jefferson and George Washington are known to have tipped slaves (Althouse, 2015; Thomas Jefferson Encyclopedia, 2024), so some form of tipping has existed in the United States for its entire history. Nevertheless, tipping was rare in the U.S. outside of major cities prior to 1840 and did not become common until after the Civil War, when wealthy U.S. travelers to Europe supposedly brought the custom back home with them. Around this time (1885 to be specific), the NY Times reported that the average tip to waiters in the U.S. was 10% of the bill while that in Europe was 5%. By the early 1900s, tipping appears to have become widespread in America. A now classic 1916 anti-tipping book—*The Itching Palm*—claimed that nearly one in ten Americans worked in occupations for which tips were a part of the compensation.

After the Civil War, the Pullman Company employed as porters many Southern blacks, who depended on tips to make a living because they were paid very little in wages. This led William Scott, the author of *The Itching*

---

[1] Seagrave's (1998) book is the most detailed history of tipping in the U.S. that I am aware of. Unless otherwise indicated, the historical information presented in this section is from that book. However, I must note that the author showed himself to be a poor evaluator of contemporary social science research when he unfairly disparaged my work and integrity. He criticized one of my studies (i.e., Lynn, 1988)—writing that I "*conveniently ignored the fact the most studies on tipping found that bill size had no effect on percentage tipped, not the opposite as he* (meaning me) *decided*" and he accused me of "*using inappropriate statistical methods to achieve a result that he* (meaning me) *believed should exist*" (Seagrave, 1998, pg. 144). Both claims are incorrect and I stand by the methods and findings of the study he criticized.

Palm, to claim that "*It was the Pullman company which fastened the tipping habit on the American people and they used the negro as the instrument to do it.*" This and other contemporaneous remarks, along with the post-Civil War expansion of tipping, are often used to taint tipping as a form of structural racism. A 2018 Civil Rights "Fact Sheet" went so far as to claim that "*Tipping was designed to keep African Americans in an economically and socially subordinate position*" (Li et al., 2018). However, such claims are undercut by the ideas that (i) tipping in the U.S. predates the Civil War, (ii) many whites, as well as blacks, worked for tips, and (iii) tipped workers presumably received as much or more total compensation as they could get from other work available to them (else they'd have taken those other jobs). With respect to the later point, black porters who worked under both an older tipping system and a newer system in which they received higher wages but no tips testified that they preferred working under the tipping system (Wilk, 2015). As we have seen in Chap. 7, racism does affect tipping, but it would be more accurate to label some tippers (not the custom itself) as racist.

Also allegedly contributing to the growth in tipping following the Civil War was hotels' movement at this time away from a business model in which communal meals were included in the price of a room (the American Plan) to a model in which individual meals were priced and charged separately from the room (the European Plan) (Mentzer, 2013). Under the American Plan, hotel managers resisted tipping because they viewed it as a way customers could bribe employees for extra portions, but this concern was abated under the European Plan by the fact that meals were prepared and served individually making it harder for servers to be overly generous with portions. Prohibition's banning of alcohol in 1919 hastened the movement to the European Plan (and with it tipping) as hotel bars were converted to "lunch rooms" and as loss of alcohol profits necessitated greater ability to separately access and manage the profitability of rooms and meals (Mentzer, 2013).

Historical Trends in U.S. Tip Amounts

There have been no efforts to systematically and consistently record U.S. tipping customs and behavior over time. However, it is generally accepted that the customary restaurant tip in the U.S. increased from 10% of the bill in the early 1900s to 15% in the middle of the century, and again to nearly 20% at the end of the century and the beginning of the next. Consistent with this, I recently analyzed tipping percentages from academic studies of restaurant tipping and found that tipping rates have increased over the past half-century (Lynn, 2025; see Fig. 11.1). Unfortunately, exactly why this increase in tip percentages occurred is unclear.

One theoretically interesting possibility is that tipping is used to buy social position and competition increases the prices of those positions over time (Lynn, 2015). Consumers must leave above average tips to buy better than typical service and/or high status and these above average tips cause servers to give less attention and status to average tippers who must then increase their tips to avoid loss of service and/or status. Avoiding such losses among the masses by tipping more raises the average tip, which requires high-position seekers to tip even more—thus starting the cycle over again. Thus, tip rates may increase over time because tips are used to buy social position and there are more people seeking higher service/status than people willing to accept declining service/status.

Another possibility is that rising tip percentages reflect other macroeconomic trends. For example, restaurant tips tend to be higher in larger more densely populated areas (McCrohan & Pearl, 1991) and the U.S. population has become less rural and more urban over time (Greenfield, 2013). Increased use of credit cards and other forms of electronic payment could also explain the rise in tip percentages, because credit card payment is associated with larger tip percentages (Lynn & McCall, 2000). Knowing which, if any, of these processes underlie past increases in tipping rates is important because it would tell us how likely the trend is to continue. Thus, testing these different potential explanations for the observed increases in restaurant tip percentages over the past half-century seems like a worthwhile topic for future research.

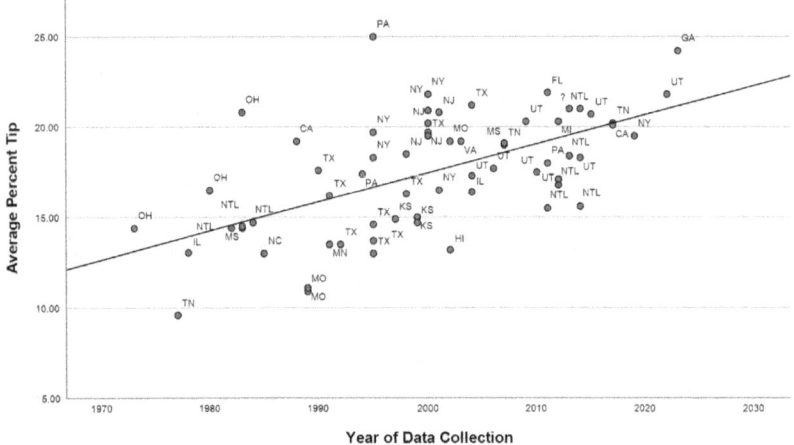

Fig. 11.1 Graph of average percent tip in academic studies (labeled with location of study) by year of data collection. *Source* Lynn (2025)

Historical Trends in Anti-tipping Sentiment

Although the United States is widely recognized as the most "pro-tipping" country in the world, the country also has a long history of opposition to tipping. In his 1916 book, William Scott wrote that tipping was an immoral and un-American vestige of European feudalism that demeaned both the recipient and giver. Around that same time, travel organizations (e.g., the Commercial Travelers' National League and the United Commercial Travelers of America), consumer groups (e.g., the Anti-Tipping Society of America, and the Society for the Prevention of Useless Giving) and even some labor unions (e.g., the Hotel and Restaurant Employees International Alliance and the International Hotel Workers' Union) actively campaigned against the practice. These efforts had some effect, with the states of Arkansas, Iowa, Mississippi, South Carolina, Tennessee, and Washington passing laws between 1909 and 1915 that prohibited the giving and/or taking of tips. Although all those laws were struck down or repealed by 1926, dissatisfaction with tipping has remained widespread over the ensuing years. The recent increases in the amounts people are asked to tip (tip-flation) and expansions in the numbers and types of services asking for tips (tip-creep) described in Chap. 10 appear to have fueled a resurgence in anti-tipping sentiment (tip-fatigue). As also mentioned in that earlier chapter, surveys I conducted found that agreement with the statement "I would like to see tipping abolished" increased from 32% in 2016 to 52% in 2022.

Future of Tipping

The recent tip-flation, tip-creep, and tip-fatigue noted above and in Chapter 10 highlight the potential for change in tipping practices and raise questions about the future of tipping. Will tip amounts continue to go up and the services receiving tips continue to expand? If so, for how long and how much? Alternatively, will the resulting backlash of anti-tipping sentiment halt these phenomena, or even lead to the abolishment of tipping altogether? The honest, if unsatisfying, answer to these questions is that neither I nor anyone else knows. The processes involved are too complex and the quality of data about those processes is too low to say with any degree of confidence what the future holds for tipping. Nevertheless, some educated guesses about these issues are offered below.

Rising Tip Rates

My previously discussed study of restaurant tip percentages over time found that the mean tip percentage increased linearly with year of data collection. There was no reliable evidence of a slowing down of growth over time (Lynn, 2025). That said, it is hard to imagine that such increases can continue indefinitely. While rising tip percentages are a short-term boon to employees and facilitate staff recruitment and retention, they also anger consumers and increase the total costs of services—both of which will eventually reduce demand. In the case of restaurants, increases in tip percentages will also exacerbate the pay disparities between front-of-house and back-of-house staff, which increases inter-staff conflict. At some point, businesses will have to stop escalating the amounts they ask consumers to tip and/or consumers will have to stop their own escalation of tip percentages given, but exactly what that point is and when it will be reached is anybody's guess.

Expansion of Tipped Services

Recent increases in tip requests from previously non-tipped workers (the tip-creep discussed above) gives the appearance that tipping is expanding into new service contexts. There is little doubt that those requests induce at least some consumers to leave tips where they would not have otherwise been given, so there is some truth to the apparent expansion of tipping. However, we saw in Chap. 10 that the expansion is not as great as many assume. Just because businesses and their workers are asking for tips does not mean that most consumers are giving them. Remember that a 2023 YouGov survey found that only 22% of U.S. consumers usually or always tip for restaurant carryout and only 48% usually or always tip at coffee shops despite the ubiquity of tip requests from these workers (Gillespie, 2023). Since roughly half of those numbers reflect only occasional tipping, they indicate that the vast majority of service encounters in these contexts go untipped. Thus, consumers wishing to resist tip-creep can take comfort from this fact and rest assured that any anger or disappointment created by their refusal to tip will be muted by the fact that most other consumers also refuse to tip in these service contexts where tipping is not traditional.

Also remember from Chap. 6 that consumers' motivation and tendency to tip a service occupation are greater when the work is low status/pay, customized, easy for customers to evaluate, and involves workers who are having a less good time than their customers are (Lynn, 2016, 2019, 2021).

In the short term, existing services with many of these characteristics are probably already tipped while those with few of these characteristics are probably not, and never will be, tipped. Those services with an intermediate number of these characteristics may be tipped by some consumers but are unlikely to ever be tipped by a majority as bartenders, waiters, and pizza delivery drivers are. Indeed, this seems likely to explain why fewer than half of consumers in the U.S. today routinely tip baristas, restaurant carryout workers, and other counter-service staff despite efforts to encourage such tipping.

In the long term, new services will no doubt emerge. Whether or not they will become tipped services also depends on their nature—those possessing many characteristics of already tipped services stand a good chance of being added to that list of services, but those with few of the characteristics do not. Thus, some long-term tip-creep seems inevitable, but how much depends on the nature of the new services that the future brings us, which is hard to predict.

Tip-Fatigue

The recently experienced tip-fatigue among many consumers in the U.S. raises questions about whether it might eventually lead to the abandonment of the custom. Although I cannot say for sure, that possibility seems unlikely to me. As described earlier in this chapter, tipping has been around in one form or another for centuries and it has flourished in the U.S. despite many efforts to squash it. The past does not have to repeat itself—change can and does happen—but the economics of tipping in the U.S. restaurant industry (where most tipping takes place) makes change unlikely.

Eliminating tipping would be difficult in U.S restaurants, because low profit margins mean that restaurants abandoning tipping must replace it with either automatic service charges or higher menu prices. Neither option is attractive. U.S consumers dislike service charges, which they see as mandatory tips, even more than they dislike tipping. Although more accepting of service-inclusive pricing as a concept, consumers judge no-tipping restaurants with higher service-inclusive menu prices as more expensive than tipping restaurants with lower menu prices (Lynn, 2017). As a result, all but the most upscale restaurants that have tried to abandon tipping experienced a decline in their online ratings (Lynn, 2018; Lynn & Brewster, 2018). Add to that the likelihood that abandoning tipping would lead a restaurants' best servers to leave for tip earning opportunities elsewhere and the economic incentives for individual restaurants to keep tipping seem overwhelming (Lynn, 2017). Many of these competitive, economic obstacles to the abandonment of tipping could be mitigated by joint action from all or most restaurants, but such collective action would run afoul of anti-collusion and price-fixing laws. We have covered these issues in more detail previously, but this brief recap of them explains why I am skeptical that the U.S. will ever abandon tipping. If I am right, and tipping is here to stay, then the information in this book is all the more important, so congratulate yourself on having read it and recommend it to others.

References

Alexander, D., Boone, C., & Lynn, M. (2021). The effects of tip recommendations on customer tipping, satisfaction, repatronage, and spending. *Management Science, 67*(1), 146–165.

Althouse, A. (2015). https://althouse.blogspot.com/2015/02/tipping-as-american-practice-stretches.html. Accessed May 21, 2024.

Azar, O. H. (2004). The history of tipping—From sixteenth-century England to United States in the 1910s. *The Journal of Socio-Economics, 33*(6), 745–764.

CBS Boston. (2016, January 27). Zagat Survey: No on tips better than Boston Diners. https://www.cbsnews.com/boston/news/zagat-survey-dining-boston-tipping-restaurants/. Accessed June 4, 2024.

Chandar, B., Gneezy, U., List, J. A., & Muir, I. (2019). *The drivers of social preferences: Evidence from a nationwide tipping field experiment* (No. w26380). National Bureau of Economic Research.

Denn, R. (2006, November 7). On dining: Zagat survey: We will pay more but we tip less. https://www.startribune.com/zagat-puts-la-belle-vie-on-top/133111168/. Accessed June 4, 2024.

Foster, G. M. (1972). The anatomy of envy: A study in symbolic behavior. *Current Anthropology, 13*(2), 165–202.

Goh, F. W., Jungck, A. C., & Stevens, J. R. (2021). *Pro tip: Screen-based payment methods increase negative feelings in consumers but do not increase tip sizes. European Journal of Behavioral Sciences, 4*(4), 1–21. https://doi.org/10.33422/ejbs.v4i4.678

Gillespie, L. (2023, June 8). Survey: 66% of Americans have a negative view of tipping. https://www.bankrate.com/personal-finance/tipping-survey/. Accessed November 20, 2024.

Greenfield, P. M. (2013). The changing psychology of culture from 1800 through 2000. *Psychological Science, 24*(9), 1722–1731.

Haggag, K., & Paci, G. (2014). Default tips. *American Economic Journal: Applied Economics, 6*(3), 1–19.

Li, H., Chaterjee, E., & Brown, C. (2018). *Fact sheet: The history of the tipped minimum wage*. The Leadership Conference Education Fund and the Georgetown Law Economic Security and Opportunity Initiative. https://civilrightsdocs.info/pdf/minimumwage/History-Tipped-Minimum-Wage.pdf. Accessed May 26, 2024.

Lynn, M. (1988). The effects of alcohol consumption on restaurant tipping. *Personality and Social Psychology Bulletin, 14*(1), 87–91.

Lynn, M. (2015). Service gratuities and tipping: A motivational framework. *Journal of Economic Psychology, 46*, 74–88.

Lynn, M. (2016). Why are we more likely to tip some service occupations than others? Theory, evidence, and implications. *Journal of Economic Psychology, 54*, 134–150.

Lynn, M. (2017). Should US restaurants abandon tipping? A review of the issues and evidence. *Psychosociological Issues in Human Resource Management, 5*(1), 120–159.

Lynn, M. (2018). The effects of tipping on consumers' satisfaction with restaurants. *Journal of Consumer Affairs, 52*(3), 746–755.

Lynn, M. (2019). Predictors of occupational differences in tipping. *International Journal of Hospitality Management, 81*, 221–228.

Lynn, M. (2021). The effects of occupational characteristics on the motives underlying tipping of different occupations. *Journal of Behavioral and Experimental Economics, 95*, Article 101783.

Lynn, M. (2023). How did the Covid-19 pandemic affect restaurant tipping? *Journal of Foodservice Business Research*, 1–20.

Lynn, M. (2025). How have U.S. restaurant tips changed over time? *International Journal of Hospitality Management, 124*, 103969.

Lynn, M., & Brewster, Z. W. (2018). A within-restaurant analysis of changes in customer satisfaction following the introduction of service inclusive pricing or automatic service charges. *International Journal of Hospitality Management, 70*, 9–15.

Lynn, M., & McCall, M. (2000). Gratitude and gratuity: A meta-analysis of research on the service-tipping relationship. *The Journal of Socio-Economics, 29*(2), 203–214.

McCrohan, K. F., & Pearl, R. B. (1991). An application of commercial panel data for public policy research: Estimates of tip earnings. *Journal of Economic and Social Measurement, 17*(3–4), 217–231.

Mentzer, M. (2013). The payment of gratuities by customers in the United States: An historical analysis. *International Journal of Management, 30*(3), 108–120.

Santayana, G. (1905). *The life of reason*. Scribners. Available at: https://www.gutenberg.org/files/15000/15000-h/15000-h.htm#vol1. Accessed June 16, 2024.

Seagrave, K. (1998). *Tipping: An American history of gratuities*. McFarland and Co.

Schein, J. E., Jablonski, E. F., & Wohlfahrt, B. R. (1984). *The art of tipping: Customs & controversies*. Tippers International, LTD.

Scott, W. (1916). *The itching palm: A study of the habit of tipping in America*. The Penn Publishing Company.

Thomas Jefferson Encyclopedia. (2024). https://www.monticello.org/research-education/thomas-jefferson-encyclopedia/route-poplar-forest/. Accessed May 21, 2024.

Warren, N. B., & Hanson, S. (2025). Tipping privacy: The detrimental impact of observation on non-tip responses. *Journal of Business Research, 186*, Article 115008.

Warren, N. B., Hanson, S., & Yuan, H. (2021a). Who's in control? How default tip levels influence customer response. *Marketing Science Institute Working Paper Series, 21*(126).

Wikipedia. (2024a). Drinksilver, https://en.wikipedia.org/wiki/Drinksilver, accessed 5/21/24.

Wikipedia. (2024b). Trinkgeld. https://de.wikipedia.org/wiki/Trinkgeld, translated by Google. Accessed May 20, 2024.

Wilk, D. L. (2015). The red cap's gift: How tipping tempers the rational power of money. *Enterprise & Society, 16*(1), 5–50.

Zagat. (2018). Zagat releases 2018 dining trends survey. https://zagat.googleblog.com/2018/01/zagat-releases-2018-dining-trends-survey.html

GPSR Compliance
The European Union's (EU) General Product Safety Regulation (GPSR) is a set of rules that requires consumer products to be safe and our obligations to ensure this.

If you have any concerns about our products, you can contact us on

ProductSafety@springernature.com

In case Publisher is established outside the EU, the EU authorized representative is:

Springer Nature Customer Service Center GmbH
Europaplatz 3
69115 Heidelberg, Germany

www.ingramcontent.com/pod-product-compliance
Lightning Source LLC
LaVergne TN
LVHW020132080526
838202LV00047B/3924